A VULGAR I

COURAGE AND CARNAGE AT THE ALROSA VILLA

by Chris A.

Crystal River, Florida
www.MJSPublications.com

Portion of proceeds to benefit the Anthony Bray College Fund.

Contact us at:
MJS Music Publications
611 NE 5th Terrace, Ste. #3
Crystal River, FL 34428
(352) 563-1779
http://www.MJSPublications.com

 Published by MJS Music Publications, LLC. 611 NE 5th Terrace, Ste. #3, Crystal River, FL 34428. First paperback edition, 2007.

Catalogued with the Library of Congress.

ISBN 0976291770

Cover by Deege

A Vulgar Display of Power: Courage And Carnage At The Alrosa Villa, the book written by Chris A. and released by MJS Music Publications in 2007, is the true story of events leading to the murder of ex-Pantera guitarist Dimebag Darrell Abbott, band security member Jeffery "Mayhem" Thompson, venue security member Erin Halk, audience member Nathan Bray, and any other entities associated with the event.

Edited by Mark John Sternal.

Written in memory of

Jeffery Thompson
Erin Halk
Nathan Bray
Darrell Abbott

Dedicated to

Anthony Bray
Seth Thompson
Micah Thompson
Martin Thompson
Chris Halk
Andy Halk
Danielle Clark
Vincent Abbott

Table of Contents

Acknowledgements

I'm overwhelmed by all the incredible people I've met and spoken with as I've written this book. From fans to family members, cops to rock stars, you wouldn't be reading this were it not for all these interested, tolerant and very cool people. I am in debt to so many who saw fit to trust me with stories and remembrances of their lost loved ones. Special thanks go to Frank & Marilyn Thompson, Seth Thompson, Martin Thompson, Micah Thompson, Danielle Clark, Eric Clark, Ferris Clark, Margie Carvour, Kerri Bray, Gene Bray, Theresa Bray, Rick Cautela, John Cautela, Diane Colasante, Marsha Bayliss and Mary Clark. I also am grateful for the assistance provided by Detective William Gillette and Officer James Niggemeyer of the Columbus Police Department. Officer Niggemeyer's foreword is thoughtful and moving. Thanks as well to Joe Bowman for proofreading my first generation chapters. I am indebted to my writing mentor, editor Al Pahl, for nearly 20 years of encouragement and friendship. I was graciously provided photos by three incredibly talented professional photographers – Amirali Marandi, Frank White and Chad Lee, who was a close friend of Dimebag. Additional artwork was provided by Bob Tyrrell. Danny "Deege" Dunford contributed his stellar graphic skills to create the cover of this book. Mark John Sternal, Jeanne Sternal and Stephanie Stokes from MJS Music Publications have been behind this project from day one. Mark's willingness to help turn my vision for this book into reality can't be overstated. I must also thank Debbie Depoyster, Ursula Porter, Anne Powers and Lisa Ziolkowski for holding down the fort at the office this past year as I focused on writing this book. Thanks as well to my incredibly cool wife, Connie, who generously supported me as I devoted my time over the past 14 months to tell this story. While I've attempted to keep track of all those who helped me, I'm sure that somehow I've forgotten someone very important and you have my apologies.

-ii-

Evan Agee
Tim Armold
Lt. Nick Armold
Zack Baer
Thomas Ball
Marsha Bayliss
Lucas Bender
Charles Blakeman
Bryan Blaylock
Matt Bowden
Scott Bowersmith
Joe Bowman
Judge Michael
Brady
Gene Bray
Kerri Bray
Theresa Bray
C. Mark Brinkley
Jeff "Stinger"
Brown
Suzy Carney
Tiffany Caron
Nick Catanese
Rick Cautela
John Cautela
Juliya Chernetsky
Rich Cencula
Danielle Clark
Eric Clark
Mary Clark
Charles Cochran
Diane Colasante
Chris & Mandy
Craig
Mike Craiglow
Joe Dameron
Jessica Deel
Debra Depoyster
Josh Drake
Mandy Drake

Abby R. Dritz
Danny "Deege"
Dunford
Vicki Farmer
Brian Fielder
Linda Gabriele
Detective William
Gillette
Floyd Golden
Mark Green
Lt. Col. Dave
Grossman
Andy Halk
Joe Heden
Nathan Heiberger
Allison Henthorn
Lt. Noah "Tony"
Hetrick
Tracy Hill
Shannon Hopps
Ross Irwin
Ronald Jenkins
Officer Ron Jester
Jason Jewett
Lee Kelly
Borivoj Krgin
Karl Kuenning
Chad Lee
Eric Loy
Erin Ludewig
Tom Lyke
Amirali Marandi
Linda McAlister
Eric McGuire
Kevin McMeans
Deb Mikesch
John Muirhead
Chris Owens
Al Pahl
Scott Patrick

Steven Patrick
Billy Payne
Jason Perlman
Anson Petty
Brian Poindexter
Tim Rabe
Jeff Rasco
Dean Reimund
Scott Robinson
Tony Rombola
Mike Settlemeyer
Brian Simakis
Michael "Mongo"
Smith
Jeanne Sternal
Mark John Sternal
Nelson Stewart
Ty Stewart
Stephanie Stokes
Corey Stringer
Zack Sullivan
Frank Thompson
Marilyn Thompson
Martin Thompson
Seth Thompson
Bob Tyrrell
Adam Vanover
Aron "Smike"
Vanover
Tonia Waldron
William Weaver
Michael Wharton
Frank White
Randy Wothke
Sharon Wothke
Zakk Wylde
Dean Zilinsky
Lisa Ziolkowski

Internet Acknowledgements & Resources

The Alrosa Villa	www.alrosavilla.com
Big Vin Records	www.bigvinrecords.com
Black Label Society	www.blacklabelsociety.com
	www.blacklabelsociety.net
Bob Tyrrell, Night Gallery	www.bobtyrrell.com
Brandy Campaign	www.bradycampaign.org
Columbus Dispatch	http://www.dispatch.com
Columbus Division of Fire	http://fire.ci.columbus.oh.us
Columbus Police Department	www.columbuspolice.org
Damageplan	www.damageplan.com
	www.damageplan.net
Dean Guitars	www.deanguitars.com
Franklin County Clerk of Courts	
www.franklincountyohio.gov/clerk	
Godsmack	http://www.godsmack.com
Guitar Digest	www.guitardigest.com
In Tune Guitar Picks	www.intunegp.com
Killology Research Group	www.killology.com
Marandi Productions	www.mirandiproductions.com
Mistress Juliya	www.juliya.net
National Instant Background Check	www.fbi.gov/hq/cjisd/nics.htm
Nick Catanese	www.nickcatanese.com
Pantera	www.pantera.com
Roadie Net	www.roadie.net
Rock Concert Photos	www.rockconcertfotos.com
The Rogues	www.therogues.com
The Scarborough Renaissance Festival	www.scarboroughrenfest.com
Scizophrenia.com	www.scizophrenia.com
Scottish Mayhem	www.scottishmayhem.com
Sinaria	www.sinaria.com
Smoke	www.smoketheband.com
Take 2 Productions	www.take2productionsinc.com
Trenam Kemker Lawfirm	www.trenam.com
UK Chapter, Black Label Society	www.uksdmfs.com.nr
Volume Dealer	http://www.volumedealer.net
Worthington Fire Department	http://wfd101.com/

Foreword By Officer James Niggemeyer

Wednesday, December 8, 2004, a day etched in the hearts of so many; a day that destroyed so many lives.

Albert Einstein said, "The world is a dangerous place to live; not because of the people who are evil, but because of the people who don't do anything about it." These words speak volumes about Erin Halk, Jeff Thompson, and Nathan Bray. Unarmed, yet undeterred, these men chose to make the world a less dangerous place to live. Without their courage and determination, I probably would never have had the opportunity to put an end to the tragic situation.

Many have called me a hero; others say I was just doing my job. The dictionary defines a hero as a person noted for feats of courage or nobility of purpose, especially one who has risked or sacrificed his or her life. All I know is that Erin Halk, Jeff Thompson, and Nathan Bray will be heroes to me forever. I just feel very fortunate to have been able to end the deadly rampage, without the hostage or anyone else being injured subsequently.

So many people became victims to the events that unfolded on December 8, 2004. A victim is a person who is harmed or made to suffer as the result of an act or circumstance. Jeff Thompson, Erin Halk, Nate Bray, Darrell Abbott, Chris Paluska, and John Brooks were victims. I am also a victim, as are the surviving band members, the police and rescue personnel, the witnesses in the crowd, the relatives of those involved, and all those who lost an idol. As a victim, I've been through the therapy, nightmares, medication, alcohol, and tears most other victims experienced. I just hope that, in time, all the victims will still be able to live life to the fullest.

The author of this book has interviewed victims who lost a loved one, victims involved in the tragedy, victims who were witnesses at the concert, and victims who lost an idol. The author has spent countless hours collecting and reviewing reports, videos, and anything related to the events that unfolded. His relentless pursuit of the truth is remarkable.

December 8, 2004 is a day we all wish we could change, a day we all wish we could forget, but it's a day that will live in our hearts forever.

- James Niggemeyer

Author's Introduction

December 9, 2004 was a cool but bright, sunny morning in Ohio as I made my daily journey from my home near Dayton to my office in Miamisburg. I had just left the village limits and was fiddling with the volume on my truck radio when I heard the newscaster say.... *"Guitarist Darrell Abbott and three other people were murdered last evening at the Alrosa Villa Nightclub in Columbus...."* My mind started to whirl. Did he mean Darrell Abbott, as in "Dimebag" Darrell Abbott? No way, it couldn't be possible... could it? I continuously changed radio frequencies seeking more news or clarification about the incident. It simply couldn't be true. Why would anyone harm Dimebag? When I got to my office I immediately logged onto my computer and went directly to Yahoo News. There it was.

"Ex-Pantera Guitarist Dimebag Darrell Abbott was murdered on-stage during a performance in Columbus, Ohio."

I sat back in my chair, my heart sinking as I tried to soak in the news. I owned the *Cowboys From Hell* album, but I'd never seen Pantera. I'd never met Darrell or ever heard of Damageplan. What I did know about the man was his fierce, fiery, "take-no-prisoners" metal guitar prowess. I also had heard he was a really great guy. I had heard how he would go out of his way to shake a hand, sign an autograph, or share a drink with someone who admired him or simply wanted to say hello. I'd seen his mischievous eyes and clearly personable "Dime" face on MTV, VH1, and on the heavy-metal show Uranium. His natural smile and scarlet-tipped beard pitched many guitar-related products within the pages of guitar magazines and publications. How could this musician, with his "Rock 'n' Roll All Night and Party Everyday" nickname, who lived for the stage and adored his fans, be intentionally gunned down during a gig?
It made no sense to me.

As the days passed, bits of the story were made public. It seemed the person responsible for taking Dimebag's life, and the lives of Nathan Bray, Jeffery Thompson, and Erin Halk had suffered from some sort of delusional mental affliction. Facts were scarce and rumors were rampant in the traditional media as well as the underground news/rumor mill of the metal music scene.

More time passed and I learned only snippets of information about the person responsible for the murders. I knew his name, his hometown, and the fact that he had been a U.S. Marine. I had also read that his mother had purchased the gun he used in the shooting. As for a motive, some speculated that perhaps Pantera's breakup had driven the killer over the edge.

While some people were uninterested in the killer's background I felt the urge to try to understand more about the man responsible for bringing so much misery to so many. I was skeptical about "Pantera's breakup" as the impetus behind the murders. It had to be deeper than that, and I simply felt too many pieces of this tragic story were missing. I wanted to know, if it was possible to find out, what made a person seemingly just go off the deep end? What would drive a person to callously and so publicly execute a fellow human being, especially one that he had apparently never met, yet supposedly had idolized at some point in his life?

Another specter of the murders haunted me. As a rock star, Darrell Abbott was *the* focus of the media, yet three other people were murdered too. Jeff Thompson, Erin Halk, and Nathan Bray died while trying to save lives or help others. Such heroism is the stuff of legends; it reminds us of the true humanity of man in the midst of gross, inhuman acts. I wanted to know more about these people. God knows they were loved, appreciated, and needed by others. I was amazed that their heroism and courage had been reduced to just afterthoughts and/or sidelined in so many news stories or accounts of the tragedy. Surely there had to be more to these men than the fact that they died tragically at the Alrosa Villa. I was determined that if their families and friends were open to my intrusions and questions, I would tell their stories.

From the beginning, I wanted to do justice to the memories of those who died at the Alrosa Villa. I had no illusions about the difficulties I would face as I ventured into this story. I am in humble awe of the support and encouragement of the victims' families and others integral to the tragic events that unfolded. They opened up their homes and their hearts to me. I've worked closely with them to ensure accuracy and an honest representation of the lives of their loved ones. I'm privileged to have the opportunity to share the stories of Erin Halk, Jeff Thompson, and Nathan Bray. My deepest regret is that my words barely scratch the surface of what made these men so remarkable and so loved.

From the start I knew there would be people who would question my motives and criticize my efforts. Sure enough, before I'd even written a word, I was accused of trying to profit from Dimebag's death. Initially, I tried to reply and "explain" but it soon proved useless. Sadly, while I have been working on the book over the months the intrusions have continued in the form of vicious e-mails, vile name calling, lies, and even threats from a few self-serving, agenda-driven zealots. Bear in mind, these are people I have never met; people who have never read a word of what I've written. Worse, perhaps, than their shallow pathetic words, is that this vocal minority have poisoned the opinions of a few people who have moving memories of the people involved, or insights into the tragic event itself. It's a shame their stories aren't included here and I hope that after this book is published they will recognize they were manipulated, and contact me after the fact. Perhaps I can include their memories in an updated edition one day.

I'm not a journalist; therefore, I'm not compelled to be objective. But this was precisely my goal as I wrote this book. I suspended any hint of preprogrammed bias and I've tried to let the facts and circumstances lead this story, without interjecting too much of my own opinion while describing what unfolded. I do offer some opinions, but they are based on careful analysis of the facts and evidence. If there are any inaccuracies, they are unintentional.

I am confident the interviews, analysis, reviews, and research I've done will clarify many issues and dispel some of the distortions of the past two years. I've done my best to write an accurate representation of the people and events involved. It is my hope that the words following this foreword will catch the attention of a parent, friend, or teacher of someone who is drifting aimlessly into the frightening abyss of mental instability. In addition, I hope the courage and heroism demonstrated by Jeffery Thompson, Nathan Bray, and Erin Halk will never be forgotten. It is the recognition of their inspirational sacrifice that merits contemplation and emulation. In both life and death, these great men left a powerful legacy of selflessness and love for their fellow man.

---Chris A.
---Dec. 22, 2006
chrisa@core.com

Chapter 1

Message in Blood

"It's a message in blood,
It's your cryptic warning
Within the message in blood
Marks the years of pain
And your godforsaken ending to life."

Message in Blood
Cowboys From Hell
-Pantera

December 8, 1980

Just after 10:30pm on a Monday, a black limousine pulls to a halt alongside the curb in front of the main entry gates of a castle-shaped high-rise known as "The Dakota" in New York City. The building's doorman quickly walks to the vehicle and opens the rear door. Yoko Ono smiles as she steps from the vehicle. Due to the chill of the evening, she heads briskly toward the building. She nods and acknowledges a few fans who, even at this late hour, wait in the hope of catching a glimpse of her and her famous husband.

A few steps behind her, former Beatle John Lennon heads toward the building, carrying several cassette tapes. As he approaches the apartment building, his gaze falls upon a chubby young man with glasses, standing with his hands in his pockets. Their eyes meet but the two men do not exchange words.

As the iconic Lennon strides past, the man suddenly addresses him, "Mr. Lennon?"

As the words leave his mouth, he simultaneously produces a .38 caliber revolver, drops into a combat crouch and aims directly at the man best known for music and peace. He quickly fires two shots. Both rounds strike Lennon in the back. Before Lennon's body has time to react to the searing projectiles, the shooter unleashes a trio of additional shots. One round goes astray, but the other two bullets strike flesh, inflicting more grave injuries. Police officers soon converge on the scene and bundle Lennon, now bleeding profusely, into a squad car. The musician is rushed to the trauma center of Roosevelt Hospital, only 13 blocks away, but despite exhaustive efforts to save him, the damage is too extensive; the blood loss is too extreme.

The man who has become a musical legend in his own lifetime—and who is known not only for his music but for extolling the virtues of love and peace—is gone, ruthlessly taken from the world in a senseless barrage of gunfire.

The news of the shocking murder spreads like wildfire around the globe. A dark pall of shock and grief envelops those who were touched by the man and his music.

December 8, 2004

Twenty-four years later, almost to the minute, a deranged gunman's mindless rampage would again shock millions, as he violently took the lives of a beloved guitarist and three brave men who tried to come to his aid. This time, the scene of the crime would be 500 miles away, in Columbus, Ohio.

Once again, the world faded to black.

Dime Time

Every opportunity I had to hang with Dime was a pleasure. He would always light up a room. He was always positive and was just simply a kick-ass guitar player. He will be forever missed. My Heart goes out to Vinnie, Keri F'n King, Zakk, and everyone who was close to him.

-Bert LeCato

President, In Tune Guitar Picks, Inc.

Bert LeCato with Dimebag. Photo courtesy of Bert LeCato.

Dimebag Darrell Abbott. Bogarts, Cincinnati, OH. April 4, 2004.
Photo courtesy of Amir Marandi - www.Marandiproductions.com

Chapter 2

Walk

"You can't be something you're not
Be yourself, by yourself
Stay away from me."

Walk
Vulgar Display of Power
-Pantera

Vine Street is located two blocks west of the University of Cincinnati. It is home to a seedy cluster of ethnic restaurants, guitar shops, music stores, sex shops, and a myriad of taverns. One tavern is even equipped with coin-operated washers and dryers for thirsty dorm-residing U.C. students who have run out of clean clothing.

Bogarts on Vine Street in Cincinnati, OH. Photo by Chris A.

It's also home to Bogarts, a rock-'n'-roll venue housed in a 19th-century brick building. Vacant during the day, the 1,500-person hall comes alive at night when heavy-metal bands and their head-banging fans journey to the Queen City. The facility is bare and basic. The stage is elevated about five feet above the main floor. In front of the stage is a waist-high steel fence that provides a three-foot buffer between the stage and the fans. Between that fence and the stage, venue security personnel and rock-'n'-roll photographers have room to monitor the crowd and work the show. Towering black columns of speakers flank each side of the stage and lighting racks crisscross the rafters above and in front of it. Black paint adorns the walls and ceilings, giving the interior a sinister, somber appearance appropriate for heavy metal. Most of the venue comprises an open floor for the general-admission audience. Behind the main floor, opposite the stage, is a slightly elevated area with a bar and a few tables and chairs. Above the rear bar area is a balcony.

Bogarts is a magnet for fans of hard-rock and heavy metal because it attracts new bands thirsting for opportunities to introduce their music. It also attracts older, established bands that still have the drive to perform for smaller audiences or whose popularity has waned. On April 4, 2004, the headline act fit nearly all of these variables.

Like a phoenix struggling to rise, the heavy-metal band *Damageplan* had been rekindled after the breakup of the 1990s heavy-metal icon *Pantera*, a wildly successful and popular speed-metal band. *Pantera* had been formed in 1982 by teenage guitarist "Diamond" Darrell Abbott[1] and his drum-playing brother, Vinnie Paul Abbott. The band's early releases were unremarkable, glam-rock albums that failed both musically and commercially. But in 1990, something clicked with the addition of Rex Brown on bass, and vocalist Phil Anselmo. The musical chemistry was there, but, more important, *Pantera* scrapped the glam-rock rubbish and replaced it with straightforward, hell-bent-for-leather, thrash metal.

Pantera's explosive success was detonated by the release of the album *Cowboys From Hell,* arguably one of the greatest metal albums ever pressed, The album showcased a frenzied guitar attack, concussive drums, pummeling bass, and brooding, dark vocals. Gone was the spandex, the poofy, teased hair, and glam regalia; replaced instead with camouflage pants, black T-shirts, tattoos, menacing lyrics, and a "screw-the-world" attitude. *Pantera* had found its real identity; more important, it had found an audience! With trend-setting heavy-metal bands such as Metallica becoming mainstream and "softening" their sound, *Pantera* unashamedly took up the banner of hard-core metal. Success followed. Before long, *Pantera* was being hailed as the "heir apparent" in the world of heavy-metal music.

In 1992 the band released the album *Vulgar Display of Power.* This work solidified the reputation of *Pantera* as the world's dominant metal band. For the next few years, the band continued to promote its albums and perform intense shows to millions of fans around the world.

In 1994, their next release, *Far Beyond Driven*, worked

---

[1] See Footnotes section starting on page 304.

its way to the top of the Billboard charts. There was no denying it, *Pantera* was the real deal and was setting the standard for aggressive, ass-kicking heavy metal. However, as nature demonstrates, what goes up must come down, especially in the music business. Even *Pantera* wasn't immune to the pressures of "popularity gravity" and commercialism.

Pantera: Phil Anselmo, Dimebag Darrell Abbott, Vinnie Paul Abbott and Rex Brown. Photo by Frank White Photography and Photo Agency (973)384-9133.

Their next release, in 1996, *The Great Southern Trendkill,* had fans scratching their heads. The music seemed detached and disjointed, with much of the trademark "honest" aggression seemingly fabricated. To some hardcore *Pantera* fans the record gave the impression that perhaps the band was trying too hard to top its earlier successes. The perplexing record sold poorly compared to earlier *Pantera* discs. Accompanying the commercial disappointment were disturbing allegations of heroin abuse by front man Anselmo. Divisive cracks were forming on many levels in *Pantera*'s foundation. Within the *Pantera* family, the Abbotts and Phil Anselmo were at war. Anselmo's behavior, a consuming ego, and self-destructive heroin addiction were destroying his relationship with friends and band mates. It was a recipe for disaster.

In 2000, despite the infighting and discomfort, the band attempted to pull it together and released *Reinventing the Steel*. It was a great improvement over *Trendkill*. The overall spontaneity and conviction of the record harkened back to the style and quality of earlier releases. With all the bickering in the press, *Reinventing the Steel* gave fans hope that *Pantera* was back on course.

Despite the new record, within the *Pantera* family there was palpable tension as Anselmo's relationship with the Abbotts continued to disintegrate. The brothers tried to cope with the situation but vocalist Anselmo continued to frustrate them. His erratic behavior, uncontrolled anger, and heroin-fueled outbursts, compounded by intense, chronic back problems seemed to push him over the edge.

Then, one day, it happened. Anselmo simply walked away from the band. He told Dimebag and Vinnie Paul he needed a break to focus on improving his health, and implied he would be back. Hoping the situation would improve, the Abbotts decided to give him time to detoxify, heal, and refocus. What they didn't know was that Anselmo had no intention of returning to *Pantera*. It was over. *Pantera* was history. Over time, *Pantera* fans and the Abbotts had to face the facts: *Pantera* had imploded. Hardcore fans and the Abbott brothers were shocked and disheartened. One of the most popular metal bands of the 1990s was gone.

While *Pantera* may have ceased, Dimebag Darrell never disappeared. He continued to be regarded as a pioneer of thrash and heavy-metal guitar. Recognized for his speedy, stellar playing, several instrument companies sought him out and offered him endorsement opportunities, including signature-model guitars.[2]

In 2003, Dimebag and Vinnie Paul felt the urge to return to what they loved, recording and performing. After two years sitting on the sidelines, the brothers decided it was time to break in Dimebag's home-recording studio. The new project required a vocalist and a bass player. They hooked up with Pat Lachman, a close friend of Dimebag. Lachman was working as a guitarist with Rob Halford, vocalist of *Judas Priest*, during one of Halford's solo projects. Eager to work with the Abbotts,

Lachman unstrapped his guitar in favor of the microphone. He became the vocalist and front man for the new endeavor. The lineup for their new band was completed when bass player Robert Kakaha, known as "Bobzilla" joined.

Damageplan. Right to left: Pat Lachman, Vinnie Paul Abbott, Bob "Bobzilla" Kakaha and Dimebag Darrell Abbott. Photo courtesy of Chad Lee - www.rockconcertfotos.com

The music was heavy, fast, aggressive, and gritty. Lachman's voice was dark and his growl added to the overall tone. The result was music similar, yet quite different, from the "good old days" of *Pantera*. Initially, Vinnie and Dimebag planned to change their direction, trying to avoid a "*Pantera*" sound. However, as the Abbott brothers eventually realized, when Vinnie and Dimebag played together it sounded like . . . well, Vinnie and Dimebag. The brothers remained true to themselves. Rather than turn their backs on their *Pantera* roots, the duo opted to embrace their musical heritage.

The new band was dubbed *Damageplan*. In February 2004, the band released *New Found Power* on the Elektra label. *New Found Power* didn't set any sales records but as former *Pantera* fans gave the disc a spin, many found it to be a good CD. The music clearly showed that Dime and Vinnie could still rock.

In support of *New Found Power, Damageplan* took to the road. They hooked up with metal bands such as *Hatebreed, System of a Down*, and several others for the 2004 MTV2 Headbangers Ball Tour. While the brothers were excited about taking their new band and music on the road, they quickly discovered the glory days of *Pantera* were well behind them. In its heyday, *Pantera* routinely sold out 10,000-seat arenas. While *Damageplan* performed at huge venues, these gigs typically occurred in large multi-band festivals. Even with the drawing power and name recognition Dimebag brought to the table, it didn't alter the fact that *Damageplan* was a new band with new music. It was back to square one for the ex-Cowboys From Hell. Instead of stadiums packed with tens of thousands of screaming fans, they now appeared at venues attended by a few hundred to a few thousand. It was a sobering experience, and starting over was tough for Dimebag and Vinnie Paul. On the other side of the coin, fans were thrilled to see the Abbott brothers and their new band live at a small venue! That's how it was for Tiffany and Roger Caron from Westerville, Ohio, who traveled to Bogarts that Sunday afternoon. Hardcore heavy-metal fans, they rarely missed the opportunity to attend a concert. They were especially excited about the chance to see *Damageplan*. They were positioned in the rear, elevated area in front of the bar. It was a good place to watch the show and meet band members. This area of Bogarts is where loyal crew members sell band merchandise. Many of the up-and-coming bands would trek to this part of the venue after their performances to meet fans, sign autographs, and help sell band-related merchandise. The night was a success for the Carons and many other fans. Members of *System of a Down* and *Hatebreed* actively socialized with fans after their performances.

The Carons were not the only ones to travel from the Columbus area to attend the concert. While they were excited and thrilled to have the opportunity to see *Damageplan*, one young man didn't share those feelings. Standing six feet, six inches tall and weighing over 250 pounds, a 24-year-old former Marine snaked his way through the standing-room-only throng of fans crowding the main floor. His immediate mission was to get as close to the stage as possible. His mind was consumed by anger and hostility, brought on by demons in his head. In his twisted thoughts, Dimebag and Vinnie Paul Abbott had betrayed him. For years he had suffered in virtual silence "knowing" what others couldn't fathom. He believed *Pantera*, and especially Darrell and Vinnie Paul Abbott, had abducted his thoughts, and used them as inspiration for *Pantera*'s lyrics. In his disturbed mind, he believed *Pantera* monitored his movements and activities and somehow read his mind. He believed the band spied on him, filmed him, and intercepted things he wrote or said to friends and relatives. For years, *Pantera* had stolen his innermost thoughts, yet they had never acknowledged him, thanked him, or given him the credit he deserved.

During this man's life, he had tried to tell others about the intrusion into his mind but was summarily dismissed and called "a nut job." He had no doubt he was as important to *Pantera* as Dimebag Darrell, perhaps even more so. After all, it was his life that had inspired the dark angst of the lyrics. The reality was that this brooding young man suffered from delusions, paranoia, and severe mental illness. The demons in his head had propelled him to Cincinnati. He would finally confront the Abbotts. Tonight he would deal with Dimebag and Vinnie Paul. He would make damn sure they knew exactly who was responsible for their past success.

As the hands of the clock passed midnight, the house lights were dimmed and the crowd roared its approval. Dimebag Darrell and his new band, *Damageplan*, launched an aural assault on Bogarts. Dimebag prowled the stage, tossing back his long dark hair as he provided the elemental "crunch" which made him a heavy-metal icon.

In the world of heavy metal, it's common to see a fan climb on stage and take a celebratory leap of faith; a "stage dive" into the crowd. Within 30 seconds of *Damageplan*'s opening number, the former Marine quickly scrambled between

Dimebag and Patrick Lachman breaking into the first tune of
the show at Bogarts, Cincinnati, OH. April 4, 2004. Photo
courtesy of Amir Marandi - www.Marandiproductions.com

a gap in the barrier. He stepped onto the side of a ladder lying
in the photo pit and climbed onto the Bogarts stage. Rock
photographer Amirali Marandi, stationed in the photo pit in
front of Dimebag Darrell, and Tiffany Caron in the audience
watched the intruder pull himself onto the stage. Both expected
him to turn and dive into the audience. Instead, the man ran
directly toward Dimebag Darrell Abbott, screaming inaudibly as
he advanced. For Tiffany Caron and Marandi, the situation was
taking a bizarre, sinister turn. The man wasn't about to stage
dive; nor was he a fan looking to touch his hero. The large man
heading directly for Dimebag had menace and hate in his
eyes.

Security personnel saw the sudden intrusion and swung
into action. Three security men intercepted the intruder, diving
upon him to prevent him from fulfilling his potentially violent
objective. Trying to escape, the man latched onto the set cart,
holding Bobzilla's amplifier rig. He held on tenaciously, refusing
to let go, as the security men tried to yank him from the stage.
In a last-ditch effort to escape their grasp, he grabbed a

lighting rack, and brought it crashing to the stage. The intruder's size, strength, and maniacal determination made him a formidable adversary. Security's attempt to stop him degraded into a fistfight on stage, with a pile of security men trying to pin the trespasser down. The band played on, watching the melee and shaking their heads in disbelief as the battle continued throughout the song. Eventually the man was subdued. As he was being dragged off stage, *Damageplan*'s front man, Pat Lachman, remarked, "Ladies and Gentleman, we'd like to introduce you to

Lachman, (foreground) and Bobzilla, watch as security personnel pounce on Nathan Gale. Bogarts, Cincinnati, OH. April 4, 2004. Photo courtesy of Amir Marandi - www.Marandiproductions.com

the fifth member of *Damageplan*." He paused and then quizzically added, "Who the f**k was that guy?"

As Lachman's words echoed through the venue, the intruder was dragged to the rear of the stage and ungraciously transported down the steep flight of stairs leading to the ground floor. He was then hustled out the rear stage door.

Once in the parking lot behind the venue, by all indications, a severe beating was dispensed as security personnel pummeled the trespasser who had resisted so fiercely.

Bogarts contacted the Cincinnati Police Department via 911 to report the incident. Dispatchers sent Officer Longworth to the scene of the disturbance where venue personnel identified the detained man as the cause of the problem. It didn't take long for Officer Longworth to determine that there was no shortage of witnesses, and that there seemed to be a case for charges relating to trespassing, endangering others, and inflicting criminal damage.

The rear stage door and loading dock area behind Bogarts, Cincinnati, OH. Photo by Chris A.

However, Officer Longworth had a problem. Neither *Damageplan* nor Bogarts were interested in pressing the charges necessary to arrest the man. Longworth took notes and later used them to complete an incident report. With no formal complainant on the scene willing to step up and press charges, Longworth had no choice but to release the suspect. The once-combative man was barred from re-entering the venue and told to hit the road.

Damageplan continued its show as the venue and band security members returned to normal duties. Officer Longworth pocketed his notes and climbed back into his patrol car to continue his shift. Later that morning, Longworth turned in his Cincinnati Police Incident Form. It provided cursory details of the incident, the potential charges, the role of the suspect, and the fact that he was unable to generate a formal complaint. The report was forwarded to the investigative unit for follow-up. Over the next few weeks, the Cincinnati Police Department tried to prosecute the intruder. To their credit, Cincinnati Police even contacted the Texas-based owners of the lighting rig damaged on stage. However, the result was the same. As with the band and the venue, The Gemini Lighting Company declined to press charges. It simply wasn't worth the trouble. On May 3, 2004, less than a month after the incident at Bogarts, the case was closed.

Cincinnati Police identified the intruder as 24-year-old Marysville, Ohio, resident, Nathan Miles Gale. On this night, he was fortunate to escape the punishment of the legal system. Instead, he licked his wounds from the beating meted out at Bogarts and strode into the darkness of the early spring morning.

For *Damageplan* it was back to business as usual. The next day they continued to rock on their tour and the incident at Bogarts was soon forgotten.

Unlike the rock stars and roadies from *Damageplan*, Gale would certainly not forget the humiliation and the beating he had endured.

Dime Time

When it comes to metal, *Pantera* was always my favorite band. Don't get me wrong, I love Metallica and Megadeth as well, but *Pantera*'s music was very honest and real to me. The first time I met Dime was in 2003. It was four years into my *Uranium* career and, with the exception of Ozzy Osbourne and Dimebag, I'd met everyone who was anyone in metal. As I walked up to his tour bus to do the interview, I was a mess. I mean, I'm a professional at interviewing bands, but Dimebag was one of my true idols. I hoped and dreamed that he wouldn't disappoint me. I mean, I had this vision of what he was like and I was thinking: "Please, please let this guy be everything I hoped he would be." As I got to the bus, Dime threw open the door and with a huge grin said: "C'mon in girl! We're not doing a damn thing, let's drink some booze and get f**ked up!" He had a tray with about 30 Black Tooth Grins already poured. He told me he watched my show and that he thought it was radical. I was nearly pissing my pants. I mean, Dimebag knew who I was. We drank a few shots and he introduced me to Rita and Vinnie. He personally showed me around his totally rock 'n' roll house, which was awesome. I've never met a guy who was so much fun to be around. He was a ball of joy, so positive, so happy. He reminded me of a 14-year-old metal obsessed kid in a rock star's body. His spirit was so infectious. I mean, Dime wanted everyone around him to be happy and content and he tried to fill everyone with joy. He was so much fun, so polite, and he really loved metal. He was amazing and way more than I could have ever hoped for. After that day, he never forgot me, and I was blessed to have had several other opportunities to hang out with him and to call him my friend.

I got into metal when I was 12 and it saved my life in so many ways. Where I lived, most people weren't into metal and they looked down on people like me as if we were freaks. Listening to bands like *Pantera* got me through the difficult days while I was growing up. They let me know I wasn't alone in what I enjoyed and in how I felt. Besides the music itself, what I love about metal is the respect and camaraderie metal fans share. Dimebag epitomized all that is good in metal, and I miss him with all my heart.

– Mistress Juliya

Right: Mistress Juliya. Television personality, heavy metal fan and a truly passionate spokesperson and proponent of all things metal. Photo by Chris A.
Below: Dimebag live in Chicago, IL. April 7, 2004. Photo courtesy of Chad Lee - www.rockconcertfotos.com

Chapter 3

I'm Broken

"The Early Life Of Nathan Gale"

"Look at me now. I'm broken."

I'm Broken
Far Beyond Driven
-Pantera

Seven years removed from the end of World War II, the Martino[1] family lived and worked in the gritty southside Chicago suburb of Roseland. It was one of the seventy seven official suburbs of the city, a growing community centered on 107th Street, with Lake Calumet just to the southeast. First settled in the 1840s by Dutch immigrants, the Roseland district sits on a slight plateau above other neighboring suburbs. In the 1930s, several gangsters and other violent criminals called the Roseland neighborhood home.

In the 1950s and 60s, the demographics of the community began to shift. Roseland's white Dutch immigrants began to abandon the urban neighborhood as black families moved in. The impetus for this "white flight" was a mixture of racism, ignorance, and fear of crime, racial chaos, and the building civil rights movement, all of which were used as scare tactics by real estate agents to entice middle-class white families to "invest" in new communities. Soon, families who had the means to relocate to the newly established suburbs moved out of Roseland. Those who didn't would find themselves in the minority as black families quickly accounted for more than 80 percent of the community.

The Martino family was one of those that did not have the financial means to leave Roseland—nor did they wish to. This was the neighborhood where Mary Martino was born in 1952. The youngest of seven children, Mary was the daughter of hard-working middle-class parents, proud people with a strong work ethic. Milo Martino was a cook—or to be more precise—a chef. While anyone could sling hash or fry up a burger, Milo was highly skilled at his craft. He often struggled to make ends meet, but his culinary abilities kept him employed. His wife Maryanne took care of the children and managed the household but would occasionally work outside the home to help bring in a few extra dollars.

For the Martinos, the racial makeup of the neighborhood wasn't an issue; the family was strongly focused on making enough money just to put food on the table. Despite the

---

[1] Chapter 3 footnotes begin on page 305.

economic boom in the United States following WWII, it was still difficult for a chef, even a good one, to make a decent living. To help make ends meet, Maryanne went to work at the same restaurant where her husband cooked, but the Martinos eventually decided to pursue the American Dream. Working for others was fine, but to get ahead—really ahead—they decided to start their own restaurant.

The couple scrimped and saved toward this goal until, through hard work and diligence, they were able to open a small family diner. However, times were changing rapidly and competition was heavy. It was the dawn of the fast-food industry, and the rivalry of these new eateries prevented the Martinos' restaurant from garnering any real success. Milo and Maryanne soon realized the business wasn't making headway and made the difficult decision to close the diner. It was a tough blow.

The Martinos transitioned back to being employed by others, eventually finding work at the restaurant inside Gately's Department Store. Gately's provided an element of stability and success, as Milo was quickly elevated from his cooking duties to manager of the entire kitchen staff. Maryanne also was successful, rising to hostess for the restaurant and manager of the dining area. During weekends and in the summer, when school was out of session, 10-year-old Mary would also help out at the restaurant. Besides lighting up the establishment with her smile and little-girl charm, she pitched in to help clear tables and wash dishes.

By the mid 1960s, the hippie culture was in full swing and the nation was divided by the conflict in Vietnam. Now a teenager and old enough to wait tables and do some of the short-order cooking, Mary began working part time at Gately's for pay. She worked hard at the eatery and dreamed of better days, dreams inspired by the real-life nightmares she observed in the rough-and-tumble neighborhood of Roseland. Mary saw first-hand the damage drugs can do to a community and quickly developed a disdain for illegal drugs and the problems they caused. She hoped to join a police department and help stamp out this growing public menace. But like that of her parents, Mary's dream was not meant to be.

In 1972, the Martino family saved enough money to move from Roseland to the southwest suburb of Calumet City, better known by its residents as Cal City or the "smiley city" because the city had painted bright yellow smiley faces on its water towers in 1970, spawning a "smiley" craze that took hold across the U.S. Living in Calumet City was a great improvement for the family. The new home was in a better neighborhood and provided the a better way of life.

Despite the move, the family continued to work in the old neighborhood at Gately's. Mary, now 20 years old, caught the eye of a young man at the department store's restaurant. He saw Mary several times a week during his lunch break and eventually built up the courage to talk to her. He was Gerald Gale, a 25-year-old salesman who worked in the auto parts business. Soon, he was showing up at the restaurant nearly every day, hoping to catch a glimpse or spend a few moments talking with Mary. Eventually, he asked her if she would like to join him for dinner and a night out on the town. Mary happily accepted his invitation, and the couple soon fell in love. Not long after, they were married.

Unfortunately, what Mary had hoped would be a blissful marriage became much less than that. She discovered that her husband was an alcoholic: He drank far too often and far too much. She often spent her evenings alone in the family's apartment, while Jerry was out with his friends drinking. Before the marriage was a year old, Mary was pregnant and, in 1974, gave birth to her first son, Charles. Two years later she had another son, Jonathan.[2] Mary wanted to remain at home and care for her children, but the economics of the household required that she continue to work. She found herself in the difficult position of having to balance childcare and work.

Over time, the couple's relationship deteriorated. Mary did her best to keep the family together for the sake of her children, while Jerry sank deeper into alcoholism. When he was drinking, Jerry's mood and behavior became erratic, and Mary had to watch her words carefully, as almost anything could set him off. The slightest misstep was followed by an explosive altercation and, often, physical abuse.

As the years slipped by, Mary focused on caring for her two boys and working hard while her husband, consumed by alcohol dependence, neglected his responsibilities. For years, Mary kept her silence and accepted Jerry's abuse. Eventually, however, she discovered that her husband had engaged in multiple affairs and, to make matters worse, that she was pregnant again. Jerry's infidelity was the final straw, and Mary realized that she couldn't take any more of his deceit and abuse. Despite being pregnant, she mustered up the courage to file for divorce. No longer would she placate the self-centered man who held her in enough contempt to see other women behind her back.

Mary's life had become extremely difficult, and trying to balance such heavy responsibilities was taking a heavy toll. Despite her disgust for Gerald's behavior, she was sad about the failed marriage but persevered in her determination to leave it. On September 11, 1979, one month after her divorce was final, Mary's third son was born. Nathan Miles Gale weighed a whopping 11 pounds, 11 ounces. The child was born with pneumonia but, after a week's stay in the hospital, he was released to his mother in good health.

As a courtesy, Mary contacted her ex-husband to tell him that his third son had been born. Jerry's reaction to the news left Mary incredulous. He refused to acknowledge that Nathan was his son, accused Mary of adultery, and made it very clear that he would have nothing to do with the child. For once, Gerald Gale held true to his word. Throughout Nathan's life, he rarely saw his father, although Gerald maintained relationships with his elder sons. While his father may have excluded Nathan from any affection, Mary was the opposite. She doted on, and genuinely loved her new little boy.

Nathan was a good-natured child. Like most children, he was bright-eyed, playful and full of life. Despite his bout with pneumonia, he was healthy and suffered no physical or psychological defects from the illness. As is often the case with young children, Nathan was restless and often resisted sleeping at times. He was slow in learning toilet training, but from a developmental standpoint, he appeared to be a completely normal child.

Still working at Gately's restaurant, Mary was fortunate that management didn't mind if she occasionally brought her sons to work with her. The three boys were well behaved, outgoing and playful with people they met. As challenging as life was for Mary, she shielded her boys from the difficulties of raising three kids on her own, so the boys were happy, well adjusted and extroverted. Nathan, in particular, seemed to be a happy little boy, often smiling and laughing as he followed his older brothers around the family home and the restaurant.

In 1980, Mary met John Clark, a long-haul truck driver. Like Mary, John was alone; his wife had been killed in a vehicle accident, leaving him to raise their five children. Mary and John felt a connection and eventually moved in together. For Nathan, having John in the home was a breath of fresh air. John truly liked the boy, and Nathan didn't mind sharing his love and affection with the man that was, in many ways, the father he had never had.

Although Mary believed she had found a responsible man with whom to share her life, she soon discovered otherwise. When John was driving, she may as well have been a single mother—but now with eight children to look after instead of only three. When John was on the road, Mary was frazzled and overworked. She was the disciplinarian and worked hard to instill a sense of right and wrong in the kids; when one of the children misbehaved, the punishment was either a spanking or banishment to a corner of a room.

In 1983, John and Mary relocated to the sleepy west-central Ohio town of Bellefontaine. Money was still tight, so Mary worked to bring more income into the household. She went to work as a school bus driver but the schedule was too rigorous with eight children to look after. She eventually became a volunteer dispatcher for the North Lewisburg Emergency Medical Technician Responders and worked as a baby sitter for additional income.

Even with the chaos of eight children sharing a residence, things were better in the small Ohio town. Nathan's behavior seemed typical and, as he got older, he showed no signs of childhood developmental problems such as bed-wetting, difficultly sleeping or persistent daydreaming.

However, he did have one physical condition that affected him tremendously. When he was three years old, Mary noticed Nathan was squinting. Concerned about his vision, she took him to an optometrist who discovered that Nathan's vision was exceptionally poor and recommended prescription glasses as thick as Coke-bottle bottoms to correct his vision.

In 1984, four-year-old Nathan began attending kindergarten. He was not a creative child and seemed uninterested in artistic or musical activities. In comparison to his older brothers, his cognitive development was considerably slower, but Mary reasoned that the disparity was because he started school early. He continued to struggle in kindergarten and had a great deal of difficulty completing the tasks and activities recognized as appropriate for a child in kindergarten. This was a trend that would continue throughout his schooling.

On several occasions, school officials, with Mary's consent and cooperation, tested Nathan for learning disabilities, but no abnormalities or traits indicative of a learning disorder were discovered. As a precaution and to give the boy time to develop further, Nathan was held back for a second year of kindergarten. Still, as he continued through elementary school, his academic performance was remained below average. Each grading period, Nathan would come home with his report card and sheepishly hand it to his mother. He knew his grades would disappoint her and, indeed, Nathan's poor grades continued to frustrate Mary.

When not in school, Nathan, like many boys in the 1980s, was attracted to the cartoon world of the Teenage Mutant Ninja Turtles. He displayed a keen interest in the shows, movies and commercials featuring the faux samurai-like turtles. It was also the dawn of the computer era, and Nathan and his brothers enjoyed playing with the video-game system of the day, Atari. The boys also enjoyed wrestling, baseball and football. Despite the fact that Nathan's brothers, Charles and Jonathan, were years older, they never excluded him from their games. While Nathan may have been the youngest, physically he was big for his age, especially through adolescence. He wanted to play basketball, but Mary's concern about knee injuries led her to persuade him not to play. Other than that, she encouraged Nathan to play, run and participate in athletics.

In 1985, after living together for many years, John and Mary married. Nathan Gale finally had a father, at least when John wasn't on the road. One of the benefits of John and Mary's marriage was that the children, including Nathan, were never left unsupervised. The family had grown close and everyone worked together to keep an eye on each other.

As a youngster, Nathan Gale showed no overt signs of hostility, depression or dementia. Certainly, he could have done better academically, but school apathy isn't unusual for children. At home, things were going pretty well.

In an effort to better herself financially, Mary pursued several career paths. In 1992, she became a real estate agent, but business was slow and she eventually gave up the effort. As money became tighter and tighter, John spent more time on the road to bring in more money. Sadly, the marriage began to crumble as Mary struggled with the challenges of adolescent children with John seldom around to help. She and John divorced and, once again, Mary and her children were alone.

In retrospect, the first 10 years of Nathan Gale's young life had many difficulties. His father rejected him, his performance in school was limited and his family often struggled financially. Despite the hard life, though, his mother did her utmost to keep the family together and provide for her children. She worked multiple jobs and tried to instill a sense of responsibility and an understanding of right and wrong in her boys. She did her best to help Nathan any way she could. Faced with these hardships but supported by his mother's efforts, Nathan seemed to be okay.

But things would soon start to unravel.

Dime Time

It was December 4, 2004. Damageplan was playing the Starland Ballroom in New Jersey, which is close to where I live. The place was packed, and everyone was having a really good time and many malt beverages were consumed. There was a point in the show where Dime was doing his solo, a moment burned into my memory forever. All the lights were out except for the spotlight on Dime. He started to play, and man, I got chills just hearing him. This was the first time I had ever seen Dime play live. Of course, I figured that there would be many more concerts to come. Sadly, I was wrong. Although I never got to meet the man, being a member of various Internet message boards afforded me the opportunity to come to know him through other fans. I got the news of Dime's passing a few days later while at work. The news hit me like a damned sledgehammer. My tribute bracelet never leaves my wrist. Dime lives on, eternally captured in the music he left us and in the memories of those close to him. He is truly missed.

– Tom Lykes, fan

Dimebag Darrell Abbott. Photo courtesy of Amir
Marandi - www.Marandiproductions.com

Chapter 4

Erin Halk: One of the Misfits

"Look to this day, for it is life. The very life of life. In its brief course lie all. The realities and verities of existence, the bliss of growth, the splendour of action, the glory of power -- for yesterday is but a dream, and tomorrow is only a vision, but today well lived, makes every yesterday a dream of happiness and every tomorrow a vision of hope. Look well, therefore, to this day."

"Twenty-Four Hours a Day"
-Kalidasa

Oh, dance in the dark of night,
Sing to the morning light.
The dark Lord rides in force tonight
And time will tell us all.

Battle of Evermore
-Led Zeppelin

Erin Halk, United States Marine. Photo courtesy of the Halk family.

"Erin... Erin Halk," bellowed the teacher as she called roll on the first day of school. A sixth-grade boy in a blue Oxford shirt sitting in the back row piped up, "Here," as he thrust his arm into the air. "Well, young man," replied the teacher, "it appears that we spelled your name wrong on the roster. It should be A-A-R-O-N, shouldn't it?" she queried. Annoyed, the young man sighed. His body language clearly showed his frustration with the question. Even at his young age, he'd heard this before. "Nope. My name is spelled E-R-I-N. It's the Irish way to spell it, just like 'Erin go Bragh,'" retorted the boy, comparing his name to the anglicized version of the Gaelic phrase meaning Ireland Forever. "Well, yes sir," laughed the teacher. "Erin with an E it is! And I won't make that mistake again."

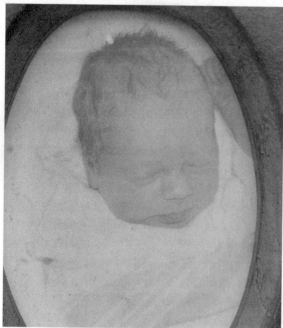

Erin Alexander Halk, born Sept. 17, 1975. Photo courtesy of the Halk family.

That Irish pride, worn so faithfully by the boy, had been imbedded in him since birth. Erin was born on September 17, 1975, the exact midpoint of the year from Saint Patrick's Day. For Margie Halk, her son's name reflected her strong belief in honoring her immigrant Irish heritage. Despite her realization that E-R-I-N was considered a girl's name, Margie threw caution to the wind. Her son would be Erin spelled with an E as a statement of pride in her Irish roots. She hoped that he would feel that "touch of the green" in his soul as well. Being a prudent woman, Margie selected a strong, masculine middle name of

"Alexander" to alleviate the potential confusion caused by the spelling of his first name. However, any concerns about taunts or teasing related to the spelling of the boy's name soon evaporated.

Erin was a mischievous toddler who discovered how to escape his crib late at night. Rather than sit in his room and occupy himself with toys, the young lad, with bottle in hand, would scale the walls of his crib and stealthily creep into the bedrooms of his older brothers and sister. Once inside, he would create late night chaos by assaulting his elder siblings with his bottle. He would bop them on the head and scurry away, giggling. The house would erupt in a chorus of abruptly awakened and very annoyed children, yelling for their mother to capture Erin and put him back to bed. From the beginning, the boy was a hellion.

Erin's brother Chris, the eldest of the brood was born in 1965. He was followed five years later by sister Danielle, and then brother Andy in 1972. Despite the difference in ages between Erin and his older siblings, he was always a central part of the

Erin and Andy Halk with a friend. Photo courtesy of the Halk family.

children's fun. In many respects, Erin was the glue that held the family together. Being the baby of the family, his older brothers and sisters not only kept an eye on him, they also made certain not to exclude him from activities simply because he was younger. When friction between the kids would rear its ugly head, Erin never seemed to be involved in those moments of sibling rivalry. He was a social little boy who interacted well with his big brothers and big

Erin Halk on his 4th birthday. Photo courtesy of the Halk family.

sister. Without a doubt, Erin loved his brothers and sister. He had an exceptional relationship with Chris, Danielle and Andy throughout his entire life.

Erin's relationship with his siblings was solidified by misfortune. When he was five, his mother and father separated and eventually divorced. The kids were clearly saddened by the breakup, but Margie did her best to limit the negative impact the divorce would have on the kids. Fortunately, the older children pitched in and helped with the younger ones to keep the household afloat as their mother and father dissolved their marriage.

Being the only daughter, Danielle found herself filling some of the voids created when Margie had to work or run errands. An astute child, Danielle had an excellent mentor in

Sitting on Santa's lap. Photo courtesy of the Halk family.

her mother. She had learned by example what worked and what didn't when it came to managing the Halk household. Thankfully for Danielle, youngsters Erin and Andy quickly adapted when she assumed the parental role. With little prompting, the boys would implicitly follow her directions. Danielle found great joy as their surrogate mom. She viewed Andy, and especially Erin, as her own children. She was the maternal big sister and worried about "her boys" constantly.

With the divorce final and the turmoil of the situation behind her, Margie tried to resume a normal home life for her kids. She felt compelled to reassure her children that she wouldn't remarry until all the children were grown. For Erin, the divorce of his parents was a difficult situation. Once his parents split up, his relationship with his father became limited. Immediately after the divorce, he visited frequently. Over time, however, they drifted apart as Erin's dad remarried and started a new family.

Erin, the sports fan, meets Notre Dame football coach Lou Holtz. Photo courtesy of the Halk family.

Margie worked at the local government office as clerk of council. After working all day, she would pile her brood into the "luxury liner," the family's battered Ford station wagon. Packed with an assortment of "stuff" and missing its rear window, the "luxury liner" transported the family everywhere.

Life as the youngest of four kids was a blast. Erin had a knack of acclimating himself to things older children enjoyed. Thanks to his grandmother, he learned to play checkers at an early age. He soon graduated to chess, becoming quite proficient at the strategic, cerebral game. He also discovered an affection for classic rock 'n' roll, courtesy of his older siblings who would spin their *Led Zeppelin* and *Beatles* records. Like many younger kids, Erin also was a source of amusement for his brothers and sisters. Constant heckling and good-natured pleas would eventually result in Erin lifting his shirt and bouncing his little belly as he performed the "Truffle Shuffle" to the delight of Andy, Danielle and Chris.

As he grew older, Erin fell in love with sports. He and his friends soon turned the Halk backyard into a baseball diamond. It was the "kid magnet" of the neighborhood. However, it didn't take long for the kids to outgrow the backyard. As they honed their skills, the windows and patio

How Do They Do That?

Brothers Erin (left) and Andy Halk took time out from a recent Northam Park softball game to entertain the spectators with a juggling act. Andy found that in addition to concentration, sticking out the tongue made the entire feat a little bit easier. (News photo by Denise Trainer)

1. Erin in his St. Agatha baseball uniform. 2. Andy and Erin make the local paper with their juggling skills. Courtesy of the Halk family.

doors of surrounding homes suffered. Eventually, Margie was forced to banish the boys to the local park.

As much as he liked his friends, Erin loved to hang out with his big brother, Andy. They were a team. Together, they would use their imaginations to create many interesting activities. They invented a card game based on baseball and created their own language, which they called "Chub-Box." The two boys introduced their friends to "Chub-Box" and soon a select group of friends could communicate in the confusing, strange dialect. Those not indoctrinated in the lexicon were left pondering the meaning of conversations held exclusively with the fabricated language.

While Erin excelled in sports and was socially adept, school was a different story. Just getting the boy up and ready for the ride to school each morning was a chore. Erin would procrastinate and linger in bed. "ERIN!" His mother beckoned with her sharp Boston accent slicing like a knife through the silence. "GET UP!" Her calls had little effect on the oblivious boy. Eventually, Margie taught the family dog, Bogie, to act as Erin's alarm clock. The dog would jump onto his bed and bark incessantly until Erin would finally succumb to the noise. He would slowly drag himself out of bed and begin his day. While getting up was difficult, Erin

discovered that school was tougher still. Through eighth grade, he attended Saint Agatha's, a Catholic school in Upper Arlington, Ohio. Margie felt the Catholic school's focus on family, discipline and structure was good for her kids. Erin seemed to disagree with Margie's intentions. With his propensity for hyperactivity, Erin quickly discovered that school bored him immensely. His mind often wandered. He had an incredibly difficult time concentrating and focusing on any material he considered boring. Erin found sitting at his desk all day was a frustrating chore. His pastime was watching the clock, wishing time would speed up and liberate him from the torture of the classroom.

From time to time, he would quarrel with some of his teachers, which didn't help. Erin, the free spirit with a rebellious soul, had a very clear definition of right and wrong. But his point of view occasionally clashed with his teachers' ideals. Unlike many who consult a teacher with their troubles, if Erin was being treated unreasonably or felt picked on, he always sought the solace and council of his brother, Andy.

1. Erin and his four-legged alarm clock, "Bogie." 2. Erin, with braces at age 11. Photo courtesy of the Halk family.

Erin could be a defiant youth. While he was occasionally influenced by his friends, usually his own beliefs guided his actions. In his own unique way, Erin analyzed things and acted accordingly. He based his decisions on his own sense of right and wrong. Once he established his belief, he was steadfast and often headstrong, sometimes to a fault. For his family, this stubbornness was a source of frustration. However, they understood that Erin was his own man. He could apply critical thinking to the variables of life. While some people might hem and haw over a topic or an issue, Erin did not. He was confident in his decisions and not afraid to act upon them.

As his middle school years slipped behind him, he moved from St. Agatha's to Upper Arlington High School, where he quickly made friends. As much as formal education seemed challenging for Erin, there was no doubt that he was smart. In high school he discovered a passion for reading. Erin loved to read and was often found with his nose stuck in a book. He enjoyed history and was captivated by a biography of John F. Kennedy. The Kennedy book inspired Erin. Soon, he was voraciously reading everything related to JFK that he could find. Like many people, he

1. Erin Halk at around age 14.
2. Erin with his earring! Photo courtesy of the Halk family.

was fascinated by Kennedy's assassination and the resulting conspiracy theories.

Conspiracy, and the "shadowy" connotation it holds, became part of Erin's psyche throughout his life. When things didn't quite go his way, or when he felt he was unable to control a situation, he would deflect the responsibility by saying, "It's a conspiracy."

Like many teenagers, Erin felt he was an outsider who didn't fit in with many of his classmates. Erin and his friends began to call themselves "The Misfits." The boys found common ground amongst each other. They weren't jocks, they weren't wealthy, but as the misfits, they managed to get along with everyone, regardless of status or clique. Erin and his friends tried to rise above those stereotypes. They did their own thing, never following others. Erin and his band of "misfits" lived a "Rock 'n' Roll High School" lifestyle, following the typical adolescent credo of looking and being cool. Erin often quoted a 1970 *Village Voice* interview with Jim Morrison, referring to himself as "a large mammal" just as Morrison did. In fact, Erin bore an uncanny resemblance to the poet turned rock vocalist.

Wearing dark sunglasses and a sly grin, Erin hangs out with his "misfit" buddies. Photo courtesy of the Halk family.

Erin's mother, Margie, admitted that she believed she was slow to pick up on some of his adolescent acts of rebellion. His high school years ushered in his first experiments with tobacco. He started smoking cigarettes in the ninth grade. That was followed by his first tattoo. Aided by one of his "misfit" buddies, Erin declared his admiration for *Led Zeppelin* with a homemade tattoo on his upper left arm. As one would expect from a hellion, he didn't seek his mother's permission. He tried to conceal the tattoo, hoping that she would never notice the crude marking on his arm. However, a trip to the hospital ER resulting in an emergency appendectomy exposed her son's secret. At first, Margie thought the marking was ink and spent several hours trying to scrub it off his arm. After the surgery, Erin came clean and told her that it was a real tattoo. Margie was far from impressed.

From an academic perspective, Erin's grades and performance in junior high school were unremarkable. His mother recalls hardly ever seeing him do any homework. Consequently, his grades were commonly in the "C" and "D" range. He was passing, but just barely. The fact that Erin wasn't performing to his full potential was a source of frustration for his mother. She would often challenge him on his performance. They would argue and he would retreat to his room where he defiantly blasted *Pink Floyd's Another Brick in the Wall (Part 2)*, "...we don't need no education," over his stereo. "Typical Erin," Margie would say. It was just another unspoken acknowledgment that his interests lay elsewhere. He would continue to squeak by throughout school.

While in freshman orientation, Erin met a young man named Brian Simakis. During breaks in the orientation program, the boys slipped away and hung out in the parking lot smoking cigarettes, shooting the breeze, and comparing notes on rock 'n' roll. Erin, a '60s hippie throwback, professed his devotion to the classic rock era. However, Brian was a hard core metal head. As they hung out after school, they began to share their musical tastes with each other. Erin turned Brian onto bands like *Jethro Tull*, *The Beatles* and *Jimi Hendrix*. Conversely, Brian indoctrinated Erin into the world of heavy metal, introducing him to bands like *Slayer*, *Metallica* and *Pantera*. With music as their bond, the two boys became fast friends.

Like many teenage boys projecting the rebel identity, Erin and Brian, with their long hair, cigarettes, occasional marijuana use, poor grades and smart-ass attitudes, found themselves constantly under the scrutiny of the school's staff. While they avoided serious infractions, school officials were on a first-name basis with the boys for violations ranging from smoking on school property to skipping classes. They were regulars in detention and even attended the rare Saturday "Breakfast Club." Throughout high school, the boys would hang out, ride bikes, goof off, and talk about the future.

Erin's ambitions and future goals changed like the blowing winds. One day, he was aspiring to work for the Sheriff's Department. The next day, he'd be researching and fantasizing about working in the world of rock 'n' roll. Erin constantly digested books about his favorite rock bands. He also enjoyed reading biographies about '60s generational icons like Abbey Hoffman and Timothy Leary. Anyone who knew Erin well agreed that he was born 15 years too late. He had an insatiable interest and appreciation of the 1960s and was fascinated by the people and music associated with the decade.

Erin's school days were punctuated by bouts of boredom, mischief and minor rebellion. But when not in school, he could be found working. He found a job at a local Italian restaurant called Ciao's where his sister Danielle worked. When Erin discovered another opening at the restaurant, he lobbied to get his friend Brian hired. Soon, the two boys were sharing time together at school and at work. His life in the world of the employed started at 14. His first job was washing dishes and bussing tables. Eventually, he worked his way onto the cooking staff. The work was unflattering and the pay minuscule, but Erin's work ethic was apparent and management clearly appreciated his drive.

Like many teenage boys, he used the modest income from his job to satisfy his music habit. Much of his pay was spent buying CDs and attending concerts. He also spent his money on girls, fast food and hanging out with the misfits. He and Brian worked at Ciao's throughout their four years of high school. With hard work, both became managers.

As he finished high school, Erin's family slowly began going their separate ways. Erin's eldest brother, Chris, moved out of the house and Andy soon followed. Danielle met a man named Eric Clark and after a long courtship, they married. After they married, the newlyweds scrimped and saved, eventually purchasing a house in Columbus, Ohio. Regarding his future, Erin made it pretty clear that college wasn't in the cards for him. There was no way he was going to subject himself to more school just for the sake of a piece of paper. Erin's ambitions were undefined. He was confident he was going to "go places" and "be somebody." Yet, he was unable to define his vision or the vehicle that would propel him to success.

A week after Erin's high school graduation, Margie met and fell in love with Sam Carvour. Eventually, they decided to spend the rest of their lives together. They made the decision to slip away from Columbus and head to Charleston, South Carolina, where a very private wedding ceremony was performed. Margie had reservations about their trip because her father was quite ill. With some trepidation, the couple headed off to Charleston with the blessings of Chris, Andy, Danielle and Erin. The kids were very pleased that their mother had found someone and was moving forward with her life. On August 24, 1996, Margie and Sam were married. Sadly, the joy of her new marriage was tempered when Margie's father passed away two days after the newlyweds returned.

Erin and his new stepfather Sam got along great. They shared a love and appreciation for music, in addition to the horror stories of Stephen King. Margie's marriage to Sam did cause some difficulties for Erin, though. Most notably, he had to find a new place to live. Margie was selling her home and moving into Sam's house. Eventually, Erin and his buddy Brian rented an apartment together near the campus of Ohio State University.

As 1996 ended, the owner of Ciao's suddenly passed away. The change in ownership forced Erin to find a new job. He quickly accomplished that when Danielle's husband, Eric, offered him work. Eric was the manager of the Cap City Diner, and the new job was a big help for Erin. He returned to working in a kitchen and was able to continue honing his cooking skills, something he discovered he really enjoyed.

For the next couple of years, Erin worked at Cap City. He enjoyed his job, but it wasn't really providing enough income. Erin was showing signs of complacency and his mother worried that her son was slipping into an unhealthy lifestyle. Margie decided to have a heart-to-heart talk with her son about his future. She wanted him to focus on a long-term goal or career. Even though he was working and out of her house, she was concerned that Erin's life was off course. He was starting to stagnate and began seeking solace in a bottle.

The situation came to a head after Erin was arrested for several drunk driving offenses. Shocked by his behavior, Margie felt it was time to give her boy a stern warning. She knew Erin had the potential to accomplish whatever he set his mind to, but he seemed satisfied to wallow in apathy. That was not acceptable to Margie. She told Erin that she was willing to help with tuition if he chose to go to college. She suggested that if he wasn't comfortable with her assistance, he should consider joining one of the armed forces and let them help. One thing was certain – Margie made it clear she was not going to tolerate Erin's self-defeating behavior.

Margie's pep talk was a success. The conversation inspired something deep inside Erin. A few weeks later, he announced he was enlisting in the U.S. Marine Corps. For Margie, the news was a mixed blessing. Her son had taken a huge step toward his own personal independence. She was confident that the discipline and regimentation of the military would be good for him.

Erin and his grandmother. Photo courtesy of the Halk family.

Erin prepared for basic training with help from his friend Brian. He memorized the Marine Corps' Hymn and read about the Corps' history. The day before he left for basic training, he strode into his mom's living room with one of his favorite possessions, his seven-disc *Led Zeppelin* CD set. "Hey Sam, would you hold onto this for me?" he said as he tossed the discs to his stepfather. Little did Sam realize that the simple gesture of friendship would later become a gift of tremendous sentimental value.

Erin entered the Marine Corps the day after Christmas 1998. He completed basic training at Parris Island, South Carolina, and was assigned to his first duty. Unlike most USMC enlisted personnel, Erin avoided the infantry. He was going to train to become a vehicle mechanic. His mother had urged him to learn a marketable trade and he was fortunate to find himself repairing vehicles for the betterment of the U.S. Marines.

One of Erin's ambitions was to travel and the Marine Corps did not disappoint him. His first duty assignment was unbelievable. He was assigned to Marine Corps Base Hawaii on the lush, tropical paradise of Kaneohe Bay. Erin was very proud to be a Marine and to be serving his country. The camaraderie and brotherhood of the military inspired him to add a couple "real" tattoos to his body. He also decided to cover up the crude "*Led Zeppelin*" tattoo with a stylized scorpion. In the movie "*Full Metal Jacket*," a character nicknamed Joker wore a peace sign button on his flak vest. On his helmet cover, he had written "*Born to Kill*," clearly contradicting the message of the button. In the movie, a Marine General asked Joker why he displayed two seemingly contrary messages. Joker responded that it "had something to do with the duality of man." The contradictory statements struck a chord with Erin. He decided to have a peace sign and the words "Born to Kill" tattooed on his left chest. He also had the initials "U.S.M.C." permanently inked onto his right bicep.

After years of small jobs with minimal responsibility, Erin had grown up. He was now contributing to his nation's security and traveling the world courtesy of Uncle Sam. During his tenure in Hawaii, Erin made Lance Corporal and was deployed to Australia and other countries in the Far East. He felt at home in the Marines and enjoyed his adventures. However, he foolishly found himself slipping back into his misfit ways.

In high school, Erin experimented with marijuana. For the free-spirited and insightful youngster, it was a vice that appealed to him. He

1. Erin Halk, United States Marine, graduation day, 1999.
2. Marine Private Erin Halk with his mother Margie and his father Jim Halk. Photo courtesy of the Halk family.

liked the mellow high he got from smoking pot. He dug the introspective and hallucinogenic state of mind it afforded. Marijuana also offered the added benefit of awakening the next day without the hangover typical from a night of heavy drinking.

Erin knew that drug use and military service were not compatible, so he initially stayed away from the drug. Unfortunately, in the late summer of 2001, one of his fellow Marines was apprehended by the military police for a drug charge. He subsequently implicated several of his comrades for alleged drug use. Erin was one of the young Marines identified. He was immediately called in by investigators and questioned. He was forced to take a drug test, which he failed. Erin knew he had made a monumental mistake. He was relieved from his normal duties. Instead of fixing military vehicles, he found himself mowing lawns and picking up trash on the base.

During the course of the drug investigation, terrorists attacked the United States on September 11, 2001. The attack that shocked America began the mobilization of the Marines for war in Afghanistan and Iraq. This deployment involved many of Erin's colleagues. Despite his strong desire to take an active role in this war, Erin's mistake forced him to sit idly on the sidelines and wait for his discharge. He was ashamed and felt he had let his family, friends and fellow Marines down. A few weeks later, he was given a general discharge from the Marines. For the young man so proud to serve his nation, it was a bitter blow. Reluctantly, he packed up his belongings, his uniforms, decorations and mementoes, and shipped them back to Columbus. Unfortunately, these items never made it home. Especially missed was his Homer Simpson chess set, a treasure that went everywhere with Erin.

Upon returning to Ohio, Erin's sadness was very evident to his family. While there were certainly times that he felt bored and uncertain, Erin genuinely enjoyed his stint in the Marines. Now, his life was back to square one due to his own misconduct.

At home on leave with his sister Danielle, 1999. Photo courtesy of the Halk family.

Often, those discharged from the military due to misconduct blame the service and deny personal accountability. But Erin never did. He never felt betrayed or slighted by the Marines. He knew his dismissal was his own fault. He also knew that once a Marine, always a Marine. While he wouldn't be deploying to Afghanistan or Iraq with his friends, he would not forget them.

In honor of his Marine brothers and sisters, Erin continually burned red, white and blue candles. It was his way

of reminding himself and others of the sacrifice and unselfishness of his friends who were now in the Middle East. His military family was never far from his mind. As an ex-Marine, he understood the danger and sacrifices his comrades were facing. In his own way he stayed true to the virtues of *Semper Fidelis.*[1]

With no immediate job prospects and nowhere else to stay, Erin turned to his surrogate mother, his older sister Danielle. For the first month, he did next-to-nothing as he pondered his poor judgment and battled bouts of depression. He wasn't prepared for the stark reality of his mistake. Once

1. Erin on his birthday, Sept. 17, 2003.
2. Chris Halk. Erin's eldest brother.
Photos courtesy of the Halk family.

again, he was unemployed and floundering and the repercussions were hitting him very hard. He kept to himself and seemed to be void of the sense of humor and mischievous spirit that had previously defined him. Danielle reminded her brother of his unlimited potential. Like his mother before, Danielle inspired Erin with a stern pep talk. "You made some poor decisions and you've paid a high price. But, it's time to get your act together and get back to life and work." After a few weeks, her words began to sink in and reignited his drive. Erin realized it was time to pull himself up by his own

---

[1] Chapter 4 footnotes begin on page 305.

bootstraps and get back in the game. He got the message. Danielle was not going to tolerate him loafing and feeling sorry for himself any longer. He started to integrate himself back into society. To Erin's credit, many of the traits he learned in the Marines stayed with him. Prior to joining the Marines, his appearance was often scruffy and unkempt. Now he was neat and tidy and had acquired a more responsible, focused attitude.

With Danielle's urging, he found a job working at a car wash within walking distance of Danielle's home. Soon after, he was working with Danielle at an upscale restaurant called Martini's. He had hoped to be a cook, but understood that he would have to "move up the food chain." Again, he started out as a bus boy and dishwasher with hopes of quickly moving up to cooking. The promotion never came. Realizing he wasn't getting anywhere, Erin grew weary of the restaurant job and set his sights on changing his life.

Erin had never really stopped thinking about working in the music industry. His high school buddy, Brian Simakis, was an audio engineer for Live Tech, a growing company in Columbus. More importantly for Erin, Brian was establishing a reputation as a solid sound guy in the local rock scene and might be able to help him.

Brian was running the mixing board for bands and working on various audio projects in studios and clubs. Erin admired Brian's drive to be a part of the rock 'n' roll world and made up his mind that he also wanted to work in music. His best chance to break in would be as a roadie. With a few pointers from his friend Brian, Erin began to hang around people in

Erin with his mother, Margie Carvour, at Christmas. Photo courtesy of the Halk family.

the Columbus music scene, talking with local roadies and looking for opportunities to learn the trade. With his Marine Corps discipline and passion for music, Erin worked hard to break into the business. Eventually, his drive paid off.

The life of a roadie is one of hard work, low pay, long hours and few accolades. One of the first venues that hired Erin was the Newport Music Hall on the Ohio State campus. The alternative heavy metal band *Godsmack* was the headlining artist for one of his first shows. After helping unload the band's gear, the new roadie took a break with one of *Godsmack's* full-time crew members. As they kicked back and shot the breeze, Erin produced a joint and fired it up to relax. As that culture dictates, he offered to share it. Soon both men were feeling the mellow results of "tuning up."

"What's your name, man?" queried the *Godsmack* roadie to Erin.

"I'm Erin, man," he replied, offering his hand.

"No," replied the *Godsmack* crew member, as he shook Erin's hand. "What's your nickname? If you're a roadie, you've got to have a nick."

Erin considered his question for a moment and replied that he didn't have one. With a laugh, his new friend said, "Man, I'm just going to call you "Stoney" since you've been cool enough to share some of your vegetation with me." From then on, while he remained Erin to his friends and family, in roadie circles he was "Stoney."

As a roadie helping set up equipment and prepare for concerts, Erin found his niche. He enjoyed the work and loved the lifestyle. His easy-going manner fit in with his peers. While not easily impressed with celebrity types, Erin admitted he dug the "cool factor" of working in music. Each gig brought its own challenges. However, Erin's military background had taught him how to adapt and overcome. Erin's reputation began to grow; he was becoming a damn good roadie.

He felt a great deal of satisfaction and pride in his new vocation. Erin no longer dreamed about being a part of the rock 'n' roll world; he was now living it full time. His life was falling into place. He

Opposite page: Professional roadie, Erin "Stoney" Halk. Above: The smile on his face says it all. As a roadie, Erin finally found his niche. Photo courtesy of the Halk family.

was working at most of the venues in the Columbus area, including the Germain Amphitheater and the Newport Music Hall. He also secured a regular spot as a loader for a small nightclub just off Interstate 71 called The Alrosa Villa.

One evening, while hanging out with his friends at a local bar, Erin was playing an exceptionally competitive game of pool. There he captured the attention of a young lady. Little did his competitor know that Erin was quite skilled in billiards.

Erin had learned the game from his "PaPa" and participated in countless matches in his grandfather's basement pool hall. Erin crushed his opponent and won the admiration and interest of Miss Patty Zink.

Erin was a people person. His friendly demeanor and quick smile disarmed all whom he met. However, when it came to women, Erin was very shy. This time was different. For Erin, his resounding victory was the opening he needed to confidently approach the girl. She quickly found this misfit's charm quite appealing. It was obvious to those who knew him that Erin had fallen hard for the pretty girl. In fact, during his last telephone conversation with his mother, Erin spoke about how he "won" Patti in a pool tournament. He said the two would often pray together, and he let his mom know that he planned to bring her along to the traditional family Christmas Eve dinner.

Around noon on Wednesday, December 8, 2004, Erin received a phone call from one of his fellow roadies. "Hey Erin," said the voice on the phone, "can you cover for me at a gig?" He had planned a quiet evening at home but decided to step up and help out his friend. "No problem, man," replied Erin. "What's the venue and who's playing?" His co-worker replied, "It's *Damageplan* at the Alrosa Villa." He hung up the phone and tossed on his Nike jacket to ward off the cold December chill as he departed for the Alrosa Villa. For Erin, it was just another gig. He had no inkling that his rock 'n' roll dream was about to become a deadly nightmare.

Erin's buddy and nephew, Ferris Clark holds a photo montage of his uncle containing assorted photos and "working credentials" for some of the concerts Erin worked at as a roadie. Photo by Chris A.

1. Erin with his nephew Ferris. 2. Erin Halk and his family.

1. Celebrating Nana's birthday, 1998. 2. "Almost" four generations of the Halk family. Sister Danielle was pregnant with Ferris in this picture. Photos courtesy of the Halk Family.

Dime Time

I first heard about Dimebag about a year after I started playing guitar. I was playing in a heavy metal band and didn't have much interest in increasing my skills on the guitar. Once I started listening to Dimebag's playing on *Pantera* albums, I was just blown away. I instantly felt inspired and wanted to improve my own chops. The rest is history. Dimebag created an entire class of guitar players, and music is the better for it.

– Evan Agee, fan

Dime touched me so much with his love of music that I have his guitar tattooed on my leg with CFH ("Cowboys From Hell") and Respect tattooed on my stomach. Every time I look in the mirror, I am reminded of Dime and his love of life. I traveled to Chicago for the benefit that was put on by *Disturbed, Anthrax, Drowning Pool,* and *Soil*. I wept as I heard chants for Dime over and over. It was the most amazing thing I've experienced and the most amazing show I have ever been to (I've been to a lot). Every time I do a shot of Crown, I always give Dime his pull first. I'd say he touched me a little. Getcha Pull!

– Tim Rabe, fan

Live in Milwaukee, WI. July 1, 2004. Photo courtesy of Chad Lee-www.rockconcertfotos.com

Chapter 5

Clash with Reality

*"Who's piss-poor excuse
is this for a world?
It swells my hatred
day by day."*

*Clash with Reality
Cowboys From Hell
-Pantera*

It was a quiet summer afternoon in 1991 when the phone rang. Mary Clark answered and the voice on the other end of the line asked, "Ma'am, are you the mother of Nathan Gale?"

"Yes, I'm his mother," Mary replied. "Is something wrong? Is he hurt?"

He had been caught shoplifting. Fortunately for Nathan, the store owner didn't contact the Bellefontaine police department but let him off with a stern warning. Mary went to the store, thanked the owner, and picked up her boy. That was the first time, to Mary Clark's knowledge, that Nathan had ever broken the law. Nathan's excuse for his offense was peer pressure: He told his mother that his brothers prodded him to steal the candy. Mary was angry about her son's behavior and made certain he understood that what he had done was theft and that he had been fortunate not to land in jail.

Less than a year later, when Nathan was in sixth grade, he was apprehended by store security as he tried to slip past the checkout at Fulmer's Grocery Store with seven large Hershey bars stashed inside his jacket. This time, the store owner called the police before he called Mary. With his mother present, Bellefontaine Police Sergeant S.L. Stout questioned Nathan, who admitted he'd been stealing candy from Fulmer's every day for a month. He had even gone so far as to cut a slit in the lining of his jacket to help him slip out of the store undetected.

Nathan was ordered to appear at the Logan County Juvenile Court on April 6, 1992, to face a charge of petty theft. At the hearing, Nathan and his mother said they understood their rights and the charges and waived their right to legal counsel. Nathan pled guilty to the charge of petty theft. His mother was embarrassed and saddened by her son's conduct and fully cooperated with the court. Prior to the sentencing, Mary discussed Nathan's unreported infractions with the judge and asked for help in getting her son back on a straight and narrow path. Taking all into consideration, the judge, Michael Brady, convicted Nathan of petty theft and placed him on indefinite probation. Along with the delinquent tag came some heavy requirements. The court ruled that:

-Nathan was to comply with all school rules and regulations and commit no act determined to be major misconduct.
-He was to undergo and cooperate with counseling provided by a local minister and comply with the recommended courses of treatment.
-He was ordered to comply with all rules and regulations placed upon him at home by his mother.
-He was to attain a minimum grade of "C" while on probation.
-He was not to commit any further theft offenses and not permitted to enter any stores without being accompanied by his mother.
-He was ordered to pay court costs of $43.

Mary hoped that her son's run-in with the law would scare him straight. Initially, things appeared to be headed in the right direction, as Nathan began to put more effort into improving his behavior as well as his studies. His grades improved and his teacher even noted on his report card that he had been more consistent and showed a positive attitude. However, it didn't last. A year later, in February 1993, Nathan violated the provisions of his probation when he committed an act of domestic violence.[1] The court immediately issued a warrant for his arrest. He was detained by the Logan County Sheriff's department and taken to the Joint Detention Facility in Marysville, OH, where he was incarcerated as a juvenile offender. Nathan was eventually released to his mother and his probation was extended. In October of the same year, Nathan, then 14, was arrested for a probation violation and was briefly returned to the Marysville juvenile facility.[2] However, the court quickly released the boy to his mother.

Mary Clark was concerned and confused as she tried to figure out what was leading her son astray. Fortunately, she wouldn't be alone for long in her struggle to address her son's behavioral issues. Her main ally would be Logan County Family Court Probation Officer, Marsha Bayliss. With over 20 years as an officer of the court, Bayliss had helped plenty of

---

[1] Chapter 5 footnotes begin on page 305.

juvenile offenders turn their lives around. She was a graduate of North Carolina State University, and one of five probation officers serving Logan County. At the time of her interview for this book she was responsible for managing 25 juvenile probation cases. Her love of children and her desire to contribute to their well being led her to a career as a probation officer. Bayliss was also influenced by a life-changing experience when one of her young daughters died of a heart ailment. She understood that grief and sadness could impact a person's behavior and attitude. Despite her own tragedy, she remained, as she put it, "a positive person who believes the glass is half full."

Marsha Bayliss, Logan County Family Court Probation Officer. Photo by Chris A.

When Marsha Bayliss first met Nathan Gale, she felt many of the boy's problems centered on his father's rejection and that he was a kid looking for an identity. He wasn't an athlete, he wasn't a scholar, and he didn't belong to any of the usual adolescent groups. He had tried to find ways into the cliques but was always met with rejection. In her estimation, Nathan was a big kid with an aggressive streak—not a tough guy or a bully, but "a big loaf, a big baby." Her initial plan was to steer the boy towards channeling his aggression and size to school athletics. Football seemed a natural choice since, at only 14, Nathan was over six feet tall and weighed 200 pounds. Bayliss hoped the sense of male bonding and the *esprit de corps* of a team environment would provide some focus for the aimless boy. However, his antisocial attitude, defiant demeanor and attention-getting, "me first" behavior made it apparent to Bayliss that Gale was going to be a tough case.

Near the end of Nathan's eight-grade year, Bayliss received a call from Nathan's school. The school had organized a "sign sheet" for all the departing students to sign. A copy would be given to each student as a reminder of his or her classmates. However, when Nathan stepped up to sign the form, instead of his name, he wrote "F**k You," something he said he thought would be funny. It landed him in juvenile detention for three days as a violation of his parole. According to Bayliss, this was a typical example of Nathan's attention-getting behavior.[3]

Nathan's unlawful behavior wasn't limited to the incidents in his juvenile court and probation records. According to Bayliss, the boy was often picked up for minor crimes for which no police report was made. She recalls an incident in which Gale's home was set on fire. He related to authorities that it was a cooking accident and no charges were filed, but Bayliss wasn't certain that was the truth.

In 1995, because of his prior theft convictions and probation status, the court elevated Nathan's theft of a $2.49 sticker from a local store to a class-four felony. Bayliss is convinced that Nathan stole for two reasons: first, to garner attention and second, because his mother never had a lot of money. His case review was set for June 1996, until which time he was allowed to remain at home. While awaiting his court date, however, Nathan continued to find trouble. In March 1996 he was arrested for smoking marijuana at school. This was a serious violation of his probation, and he was immediately transported back to the juvenile detention facility. In addition, the court ordered random drug testing and barred him from any contact with his accomplice. While incarcerated, Nathan was caught grinding up the drug Ritalin and snorting it. A smoker since the age of 12, Nathan had also experimented with marijuana when he was about 15 years old. With his propensity to be alone, Nathan didn't have many friends, so it is hard to blame peer pressure as the impetus for his drug use.

The courtroom at the Logan County Family Court. Photo by Chris A.

When Nathan's court date for the felony theft arrived, he pled guilty, and the court ordered that he be placed in the care of the Department of Youth Services for an indefinite period of no less than six months. More significantly, he was also sentenced to 30 days at the Juvenile Detention Center. However, once again, the court suspended both punishments with the caveat that he obey the mandates of the court and comply with his probation requirements.

For Marsha Bayliss, Nathan was an enigma whose behavior was extremely perplexing. The courts continued to be very lenient, yet he persisted in to defying them.[4] She worked the case hard, trying to get to the root of his behavioral problems. Bayliss got to know Nathan's family quite well. Mary Clark was a hard-working, single mother who, when she wasn't at work, was at home taking care of her children. It was obvious to Bayliss that Mary sacrificed a great deal for her kids. Bayliss was still convinced that Nathan's problems stemmed from his father's rejection, which caused him to push people away from him. To her credit, her relationship penetrated that wall, and she was probably closer to the boy than anyone, including his mother. He even talked with her about girls and the fact that he carried a condom with him "just in case." But Nathan didn't share everything with Bayliss; he had dark secrets buried inside him.

For years, when Nathan went to bed, the darkness brought with it eerie scenes. Beginning when he was in second grade, mysterious, floating, unrecognizable faces harassed him in the dark of night. Often, the visions were accompanied by harsh, demeaning, frightening voices. According to Nathan, these auditory aberrations directed their anger towards him. Always condescending and derogatory, they told him he was homosexual and compelled him to perform solo sex acts, although Nathan did not specify what they were. The voices also encouraged him to kill himself. Nathan shared his life with the tormenting voices until he was 16 or 17 years old.[5]

When he was about 15, Nathan became fascinated with the MTV animated series, *Beavis and Butthead*. These moronic characters could best be described as composites of 1990s teenage slackers. The two boys' lives revolved around TV, fantasies with "hot chicks" and banging their heads to heavy-metal music. The popularity of the crudely animated series wasn't based on spectacular graphics or deep plots but an elemental familiarity of the behavior of its central characters. The depths of their absurd juvenile behavior, coupled with stupidity, struck a chord with many young, white, heavy-metal-loving males, who saw a bit of themselves in the boys. In Nathan Gale's decaying mind, that familiarity went to an extreme level, and he often told his mother that the show was based on his own life—that, in fact, the creator of the show was spying on him and using his life as the basis of the cartoon. Because he couldn't comprehend that many people—not just him—shared similar traits with the animated metal-heads, as far as he was concerned, it was "his life" on display. He believed he was the inspiration for the show and even relayed his frustrations with the cartoon to a judge during a court hearing. He told the judge that he was the model for the show and that the concept was "stolen" from him. The judge relayed that if he were to continue talking such nonsense, he would be "put away." After that threat, Nathan never again mentioned *Beavis and Butthead* to anyone.

Despite the best intentions of Marsha Bayliss and his mother, Gale continued on his self-destructive course. He showed a complete lack of enthusiasm for anything, and both his mother and Bayliss described him as very lazy. During the winter months, while his brothers shoveled snow from neighboring driveways to make a few extra dollars, Nathan took his dope smoking to the next level and began experimenting with harder drugs.

His mother remembers the day she was called by the school office to pick up her son and take him home. When she arrived, she found Nathan acting weird. She concluded that he was high. Nathan was sitting in a chair outside the principal's office with his arm extended. In his hand he held a soft drink can and stared at it intensely. He seemed hypnotized by the can and didn't even acknowledge her when she entered the room. Apparently, several students and teachers had become concerned by Nathan's off-kilter behavior. He had told classmates that members of the heavy-metal band *Pantera* had just visited him at the school. Mary agreed with school officials that she should take Nathan home. On the drive home, his odd behavior continued.

"Did you notice how perfectly I held that can of Pepsi?" he inquired.

Mary ignored the strange question and asked him about his "visitors." Nathan insisted that he had just met with Dimebag, Vinnie, Phil and Rex from *Pantera*; in fact, they had come to the school specifically to see him. Mary off-handedly told him he was nuts and to stop deluding himself. His response was silence and, as he had done when challenged by the judge regarding his *Beavis and Butthead* contentions, he rarely mentioned *Pantera* to his mother again.

This was the point at which Nathan Gale's descent into mental instability began to manifest itself in public, as he was no longer keeping his voices and visions to himself. Nathan's initiation into *Pantera* came when he was about 16 years old when a friend introduced him to the band's second album, *Vulgar Display of Power*. He became completely obsessed with the album's dark sound and lyrics, including songs with menacing titles like "F**king Hostile," "Rise," "By Demons Be Driven," and "Mouth for War." He played the CD incessantly, burning the lyrics into his brain. He spent hours meditating on the meaning of the lyrics, trying to dissect the messages he believed the songs contained. Eventually, his dementia convinced him that he was the impetus and inspiration for *Pantera*, and he told his mother and several schoolmates that the band had stolen his lyrics and used them in their songs. In his mind, he wasn't given credit by the band for his contributions and that infuriated him. Gale's passion for *Pantera* was evolving into something more than admiration. He was starting to hate.[6]

His mother, his probation officer, his school counselors and the courts were trying to help him, but Nathan Gale cascaded deeper and deeper into the abyss of mental illness. He was using marijuana, cocaine, mushrooms, and LSD, and his drug abuse almost certainly added to his mental decline.

After nearly six years of hard work, Marsha Bayliss and the Franklin County Court were relieved of their responsibility to help Nathan. Earlier that year, Mary Clark and her son moved from Bellefountain to Marysville, Ohio. He was now under the jurisdiction of Union County. Unfortunately, nothing changed for the boy as a result of relocating. He remained lazy and uninterested in anything or anyone but himself. Just before his 18th birthday, He was arrested by the Marysville Police Department for trespassing because he had entered a secure area near an old K-Mart. Gale claimed he and his two companions were simply looking for a clean place to skateboard, but several witnesses said they observed the trio attempt to break into the abandoned store. Gale received a

In 1997 Gale and his mother moved to the small town of Marysville, OH. Photo by Chris A.

summons for the case and appeared in court. Available records seem to indicate that the punishment imposed was suspended.

Gale continued to reside at home with his mother. He struggled with sleep and wasn't interested in finding a job. He spent his days at home, sitting around, complaining, and playing video games. As 1997 came to a close, 18-year-old Nathan's behavior became darker and darker. Around Christmas, Mary Clark had her first frightening encounter with Nathan's auditory hallucinations. At approximately 2 am, she heard a noise in her living room and crept out of bed and down the hall to investigate. She peered into the living room and saw Nathan sitting on the sofa, his knees drawn up and his arms tightly wrapped around them. Seeing that he was very agitated, Mary slowly approached her son and asked him what was wrong.

"Be quiet, Mom. They are out there, and they are watching me," came his reply.

"Who's out there?" she asked.

"They are. They are after me, and they are taping me."

Mary became frightened. Cautiously, she moved to the front window to peek outside but Nathan warned her back.

"Mom, they'll see you," he cautioned, and urged her to stay away.

Mary's initial thought was that he was reacting to a nightmare, so she sat next to her son and held him close. She could feel him shaking and could sense his fear. Over the next 90 minutes, she tried to understand what was frightening him. She cradled him and assured him that no one was watching, taping or spying on them. Eventually, he calmed down and she ushered him off to bed. He never said who "*they*" were. Mary returned to her room physically exhausted and emotionally shaken by the experience. More than ever, she was convinced that Nathan was abusing drugs.

A few months later, Mary grew weary of Nathan's slacking and ambivalence toward work, and confronted him about his erratic behavior. Nathan erupted with uncontrolled rage and, in a flash, grabbed his mother and threw her against the wall with enough force to damage the drywall. For the first time in her life, Mary Clark realized that her son could easily kill her. However, Gale immediately knew that he had stepped over the line. He released his grip, backed up and stood quietly. Having promised herself that no man would ever abuse her again, Mary called the police. When they arrived, Gale was escorted away but was not arrested. Mary made it clear to her son that, until he cleaned up his behavior, he was not welcome at her home. Gale was banished.

Over the next 18 months, Gale remained essentially homeless. He occasionally sought out odd jobs for a few dollars, but mostly he lived on the streets. He drifted about the community with no friends, no goals, and no future. Nathan Gale, the young man so many people tried to help and guide, was a doper and a loser. He was arrested on several occasions for trespassing when he was found sleeping in public locations, including in the American Legion picnic shelter. He was also arrested for unauthorized use of a motor vehicle when he senselessly climbed into the driver's seat of a stranger's car while the owner was fueling.

Occasionally, Gale would call his mom or show up unannounced at her home or place of work to ask for money or food. His mom remembers finding her son sleeping on her back porch on many occasions. He wandered Ohio briefly but eventually returned to Bellefountain, where he stayed with some of his boyhood friends. Ultimately he moved back to Marysville. Details explaining what exactly Nathan Gale did over this lost period of 18 months are sketchy. However, his continued use of drugs and heavy narcotics, coupled with the challenges of surviving on the streets, likely contributed to further mental degradation. Gale had struck rock bottom and was completely alone.

In 2000, Gale reached out to his mother for help. He told her that he understood that he had made mistakes in his life and wanted to make amends. He was considering joining the military as a way to get his life on track and asked to move back in with her. Mary told him that he would have to subscribe to her rules and stipulations and made it clear that she wouldn't tolerate any physical violence or drug use. Any violations of those two requirements would mean his instant eviction and a call to the police. Gale agreed to abide by the rules and promised her he would turn over a new leaf.

Just a few days after Gale moved back home, Mary discovered a new quirk in her son. He would incessantly pace back and forth in the living room. She said it drove her crazy and she thought it was related to drug use or a withdrawal symptom. Mary talked him into attending drug counseling sessions at The Mill Center, a rehabilitation clinic in Marysville. He attended a few sessions but gradually stopped going. Briefly, he adopted a "Goth" appearance, dying his hair and painting his fingernails jet black.

Gale's return home provided him physical safety, but his mental health demons were certainly not silenced. He told his mother that he still heard voices and still believed that he was being watched and that his thoughts were being stolen. Mary Clark felt helpless as she watched her youngest son's life fall apart; her once happy, friendly boy had decayed into a dark, moody, troubled young man with no friends and no prospects.

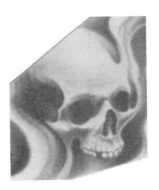

Skull drawing by Bob Tyrrell, done in pencil. Photo courtesy of Bob Tyrrell, Night Gallery - www.bobtyrrell.com

Dime Time

Dimebag Darrell tears it up in Madison, WI, July 24, 2004.
Photo courtesy of Chad Lee - www.rockconcertfotos.com

For Black Label Society's Nick *"Evil Twin"* Catanese, Dimebag Darrell Abbott wasn't simply an iconic guitarist whom he listened to in his younger days. For Nick, Dime was a friend and very important mentor who helped him acclimate to the surreal world of being a big-time rock 'n' roll guitarist.

Nick first met Dime around 2003 while on tour in Japan. The two men instantly bonded and Nick could hardly believe that he was swapping cell phone numbers with one of rock's most influential metal guitarists. As the friendship matured, whenever Black Label Society was in or around Texas, Dimebag could be counted on to show support. He liked to hang out with the crowd and would position himself directly in front of the stage. Dime would focus on his friend Nick as he traded licks with monster guitarist Zakk Wylde. Nick can remember looking down from the stage and seeing Dimebag shake his head in approval as the two Black Label guitarists tore it up. After the shows, Dime never failed to tell Nick how impressed he was with his chops. He was mesmerized by his ability to synchronize complex, blazing licks with the masterful Zakk Wylde. Dimebag's accolades filled the young guitarist with pride, but his compliments paled in comparison with the advice and counsel he shared with the up-and-coming guitarist. Dimebag loved his fans, he loved rock 'n' roll, and, unlike many "rock stars," Dimebag always managed to keep his ego in check. He realized that much of his success was due to his fans and he unselfishly shared his insight with Nick. "After they made Dimebag they broke the mold," says Catanese, a huge grin on his face as he recalls his friend. "Dimebag was a guy who loved life and loved to have fun. He cared about people and he wasn't hesitant to share his time, an autograph, or take a photo with a fan."

Nick "Evil Twin" Catanese and Dimebag Darrell. Photo courtesy of Nick Catanese.

　　Catanese remembers a phone call he received from Dimebag. "Hey Twin, what are you up to?" Dime asked.

　　"I'm playing some slots in Jersey," replied Nick.

　　"Are you up or down?" inquired his scarlet-bearded friend. With a sigh, Nick replied that he was down a couple hundred dollars.

With a laugh, Dimebag said, "Don't worry about it man, I've been down $35,000 before. Just live life and enjoy yourself."

That ability to make light of his own misfortune was vintage Dime. He loved to pump people up...even if it was at his own expense.

A few months before his death, Dimebag played a pivotal role in Catanese being offered an endorsement deal from Washburn guitars. The result was the Nick Catanese "Evil Twin" signature model guitar.

Nick Catanese live as Black Label Society plays at Ozzfest, 2006 in Columbus, OH. On the right side of his vest, under his arm is a patch commemorating his friend Dimebag. Around his neck he wears a razor blade pendant that Dime gave to him. Photo by Chris A.

"Hey brother," said Dime. "You deserve this, you earned it and I'm proud of you." That, according to Nick, was the essence of the man. He loved his family and friends, lived life with vigor and enthusiasm, and went out of his way to touch others both musically and personally. Dime's lessons clearly made their mark on the Pittsburgh native who, in very much the style of his friend, reaches out to his fans with sincere kindness. While Catanese mourns the loss of his friend, he still feels Dime's presence in his life, especially onstage when he plays the guitar.

– Interview with Nick Catanese by the author

Chapter 6

Nate Dogg

"And the memory remains."

Cemetery Gates
Cowboys From Hell
-Pantera

Dancing at the top of the key, with his long dreadlocks pulled back, the basketball player contemplated his attack on the goal. He flashed a confident toothy grin. His shoulders glistened with sweat in the warm Ohio sun. He effortlessly dribbled the ball, smoothly transitioning it from one hand to the other, always wary of the defense.

He'd been here before. He knew his opponent's weaknesses and how to exploit them. In a flash, he made his move. A quick step to the inside, then fool him with a spin to the left. Drive around him to the outside, then cut across the baseline.

With ease, he leaped into the air and scored. He swaggered backwards, taunting his opponent, a wide grin forming on his face. "Who's the man now?" he teased.

"Nate-Dogg, for a little dude you talk so much smack," remarked his friend, Johnny Poole.

"Well," Nate replied, "when you're good, you're good."

Indeed, Nathan Bray was good.

Born on February 8, 1981 in Circleville, Ohio, he had lived with his parents in southern Ohio until he was 9 years old. In 1990, his parents divorced. After the divorce, his mother re-located with Nathan and his older sister to Grove City. His father, Gene, opted to remain in Circleville.

As a child, Nathan was always active with his friends. He loved to play outside and displayed a great interest in athletics. When Mother Nature didn't cooperate, he would seek solace in his video games, but playing sports was his passion. He was a baseball pitcher who played Little League

Previous page: Nathan Bray and his son Anthony. Courtesy of Kerri Bray. 1. Nathan on his first birthday. 2. Nate Bray at around age two. 3. Nathan at age three. Photos courtesy of Gene Bray.

and, eventually, high-school ball. Despite his diminutive stature, Nate's competitive drive kept him pursuing his love and enjoyment of playing basketball. Nate wasn't bashful about his basketball skills. He always felt he was an outstanding player.

As much as he loved to play sports, it should come as no surprise that he was a passionate fan as well. When it came to college basketball, he loved the Duke Blue Devils. Professionally, Cincinnati was his town. He ardently supported the Reds and the Bengals. His passion for sports was nurtured by his Grandpa Strawser, who bestowed his love for the Reds upon Nate. Grandpa was a huge Pete Rose fan and would regale Nathan with stories of the Big Red Machine. All summer long, Nate and his grandfather could be found listening to Reds games on the radio. Grandpa Strawser didn't have cable TV but that didn't matter. They found it more fun to listen to the game and imagine the thrill together. Grandpa made sure both die-hard fans had their own "gameday" recliner. They listened to the game under the watchful eyes of Grandpa's prized 8 x 10 photo of Pete Rose. Nate loved Grandpa Strawser; in Nathan's eyes he was picture perfect.

Despite the divorce, Nate's father Gene always made an effort to spend time with him every other weekend. Nathan loved the opportunity to be with his dad. Nate thought his dad was cool with his biker lifestyle and penchant for black leather. Gene loved to ride, and he entertained his son with the glories of the open road. He also extolled the virtues of the Harley-Davidson motorcycle company. Despite Gene's limited interest in team sports, he instead

Nate in baseball uniforms.
Photos courtesy of Gene Bray.

Nathan Bray and his father Gene attend a motorcycle rally. Photo courtesy of Gene Bray.

shared his passion for motorcycles with Nathan and exposed him to golf.

On one occasion, Nate joined Gene on an alumni trip to his old school. There, his dad was talked into playing a full-court game of basketball. As his son watched in the stands, Gene was feeling the effects of trying to run up and down the hardwood. As he sat on the bench, Nate leaned over and whispered: "Dad, you suck at this!" With the gauntlet thrown down, Gene dragged himself back onto the court. Inspired by his son, he managed two quick scores, ending any doubt about his skills. Nate beamed a proud smile from the sidelines and he never said his dad sucked at basketball again.

Together, Nathan and his father took up golf. They would spend hours practicing putting and chipping skills. In time, both of them realized that this was one sport that neither was particularly skilled at. But for the highly competitive Nate, this was one game where victory didn't matter nearly as much as the companionship. Golf provided an excellent excuse for father and son to spend time together. They would visit the local driving range. Since both Nate and his father were left-handed, they would occasionally shop in search of a magic club, each time hoping the new "stick in the arsenal" would somehow enhance their incredibly average skills.

Nathan was also an avid sports card collector. As a boy, he spent almost every dollar he made at "*Home Run Hobbies*," a sports card shop on Broadway Street in Grove City. Over time, Nathan's collection grew into thousands of cards. He meticulously categorized and organized all of them. Identifying those with future earning potential was his goal. He could often be found flipping through a copy of "*Becketts*", the sports card valuation magazine.

Nate's sister was about five years older than he. After the divorce, there was often friction between the siblings. Nate's sister, who became a single mother in her mid-teens, was more apt to thumb her nose at authority. She would routinely butt heads with her divorced parents, while Nathan was the model child.

While his parents dealt with the turmoil caused by his sister, Nathan stayed focused on what his father continually reinforced as his priority — school. Nathan was constantly pushed to pursue and attain good grades. He apparently recognized the chaos his sister's behavior exerted on his parents' lives, and he made a conscious effort not to be a burden. He did his best to live by the rules. He didn't break curfew and always did his chores. While he may not have realized it, Nathan was a very responsible son.

As he grew older, his competitive drive didn't diminish. His one regret, and one that he could do little about, was his small frame. At 5'8" tall, and weighing in at 150 pounds, his size prevented him from making his high-school basketball team. Conversely, his burning desire and competitive drive, combined with his physical talents, often led to victory for Nate on the playgrounds. It also meant humiliation for the vanquished opponent.

"Nate Dogg" reveled in his triumphs and was recognized by friend and foe alike as a world-class "s**t - talker." If you lost to Nathan Bray you heard about it. He reveled in his victories and would recount his brilliance and domination for hours after the event. Whenever the opportunity presented itself, he had no conscience about slamming home the basketball with an "in your face" blast of pride as he kicked his opponent's ass. Nate was a

1. Nathan Bray absolutely loved basketball.
2. Confident, happy and ready to play ball! Photos courtesy of Gene Bray.

In addition to sports, Nathan, for a time, was a member of the U.S. Navy Junior ROTC program. Photo courtesy of Gene Bray.

scrappy competitor who refused to allow anything to limit or define him.

Throughout high school, Nate played baseball. And each year, despite the fact that his stature conspired against him, he made the team. Once, when he was a kid, he was accidentally struck in the face by a baseball bat. He lost several teeth, but it never dissuaded him from playing. His father remembered how Nate's Little League coaches said they wished everyone on the team played with the same heart and determination as his son did.

Another of Nate's passions was music. Nathan Bray absolutely loved to rock. His father was his first musical mentor. Gene, the Harley Dad, shared his classic rock heritage with Nathan. He was introduced to all things *Led Zeppelin, AC/DC, Steve Miller, Ozzy Osbourne* and *Black Sabbath*, among others. Nate wasn't interested in listening to some acoustic cat bemoaning some sad, mournful melody. He wanted to rock, he wanted to move. His greatest musical influence was yet to come. The life-changing event in Nathan's world of music came at age 13, when two friends took him to see *Pantera* in Columbus. He left the *Pantera* show in utter amazement at the power, volume and intensity of the show. He had been converted to the world of heavy metal. For Nate Dogg, no one rocked as hard as Dimebag Darrell Abbott and the boys from *Pantera*.

From then on, whenever *Pantera* was within driving distance, Nathan would make the journey. Over the years, he amassed an impressive array of "Dimebag" guitar picks — hard-won relics reserved for those fans brave enough to venture into the mosh pits in front of the stage. During the course of a show, Dimebag would flip dozens of picks into the audience. Several in Nathan's collection had sailed directly from the hand of his hero to his. Usually, scoring a "Dimebag-used" pick meant jumping into the mass of humanity and crawling on the floor of the arena. There, Nate would battle with dozens of other die-hards in hopes of snatching the thin piece of hard plastic off the concrete. It was worth the bruises to obtain a piece of Dime's gear.

In 1996, the 16-year-old high school student applied for a part-time job at a Dublin, Ohio company called "Inside Outfitters." Dennis Hoffer, the owner, was looking for someone to take care of the "grunt work" at his business. The position meant cleaning, taking out the trash and doing all the mundane chores that are absolutely essential to maintaining a good working environment. Nate applied for the job and was hired. He was assigned to work for long-time employee Bonnie Darby and given the opportunity to show his stuff.

At 16, Nathan Bray looked his age. He sported youthful whiskers on his chin and close-cropped hair, accentuating the fact that he was just a kid compared to the other employees. Not only did the job help Nate make some money, but it filled another void as well: A few years earlier Nate's father had moved to Florida. Nate missed his dad a great deal and hoped he would one day return to Ohio. In the interim, he found a good male role model in Hoffer, who took an interest in Nate and served as a mentor for his young charge.

Nate was determined not to let his age hold him back. He relied on his guiding principle: *"Do the right thing."* His innate grasp of responsibility translated into a keen work ethic. Both his supervisor, Ms. Darby, and employer, Mr. Hoffer, recognized his ability and drive. For the remainder of his high school years, Nathan Bray would spend his summers as an employee of Inside Outfitters. His hard work was recognized and in just three years, he moved from pushing a broom to becoming a lead installer of the company's window treatment products.

Unlike many students working part time, Nathan Bray didn't spend his hard-earned money frivolously. He had a very clear, focused plan and purpose for the money — a Chevrolet Cavalier. He paid cash for the vehicle and was exceptionally proud of the fact that he didn't have any car payments.

In 2000 Nate graduated from high school. Around the same time, he was thrilled to discover that his father was moving back to the Columbus area. Father and son resumed their relationship as if they had never been apart. Encouraged by both Hoffer and his father, Nathan made the decision to continue his education. In September of 2000, he entered Ohio University in Athens as a freshman. Many of his classes were skewed to his appreciation of history, with his focus gravitating toward ancient Asian cultures — most notably, the Ming Dynasty. As with his appreciation for motorcycles, Nathan's love for history and nature was something passed on by his father Gene, who was intrigued by the mysteries of American Indians. In addition to history, Nathan was very adept at mathematics. He often tutored classmates when they needed assistance. Inspired by his tutoring, Nathan decided to explore teaching. His goal was to teach high school or college level history.

When Nate had started working at Inside Outfitters, he decided to let his hair grow. By the time he started at Ohio University, he was sporting dreadlocks and a beard. In November of 2000, Nate was kicking back at a dormitory party when he caught the eye of a young lady. Miss Kerri Vuotto was immediately drawn to the cute hippy boy. With his dreadlocks and laid-back attitude, she figured he'd be a "rad" person to hang out with. The outgoing Kerri coyly approached Nathan, who was somewhat distracted. Ironically, he was hitting on Kerri's friend Betsy. Kerri wasn't to be dissuaded. Her innate beauty and charm quickly muscled Betsy out of the picture.

Kerri's hippy boy seemed a bit shy and reserved, but she found him quite interesting. She knew that she liked him and hoped the feeling was mutual. For Kerri, the evening couldn't last long enough. She was perfectly content to sit around talking to her new friend. But eventually Nate had to go home. He had a sociology test the next morning and wanted to make certain he got some sleep before the exam. Reluctantly, the pair parted ways. Soon after, the holiday break started. Kerri and Nate went their separate ways.

During the holiday break, neither Nate nor Kerri gave much thought to the other. However, as the vacation drew to a close, they both began looking forward to seeing each other again. In January of 2001, they ran into each other in the dorm. Enjoying each other's company, they started dating and soon became inseparable.

Kerri soon discovered that her "cute hippy boy" was really a hard-core, head-banging heavy metal aficionado. Nate of course made it a priority to introduce Kerri to the world of metal. In the summer of 2001, he talked her into joining him for "Ozzfest" in Columbus, where *Marilyn Manson* and *Black Sabbath* were headlining. The uninitiated classic rock girl wore a patchwork skirt to the show. She stuck out like a sore thumb in the throng of black leather, spikes, t-shirts and biker apparel, but she had a great time. Sensing her enjoyment, Nate introduced her to his favorite metal band, *Pantera*. Initially skeptical, Kerri discovered that she enjoyed most of their music, noting it wasn't just "noise" as she had anticipated. Of course, for Nathan, music and attending concerts wasn't simply a pastime — it was a passion.

In December 2001, Kerri had her first taste of Nathan's devotion to *Pantera*. Learning the band would be playing a concert at Hara Arena in Dayton, he instantly scored tickets. Soon he and several friends found themselves driving through a blizzard to attend the show. They parked the Cavalier and headed to the doors. At the door, Nathan discovered that he didn't have his ticket. In a panic he called Kerri to see if he had left it at home. She assured him he had not. Then she encouraged him to calm down and retrace his steps back to his car. Nate obeyed the composed directions of his girlfriend and slowly hiked through the snow. He meticulously scanned the snow-covered parking lot as he made his way back to his car. As he arrived at his Chevy, Nate was about to give up — but then, just below the door, he saw the corner of his ticket protruding from the snow. With his heart rate back to a reasonable rhythm, he quickly made his way back to the arena and joined with his friends. They enjoyed a night of head banging and partying with their favorite metal band. As always, *Pantera* rocked! Nathan left the show with a renewed devotion to the band, and was extremely grateful for the guidance Kerri had given him.

Kerri and Nathan relax on Christmas, 2002. Photo courtesy of Kerri Bray.

For Kerri and Nathan, it was a glorious time to be in love. The town of Athens and the campus of Ohio University beckoned with a variety of activities and places to visit. Kerri and Nate loved to hike the paths and walk the streets of the town. They enjoyed visiting local attractions, such as Old Man's Cave, and after-dinner musical shows and rock concerts. Typical of college towns, Athens was filled with a myriad of recreational opportunities and events. A favorite activity among students at OU was to hike to the peak of "Bong Hill." It afforded hikers an incredible view of Athens and the campus. Students would gather and enjoy bonfires in the warm summer evenings. After pounding back a few cold ones, they'd stagger back to the dorm when exhaustion overtook them.

For the next two years, Kerri and Nate were rarely apart at school. When you found one, you knew the other was near by. During the breaks in the school year, Nathan would return to Dublin and resume his job at Inside Outfitters.

In December, 2001, their lives changed. Kerri discovered that she was pregnant. She called Nathan with the news and also made it very clear to Nate that she wasn't about to tell her parents without him at her side.

A few moments after hanging up, Nathan telephoned Dennis Hoffer and explained his situation. His years of service, coupled with his consistent work ethic, paid off. Hoffer offered him an immediate full-time position with an excellent salary, plus benefits. To Hoffer, it was like watching one of his children come home. He'd seen Nathan work in his company as a minor, graduate high school, attend college — and now return home to Inside Outfitters as a permanent part of the company.

Nathan's decision to leave college wasn't an issue of weighing priorities. It was simply a matter of responsibility. He wanted to continue his education, but it would have to wait. He was confident he could finish college down the road. At this moment, he needed a job. He was about to have a family and he was going take care of them. Nathan vowed that Dennis Hoffer would never regret his decision to hire him as a full-time employee. He adapted well to the position and soon his

1. Kerri and Nathan unwrapping Christmas presents. 2. A pregnant Kerri and "her" Nathan. Photos courtesy of Kerri Bray.

outstanding skills made him a very important cog in the wheel that was Inside Outfitters.

His last step into manhood was the hardest. Nathan, with some gentle prodding by Mr. Hoffer, understood that his appearance could impact his credibility when dealing with high-value customers. While his long hair may have looked great in

Confident and very capable, Inside Outfitters ace installer, Nathan Bray admires the New York City skyline. Fall, 2004. Photo courtesy of Kerri Bray.

school, he accepted the fact that he now needed a more refined professional appearance. His long locks, which took years to grow, quickly fell to the barber's shears for the sake of his family and his job.

Nate was a team player and a responsible family man. Bonnie Darby always knew that when a difficult task needed to be a c c o m p l i s h e d — especially if heights were involved — Nathan could handle the situation. The only problem they ever e n c o u n t e r e d was Nathan's age. When he arrived for some out-of-state installation jobs, he discovered that he was too young to rent a car. The minimum age was 25 and Nathan was just 22. The same situation popped up with heavy equipment. Again, Nathan's age prevented him from renting the equipment, so the company would send out one of its older employees. However, once that nuisance was out of the way, Nathan would operate the equipment and knock out the job. Nathan loved working for Inside Outfitters and seemed content to work there as long as Dennis would have him. Not only was he able to support his family, but as a bonus, he was also seeing the country. On installation trips, he traveled to New York, Chicago and Seattle, among other places.

For Kerri, introducing Nate to her parents was somewhat tense. She was bringing home this scrawny headbanger and had to break the news: "*By the way, I'm pregnant and he's the father of my baby.*" However, Nathan's charm and smile quickly won over her parents. Tony and Anne Voutto instantly liked the boy. It also didn't take long for Nate and Tony to delve deeply into their shared passion, college basketball.

A recurring tra-dition developed when Kerri's father and Nate would hang out. Nathan's adoration of the Duke Blue Devils required him to torment Tony, the Kentucky Wildcats fan. The commentary always seemed to gravitate toward the famous Christian Laettner miracle shot from the 1992 Duke vs.

Kerri and Nate spend an evening with Kerri's parents Anne and Tony Vuotto and Nate's father and step-mother Gene & Theresa Bray. Photo courtesy of Kerri Bray.

Kentucky NCAA East Regional Final. Laettner's turn-around jumper put the seemingly defeated Blue Devils in the Final Four and paved the way for a second consecutive national title. Nathan's glee over Kentucky's failures had never abated since. Throughout the long college basketball season, Nathan would revel in the opportunity to telephone Kerri's dad simply to taunt him when the "Cats" lost a game. Throughout his life, Nathan's devotion to his two favorite teams never waned: he loved Duke…and whoever was playing Kentucky.

Sports were a huge part of Nathan's relationship with the man who would one day be his father-in-law. While good-natured adversarial taunts held center stage during the basketball season, Nate and Tony became allies with the dawning of each new baseball and football season. Both men shared a love and devotion to Cincinnati's Reds and Bengals.

During her pregnancy, Kerri would routinely fret and worry about the future. Yet, Nathan remained confident. He was optimistic and looked forward to his role as a parent and a husband. He finally mustered up the courage to ask Kerri if she would be his wife. She instantly agreed. As the birth of their child drew near, the young couple would sit and talk while Nathan helped Kerri relax by rubbing her swollen belly. Jokingly, Nathan would fantasize that one day his child would be the place-kicker of his beloved Bengals, remarking that kickers rarely get hurt and can have long, fruitful careers. Nate and Kerri hadn't really discussed baby names in detail, but Nathan did have a plan in the event his "son" turned out to be a daughter; Nathan was adamant that his daughter's name would be Morgan Louise Bray. Of course it wasn't a coincidence that her initials would be the same as Major League Baseball.

The power of sports and its lure was never more apparent than during the birth of Nathan's first child. Kerri, suffering the pain of labor in the delivery room, was relegated to "annoyance status" while Nate and her father watched a meaningless scrimmage between the Bengals and the Pittsburgh Steelers.

Three generations of the Bray family. Grandfather Gene, father Nathan and newborn Anthony Bray. August, 2002. Photo courtesy of Gene Bray.

Later that evening, August 9, 2002, Nathan and Kerri became parents when Anthony Bray was born. Kerri's father congratulated his daughter with a kiss and a bouquet of flowers. Like most men, Nathan was thrilled to have a son. His dream of being the father of an NFL kicker was alive and well. Kerri's father presented Nate with a congratulatory pair of Bengals tickets.

Two months later, on October 26, 2002, Kerri and Nathan were married. Their wedding took place in Kerri's parents' home. A family friend, who was a judge, officiated the ceremony. The joyous day was tempered, as the bride and groom suffered from the flu. Despite its uncomfortable effects, Kerri and Nate mustered up the strength to finish the ceremony. They then slipped away for a solitary evening in Cincinnati to celebrate the start of their new lives as husband and wife.

Life had certainly changed for the two former students. They relocated from the liberal world of Athens and moved to Columbus. Nathan worked for Inside Outfitters and Kerri worked part time at a day care center and took care of Anthony.

As most young couples discover, sharing one's life with someone isn't always easy. When she was frustrated with Nathan, Kerri would telephone her parents to vent her displeasure and relay what was pestering her. Tony would

1. Nathan and Kerri at their wedding, Oct. 26, 2002. 2. The Bray Family. Photos courtesy of Kerri Bray.

usually side with Nathan, reminding her how fortunate she was to have such a responsible young man in her life.

Nathan acclimated quickly to the role of father. He took charge and did his best to manage the household. He took a couple of weeks off from work after the baby was born and threw himself into holding down the household as Kerri recovered. He washed clothing, did dishes, changed diapers and fed the baby, all the while keeping a grin on his face.

He enjoyed his role as a father very much. Kerri was amazed that she never once had to ask for his help. With Nathan doing very well at Inside Outfitters, Kerri was able to quit her job and become a stay-at-home mom. Even with his wife home full time, Nathan never shunned his chores. Despite coming home from work exhausted, he recognized that Kerri needed a break from watching Anthony.

1. Nate and Anthony. 2. Nate was a very involved father who loved to spend time with his son. Photos courtesy of Kerri Bray.

Nighttime was daddy time. Nathan would spend a lot of time with his son. He would take his son for walks, watch TV with him, or take him shopping. Nate wanted to be deeply involved in Anthony's life. He often voiced his excitement of one day being a Little League coach. He was going to teach his son all the important aspects of sportsmanship, hoping that Anthony shared his competitive drive.

In March 2004, Kerri desired a new challenge. She proved herself a capable mother, but staying at home wasn't her thing. She talked it over with Nathan and together they agreed that she could return to work. She found a suitable day care professional to care for Anthony and quickly landed a position working for a local legal firm.

It appeared that the Bray family was doing well. Kerri and Nate were working, Anthony was healthy and the financial situation had never been better. However, there were tribulations and difficulties. Kerri and Nathan were exhausted physically, mentally and emotionally. The changes had taken their toll.

The young couple began arguing about petty issues. They had second thoughts about the marriage and were overwhelmed and confused. Eventually, they decided to take a break from each other. Nathan made arrangements to move in with his friends, Jason and Josh Jewett, while Kerri would stay in the apartment with Anthony. They felt that time apart would give them the opportunity to reflect and realize what they had together.

Even with the "separation," Kerri and Nathan were rarely apart.

1. Nathan teaching Anthony not to color on the walls.
2. Nate and Anthony. Photos courtesy of Kerri Bray.

Neither made a decision without consulting the other. Kerri's parents were dumbfounded by the separation decision and were quite vocal in their objections. They felt the opportunities for reconciliation were limited if Kerri and Nathan lived apart.

While others found Kerri and Nathan's decision foolish, the time apart was proving to be an opportunity for the couple to mature. The separation caused Nate and Kerri to open their eyes to their special relationship. They rediscovered their love

Nathan introduces his boy to the joy of riding! Photo Kerri Bray .

Grandfather Gene Bray gives Anthony a taste of a real Hog! Photo courtesy of Gene Bray .

for each other. They rekindled their friendship, something that had been lost in the confusion of the past.

During their free time, Nathan and Kerri would get together to talk and spend time with Anthony. The reality was that Kerri and Nathan's separation was a waste of time and money. Despite sleeping apart, they spent all their free time together. To all who knew them, it was just a matter of time before the two "kids" would reunite.

In November 2004, Nathan discovered that *Damageplan*, led by his hero Dimebag Darrell, would be playing at the Alrosa Villa in Columbus. He couldn't believe that his metal hero would be playing such a small venue. For just $8.00 per ticket, he had to go. He dragged himself out of bed early and headed to the Kroger store on Springtown Road to be first in line for tickets. He purchased two, one for him and one for his friend Jason Jewett. The week prior to the concert, Nathan arranged to slip away from work at three o'clock on the day of the show. He told everyone about the concert and fervently hoped that he would meet and hang out with Dimebag Darrell.   Around 6:30 that evening, Kerri received a call from Nathan just before he headed out to the Alrosa

Villa. "Hey baby!!!" he screamed into the phone, as Jason whooped and yelled in the background.

"Nathan, tell Jason to shut up! I can't hear you," replied Kerri, grinning as she heard the excitement in her husband's voice.

"Tonight is the night Kerri! Tonight I'm going to meet Dimebag!" He continued to tell Kerri of his plan to hang out at the rear of the club in hopes of meeting Dime.

Kerri had a huge smile on her face as she spoke with Nathan. She loved it when his emotions ran wild. It was clear that he was thrilled that he would have a chance to meet his guitar hero. "Well, you be careful tonight, and call me if you need a ride," said Kerri.

"I will," he replied. "I love you baby. Give Anthony a kiss for me."

Nathan hung the phone up and headed for the Alrosa Villa. Kerri placed the phone receiver back in its cradle and looked forward to a quiet night addressing Christmas cards while watching television. She had no way of knowing that she had just heard Nathan's voice for the last time.

Nathan and Anthony with Gene's Harley-Davidson. Photo by Gene Bray.

Nathan and Anthony. Baby's first Christmas, 2002. Photo courtesy of Kerri Bray.

Dime Time

It must have been in 1996 that I had the pleasure of meeting and spending some time with heavy metal's most bad-ass guitarist. I grew up in Columbus, Ohio, when the metal scene ruled the world. Bands like *Judas Priest, Iron Maiden,* and *Black Sabbath* crushed any other bands. Right out of high school, I was caught up in the metal world. In 1984, I moved to California and found a job working at the Shoreline Amphitheater built by rock promoter Bill Graham. It was absolutely the coolest job I ever had. One of the great perks of the job was that I had access to almost any show at any Bill Graham venue. In the early 1990s, when *Pantera* was just starting to break, I found myself on the guest list for the San Francisco "War of the Gargantuans" featuring *Pantera* and *White Zombie.* It would be the first time I would get to meet and hang out with Dimebag. I remember, years later, hanging out with the band on the East Coast. Things were pretty ugly between everyone at the end, but Dime and Vinnie still took time to visit. I just can't speak highly enough of those two. Brother Dime, you are missed greatly. Thanks for rocking us over the years and for sharing your wisdom.

– Brian Fielder, friend of Dime

See images of Brian and Dime on pages 200 and 201.

Above: Dimebag in Milwaukee, WI. July 1, 2004. Photo courtesy of Chad Lee - www.rockconcertfotos.com

Chapter 7

Psycho Holiday

"Now I'm far from home Spending time alone
It's time to set my demons free
Been put to the test
My mind laid to rest I'm on a psycho holiday."

Psycho Holiday
Cowboys From Hell
-Pantera

It had been a year since Nathan Gale moved back in with his mother and things appeared to be improving. He still had occasional encounters with the police but they were primarily just for traffic infractions. He had also been attending a trade school, learning automobile engine repair.

He rarely spoke anymore about the voices in his head and he no longer burdened his mother with his thoughts, ideations and fears.

On the morning of his twenty-second birthday, Gale awoke early and flipped on the television just in time to see United Airlines Flight 175 slam into the South Tower of the World Trade Center. September 11 was Nathan's birthday but it would be overshadowed by the events of the mammoth terrorist attack on the United States. As far as the attack itself was concerned, Gale knew exactly who was responsible. While the United States government pointed the finger of responsibility at the international terrorist group Al Qaeda, Gale knew that rock star Marilyn Manson had been the true mastermind of the attack. Although he never explained or articulated what would have motivated Marilyn Manson to attack the United States, according to the voices in Gale's head, Manson brainwashed the Al Qaeda operatives, causing them to hijack the airliners that fateful day. Several people who knew Gale, indicated that he had expressed a desire to kill Marilyn Manson.[1]

Over the next two months, Gale intently followed the U.S. response to the terrorist attacks on America. He watched, fascinated, as Special Forces and U.S. Airborne units entered the Islamic country of Afghanistan. Inspired by the media's coverage of the growing Middle East confrontation, he decided to enlist in the U.S. military.

He approached his mother and told her of his decision to enlist in the United States Marine Corps. She reacted as any parent would, torn by his decision. She was concerned about her son entering the armed forces. After all, the country was at war. However, she believed that this was a huge step in

---

[1] Chapter 7 footnotes begin on page 306.

Nathan's maturation. She ultimately embraced his decision and fully supported his enlistment.

In December 2001 and January 2002, Gale met with a recruiter and applied to become a United States Marine. One of the basics of applying for membership in the U.S. armed forces is the completion of a background and security information questionnaire, Department of Defense Form 1966, Record of Military Processing. Information the potential recruit provides on the application is reviewed and used to determine initial suitability for entering the military. The application poses basic questions related to drug use, prior military service and education. It seemed almost certain that Gale would be rejected based on his past drug use. However, he simply lied on the application. A specific drug question on the DD Form 1966 asks: Have you ever tried or used or possessed any narcotic (to include heroin or cocaine), depressants (to include Quaaludes), stimulant, hallucinogen (to include LSD or PCP), or cannabis (to include marijuana or hashish or any other mind-altering substance)? Gale, who would later state he had used nearly all the drugs listed, simply answered "no" to the question. Recruit applications are rarely scoured for disqualifying information. In 2001, the Defense Security Service was carrying a backlog of more than 500,000 military and civilian background investigations. Nathan Gale's squeaky-clean, falsified application was promptly approved.

On February 12, 2002, Marine Recruit Nathan Miles Gale was alone and intimidated. He was now at the U.S. Marine Corps Recruit Base, Parris Island, South Carolina. The moment he and his fellow recruits stepped off the bus, they were ordered to stand at attention on yellow combat-boot prints painted on the asphalt surface. Grim-faced drill instructors shouted commands at the stunned recruits and welcomed them to the island. It was 3 am.

Six days after entering boot camp, Gale sent his first letter to his mother. He wrote of attending a group meeting for recruits on the history of the Marine Corps. Below is a direct quote, including improper punctuation, spelling and grammar, from an undated letter Gale sent to his mother from Marine Corps basic training:

"All of Echo company, 6 platoons its about 500 people. And every body is screaming like a pep rally. Its pretty gruesome too see that many shaved heads hitting them selves chanting "Ready To Kill, Ready to Die, But Never Will."

He also laments in his letter that he has not heard from her, saying:

"It would be kind of nice to hear from you, it's kind of sad to see everyone get letters but me."

In basic training, Gale's plan was to lay low, but his plan proved difficult. On several occasions, he found himself in trouble with the drill sergeants and his fellow Marine recruits. He became the butt of jokes, as his appearance and demeanor led to him being compared to the fictional character known as "Gomer Pyle;" a slow witted, overweight, lazy and mentally unstable Marine recruit from the movie "Full Metal Jacket."[2] As frustrating as that may have been to Gale, he began his next letter to his mother with what sounded like good news:

"I'm the new guide in the platoon. I'm marching in the front row and a lot of other things. Because of it I wear a pager and carry out the orders of the drill instructors. I make sure that everybody's in line and ready. Most of them here have no respect. I hate this platoon most of them curse me out and the rest tell me to shut up. I'm getting the same treatment I did when I was on the street. I thought this was the place for people like me."

Nathan begins his letter as if he is bragging about being the new guide. Traditionally, the guide in a platoon is the tallest person and has nothing to do with merit or marching skill.

Once again, it appeared that Gale's inability to fit in was raising its head. However, while he might have been razzed a bit, overall, Gale's time at Parris Island and U.S. Marine Corp recruit training wasn't remarkably different from most recruits. But Gale did require more time than average to graduate from basic training. Because of his poor physical condition, he failed the Individual Strength Test (I.S.T.). His progress ground to a halt when he was removed from his original platoon and placed in a platoon devoted to physical fitness and weight loss. This fitness-oriented platoon, called the "Fat Farm" by the recruits, was designed to help recruits meet the minimum physical standards required to become Marines. Being shipped out to the "Fat Farm" might have also been in Nathan's best interests. His letters home indicated that his relationship with his original platoon-mates had continued to degrade.

"Dear Mom, I'm having lots of problems with the other recruits. They keep cursing at me and threatening me. I got yelled at last night for marching to a song while on fire watch. He was pretty pissed off and threw my flash light and a bottle of mouth wash across the bathroom. He keeps threatening to me that he's gonna murder me and kick my ass. I don't know if he's gonna punch me or not. He make me kind of nervous. I think he would if I couldn't kick his ass write back soon. Love Nate"

It isn't clear in this letter if Gale was talking about a voice or apparition in his head, or if he was referring to an actual person. Although the letter begins by sighting other recruits, his use of the word "he" instead of using a person's name gives the impression that perhaps the "he" is the voice or the vision in Gale's twisted mind.

When Gale wrote home about his transition to the Fat Farm, he sounded almost optimistic and upbeat. His letter spoke of how he "fled" his original platoon to "join" the Fat Farm. He lauded the attention of the drill instructors and stated that Drill Sergeant Kim was "cool." He also spoke of how the Fat Farm's drill instructors had eased up on him:

"I think they are backing off me and this is helping me out more than yelling. The drill instructor Sgt Mikinsin was a real inspiration. I think they like me because of my willingness to learn."

He continued the letter, saying:

"I have a hard time paying attention and there helping me with that. I wonder how much time I have before it all comes down on me but I think I can't suk no further."

Over time, he was able to slim down and show improvement in the physical tests. In a letter to his mom, he wrote:

"We are watching "Heartbreak Ridge" on T.V. for a lot of the guys in the platoon who passed the I.S.T. I was one of them. I went from 29 sit-ups to 46, I need 44. I was so scared that I would fail and be stuck here."

Passing his I.S.T. was crucial in departing the "Fat Farm" and rejoining a training platoon. Gale could now get back on track and complete basic training. On Day 27 of training, he wrote to his mom about new skills he was learning:

"I'm on the rifle range, we hiked 5 miles to get here, the chow is a lot nicer and we are getting more free time."

Gale had completed roughly a third of basic training and was focused on learning essential tasks, including rifle commands, marching, saluting and self-defense. Eventually, Gale completed Marine Corps basic training and was deemed qualified to wear the distinctive "Eagle, Globe and Anchor" insignia so beloved by those who become U.S. Marines. Gale had faced his greatest challenge and had survived the high-energy, high-stress, seventy-odd "training days" that make up the twelve weeks at Parris Island. It seemed that Nathan Gale had turned a corner in his life. He was no longer lost, no longer a loner. He was now a Marine.

Unlike the vast majority of Marines who would be trained as combat infantrymen, Gale, with his technical degree in automobile maintenance, qualified for training as a motor-pool mechanic. Instead of carrying a rifle and learning the intricacies of the Marine warrior, Gale would repair and maintain Marine Corps vehicles as an Organizational Automotive Mechanic.[3] His first assignment was with the 2nd Marine Division at Camp Lejune, S.C., to receive his training. He would then stay at the base as a member of the unit. With his first real job, money and formal training, the armed forces of the United States was giving Private Nathan Gale every opportunity to succeed.

In Marysville, his mother was both proud and relieved. Her youngest son had finally escaped his misguided ways and was contributing to society. Now gainfully employed, Nathan purchased a cell phone and, instead of writing letters home, he telephoned. Mother and son spoke often. By all indications, he seemed to have found his niche and was doing well. In fact, Gale's performance in the Marines was satisfactory. His military personnel records indicate that his service was typical, and that he didn't go out of his way to seek trouble. Like many young men away from home with money in their pockets, he spent most of it on several vices: alcohol, cigarettes and strippers. He also purchased a television and a video-game console. According to his mom, his favorite game was "Grand Theft Auto."

In early November, 2002, Gale phoned his mom, announcing that he was taking several weeks leave, around Christmas, and would be in Marysville in early December. Mary was thrilled to have the chance to see her young man. She swelled with pride, knowing her troublesome boy had grown up and was on the right course. With her son scheduled to visit for Christmas, Mary decided to reward his maturity and demonstrate her pride in his achievements. Since Gale had joined the military, he had expressed an interest in purchasing a handgun. Mary decided that this holiday would be the perfect opportunity to surprise her son. His weapon of choice was the Beretta M9, a 9mm pistol that was the official sidearm of the U.S. armed forces.

With that information, Mary visited a local gun shop, Scott's Sporting Goods, in search of a handgun. At the shop, she was informed that the Beretta M9 was the military version of the Beretta 92F. The shop had a nickel-plated Beretta 92F in stock. Mary decided to purchase it for her son. She inquired about the purchase procedure and was informed that she could not buy the gun for someone else, not even her son. She could pay for the firearm but would not be allowed to simply "give it as a gift." Federal law required the owner of a handgun to complete a Department of the Treasury Firearms Transaction Form. Mary paid for the gun and waited for her son to return home on leave.

In early December, 2002, Gale arrived home. He was in the best physical shape of his life, and demonstrated a maturity Mary had never before seen. Unable to hide her excitement, she broke the news about his Christmas gift two weeks early. Nathan was thrilled and, on December 9, 2002, he drove to the store to complete the required documentation to pick up the gun.

Before Gale could walk out of the store with the weapon, he had to complete ATF Form 4473, Firearms Transfer Record, and be approved via an instant background check. As he had done with his military entry documents less than a year prior, he lied on the form. Under the section entitled "Certification of Transferee," Question C asked: "*Have you been convicted in any court of a felony, or any other crime, for which the judge could have imprisoned you for more than one year, even if you received a shorter sentence, including probation?*" Gale answered "no." The next area where Gale showed clear deception was on Question E: *Are you an unlawful user of, or addicted to marijuana, or any depressant, stimulant, or narcotic drug, or any other controlled substance?* Gale again answered "no."

Beretta 92F, serial number BER319253. The weapon Nathan Gale would use to commit his horrific crime. Columbus Police Department, evidence photo.

After Gale completed the form, Joe Glick, who was working the sales counter, called the authorities, in compliance with the NICS or National Instant Criminal Background Check System.[4] The NICS is a national system that checks available records on persons who may be disqualified from receiving firearms. The FBI developed the system through a cooperative effort with the Bureau of Alcohol, Tobacco, Firearms and Explosives (ATF) and local and state law enforcement agencies. The NICS is a computerized background-check system designed to respond within 30 seconds on most background check inquiries. Store owners receive an almost immediate response for their prospective buyers. In the case of Nathan Gale, when the store telephoned the NICS, the response from the agency was to "delay" the sale. Eventually, the store re-contacted the NICS and was given the approval to proceed with the handgun sale. The reason for the initial delay was not explained.[5]

The transaction was completed and Gale took home his Christmas gift in its hard-plastic storage container. He also purchased 100 rounds of ammunition so he could break-in his new weapon. After Christmas, Gale returned to Camp Lejune, taking the weapon with him. Without authorization, he kept the handgun in his barracks. However, he told several of his fellow Marines about his gun, and soon the weapon was confiscated and shipped to his mother for safekeeping. When it arrived, she put it in her closet and essentially forgot about it.[6]

From January, 2003, until March of that year, Gale continued to work at the motor pool at Camp Lejune. He was assigned to the 1st platoon of the 10th Marine Regiment, 2nd Marine Division. In February, news came that his regiment would soon be deploying to Iraq for combat operations. However, Gale had been talking to several of his fellow Marines, telling them he was having difficulty sleeping and that he was hearing voices and seeing visions. In addition, his behavior was becoming erratic and he was increasingly forgetful. He soon found himself in trouble with his enlisted superiors. Gale had already received several written reprimands for minor violations, including missing appointments and failing to maintain the weight and fitness standards required of all Marines. Eventually, Gale's odd behavior prompted his supervisors to reassess his deployment eligibility. Senior non-commissioned officers and unit commanders determined that the complexities and danger of combat operations made taking a potentially unstable Marine to Iraq out of the question. About a week prior to the scheduled deployment, Gale was transferred out of the 1st Platoon and into the 3rd Platoon. He was also referred to Dr. Puder, the 2nd Marine Division psychiatrist, for a full mental-health evaluation. It didn't take long for Dr. Puder to determine that Gale had serious mental problems. After the initial evaluation, he immediately admitted Gale to the mental-health ward at Camp Lejune's hospital.

From the 3rd of March until the 10th of March, 2003, Nathan Gale was hospitalized in the mental-health ward. The initial diagnosis was that he was suffering from a psychotic disorder. During this hospitalization, doctors performed a barrage of tests and evaluations to assess his mental faculties and to determine what problems he had.

Doctors at Camp Lejune determined that Nathan Gale was a very disturbed young man. His conversations with staff

THE COMMUNITY COUNSELING CENTER

Located in Bldg. 41
For an appointment
call 451-2864
or
451-2876.

26 Aug 07
1100 -
ms. Blake

Licensed counselors serving
the needs of Active Duty
Personnel and their families.

A pamphlet from the counseling center at Camp Lejune where Nathan Gale was treated while in the Marines. Courtesy of Mary Clark.

psychiatrists were revealing and demonstrated the depth of his illness. Initially, when asked by doctors why he thought he had been transferred out of the 1st Platoon, he replied that he didn't know. As the questioning progressed, he stated that he was probably moved to the 3rd Platoon due to his past problems. Those problems, he explained, included hearing voices in his head and seeing visions. He told the doctors that he had experienced these phenomena since the second grade. Gale recounted how the voices told him that he was "a Beast." He also spoke of his struggles with visions and apparitions. He reported near daily visions, described as shadows looking into his room at night or faces floating in front of him. When he was faced with these visions, he reported severe anger that would lead him to break things in his room, including TVs, doors and windows. Again, Gale was experiencing *command auditory hallucinations:* voices, often demeaning and derogatory, that tell or "command" a person to do something or accomplish a task. Marine Corps psychiatrists also learned of Gale's belief that rock star Marilyn Manson had been responsible for the 9/11 terrorist attacks. He even told the doctors that the heavy-metal band "*Pantera*" had been formed because of him, but that the band refused to acknowledge that fact. He said he had been trying to find a lawyer to sue them but that no one would take his case.

Compounding Gale's mental instability was his prior drug use. This, without a doubt, seriously impacted his mental capacity. Although he lied on his enlistment documents, Gale admitted to the doctors at Camp Lejune that he had been arrested for drug use and theft prior to joining the Marines. He admitted that when he was in school he would go to school drunk and would use alcohol at school. As for drug use, he confirmed that he had regularly used multiple substances, including LSD, mushrooms, marijuana, laughing gas and cocaine. He denied any drug use while in the Marine Corps.

As a part of Gale's treatment and evaluation, he was afforded individual, group and *Milieu* therapy. During Gale's seven days of in-patient treatment, it was noted that he told very few people about his delusional beliefs. He was guarded throughout his stay. He completed psychological testing consisting of the Minnesota Multiphasic Personality Inventory (MMPI) and the Millon™ Clinical Multiaxial Inventory (MCMI). The results of Gale's tests, coupled with the information obtained from interviews and therapy, led Marine Corp psychiatrists to a conclusion: Gale was suffering from a chronic psychotic process that matched the classic symptoms of paranoid schizophrenia. Gale's paranoia was demonstrated to his doctors during an interview when a loud noise was heard outside the examination room. Gale immediately appeared anxious and asked, "Is someone listening to me?"[7]

Based on what they learned, Marine Corp doctors told Gale about their diagnosis. They explained his need for medication to help counteract the difficulties in his mind. After an in-depth discussion about the risks, benefits, side effects and alternative therapies, Gale consented to a trial of the drug Zyprexa. According to its manufacturer, Eli Lilly, Zyprexa is an "atypical antipsychotic" drug. It is believed that Zyprexa works by adjusting the imbalance of chemicals in the brain that may cause psychotic symptoms. By doing so, Zyprexa may help restore more normal thinking and mood. Gale's initial trials with Zyprexa appeared to provide him some relief, so his doctors increased his initial dosage of 10 milligrams to 15 milligrams. He was also prescribed Prozac, also called Fluoxetine, a drug used to treat and provide relief from the effects of depression. Doctors advised Gale that, if he maintained his recommended dosages of medication, he could keep "The Beast" under control.

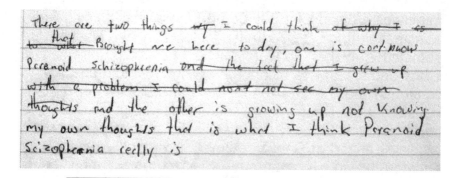

Nathan Gale writes: There are two things I could think that brought me here today. One is continuous paranoid schizophrenia and the other is growing up not knowing my own thoughts that is what I think paranoid schizophrenia really is. It isn't known when this note was written. Courtesy of Mary Clark.

Gale's treatment continued as an outpatient for the next six months. Once he was stabilized, Marine doctors debated his future in the armed forces. They classified his impairment as "moderate." However, his condition rendered him incapable of further service to the Marines. On July 1, 2003, a Physical Evaluation Board reviewed Gale's case and concurred with the conclusion of his psychiatrists. The board determined that, due to Gale's diagnosis, he was no longer fit for service in the Marines. The board also determined that Gale's condition was considered EPTS, or *"Existing Prior to Term of Service."* Doctors believed that Gale was burdened with paranoid schizophrenia long before he joined the Marines. Gale disagreed, but his own words and answers during treatment made it clear that his delusions and symptoms existed all the way back to the second grade.

The final paragraph in Gale's Physical Evaluation Board letter states:

"The formal PEB (Physical Evaluation Board) find that there is sufficient evidence to support a lifelong history of symptoms of a psychotic illness with a prodromal[8] period prior to enlistment. Accepted medical principles support that a highly structured environment, such as recruit training, minimizes the appearance of symptoms of schizophrenia. Accepted medical

principles also include the progression of symptoms in early adulthood and a positive response to antipsychotic medications."

In essence, the Marines were confident that they hadn't caused his condition. They also admitted that identifying the condition was difficult, due to the strict discipline of basic training. They also believed that Gale's medication was helping him. Perhaps the most important paragraph in the document was entitled, Recommended Medications. It stated:

"Continued psychopharmacological medication was advised. The level of medication required does not render him so sedated as to impair his psychomotor activity. He takes the prescribed medications appropriately and can be expected to continue taking them upon discharge. He has an adequate understanding of his illness and can be expected to seek professional assistance if his symptoms recur."

This single paragraph, more than any other document, makes it clear that Nathan Gale had been thoroughly counseled and informed of his mental health condition. Gale showed he was fully capable of taking his medications and was explicitly told that he needed to continue the medications when he left the service of the Marine Corps. His eventual decision to stop taking his prescriptions clearly facilitated his transformation into "The Beast."

On October 8, 2003, the Physical Evaluation Board conducted its final review of Nathan Gale's disability evaluation. The Board's final decision was that Gale was ineligible for veteran's benefits, due to his condition not being "service aggravated." He was advised of the importance of continuing to take his medication. Gale was given an honorable discharge from active duty. Just over a month later, on November 30, 2003, Nathan Gale found himself standing outside the front gate of Camp Lejune. He was no longer a Marine but a civilian again. He was alone, unemployed and forced to re-enter the cold, harsh reality he believed he had

The red and white striped door of Gale's apartment on South Fifth Street, Marysville, OH. Photo by Chris A.

escaped when he enlisted. He had served in the Marines for slightly less than two years.

In December, 2003, he returned to Ohio and moved into a small second-floor apartment in downtown Marysville, next door to his mother. For Mary Clark, Nathan's discharge from the Marines was a complete shock. He hadn't been telling her about his situation. She was unaware of his medical condition and, in fact, didn't even know that he was being discharged from the Marines. Upon his return to Marysville, Nathan downplayed the reasons that had prompted his discharge. He told his mom that, while in the Marines, he occasionally had "outbursts."

These outbursts, he explained, were fueled by an "illness." He went on to tell her what he knew about paranoid schizophrenia, and Mary did her best to try to understand her son's affliction. She began to study the characteristics of the illness. She also began to recognize behaviors in Nathan that were associated with the disease. In the past, she hadn't been able to understand his actions, but now she was starting to understand why he behaved so erratically. Nathan also told his mom that he was taking medication to control his condition, and that things were going okay.

Apparently, Gale wasn't shy when telling others about the reason for his discharge. His mother was now working as a bartender at the Marysville Eagle's Club. She remembers a time when Nathan went into detail about his discharge with a patron he hardly knew. Later, Mary quietly told him that he shouldn't volunteer information about his condition, due to the stigma attached to mental illness.

With Nathan settling back in Marysville, Mary reminded him of his aimlessness prior to joining the Marines. She made it clear to him that she was not going to help him financially or otherwise if he was simply going to lie around. She encouraged him to visit the local "Manpower" office in an effort to find a job.

He listened to his mom and applied for several jobs. In January, 2004, Gale landed a position at "Minit Lube," a small locally owned garage that specialized in automotive oil changes. Gale was a perfect fit for Minit Lube. Owner Rich Cencula knew that Gale had been a mechanic in the Marines and was aware of Nathan's "medical" issues. He quickly realized that Gale "wasn't a rocket scientist" but decided to give the veteran an opportunity.

One of Nathan Gale's final places of employment, The Minit Lube, Marysville, OH. Photo by Chris A.

According to Cencula, Gale was a good employee who worked hard and showed up on time. Rich took an interest in Nathan and they became friends. Both men were rabid fans of the Columbus Blue Jackets, a professional hockey team in the National Hockey League. On several occasions, Rich took Gale to Blue Jackets' games and offered him friendly, fatherly advice.

Gale was back to work and readjusting himself to civilian life. He kept to himself and didn't bother anyone. Marysville residents who encountered him after his return from the Marines didn't detect any anger or hostility. Most people who knew him felt he was a shy, awkward, lonely man, and completely non-threatening. He often ate lunch at "Maggie's," a small downtown diner where he seemed to enjoy exchanging chitchat with patrons and their children. He was soft-spoken and always alone.

In January, 2004, Nathan asked his mother about his handgun. It was a seemingly off-the-cuff question, asked with curiosity and no sense of urgency. She replied that she had placed it on the top shelf of her closet. Later that evening, Gale nonchalantly retrieved the gun and took it to his apartment. Despite his recent discharge from the Marines and his struggle with mental illness, Mary Clark never considered that her son could be dangerous or pose a threat to anyone.

Nathan Gale's apartment, photographed by Columbus Police, Dec. 9, 2004. Columbus Police Department, evidence photo.

When he wasn't working at Minit Lube, Gale stayed at his apartment, playing video games or working out with his weights. He also wandered the streets of Marysville, dropping in at his favorite haunts. As always, Gale continued to seek an "identity." He began to frequent a tattoo parlor across the street from his apartment. The Bear's

Den was family owned and operated by tattoo artist John Bender and his son, Lucas. To Gale, the Bear's Den was a place where he, "an outsider," could hang out and be accepted. He added to his tattoo collection by having a black "tribal" design

tattooed onto his left forearm. He also had his left ear pierced. Even in the relaxed, laid-back atmosphere of the tattoo parlor, Gale stood out. Staff and patrons found Gale's presence at the shop somewhat "creepy." Gale would try to engage strangers in conversation, and would often stare at customers or fixate on the shop's security camera. It was clear to the people working at the Bear's Den that Nathan Gale wanted to be accepted. He wanted to be their friend. While he may have been considered "odd" by the tattoo parlor's staff, he was also a customer, so his presence was tolerated. In Marysville, Nathan Gale was a riddle that no one could figure out.

Five months after his discharge, Nathan Gale's life appeared to be moving forward. He was employed. He was trying to make friends. He was becoming self-sufficient. His mom had helped him purchase a car, a red 1995 Pontiac Grand Am. He spoke of plans to enter college and improve his employment situation. To the outside world, all seemed well. What wasn't known at the time was that, at some point after returning to Ohio, Nathan Gale made a

1. The Bear's Den Tattoo Parlor, across the street from Gale's apartment. 2. Lucas Bender from The Bear's Den Tattoo Parlor, Marysville, OH. Photos by Chris A.

life-changing decision. For unknown reasons, Gale stopped taking his antipsychotic medication. Once his body weaned itself from the protective chemical balance the drug afforded, the visions and the voices returned to haunt him. Through his own negligence, the taunts and ideations of the past returned, and Gale soon found that his nemesis, "The Beast," had returned, as well.

On April 4, 2004, Gale drove to Cincinnati, Ohio, to attend a concert by the heavy-metal band "*Damageplan*," at Bogart's. Gale had a plan to confront brothers and ex-*Pantera* members, Dimebag Darrell and Vinnie Paul Abbott. No longer controlled by medication, he found that the voices and visions had reignited his hatred for *Pantera*. As Chapter Two of this book previously explained, Gale's actions at Bogart's resulted in a fight on the stage, with Gale coming out on the losing end. He never had the chance to talk to Dimebag or Vinnie Paul.

Gale's 1995 Grand Am, parked across the street from the Alrosa Villa, Dec. 8, 2004. Columbus Police Department, evidence photo.

Perhaps it was on his drive back to Marysville, angry and battered, that he decided what he would do next. Next time, he wouldn't waste time talking. Instead, he'd let his actions speak for him. He would kill them. After the encounter at Bogart's, Gale wrote:

> *"look into my Eyes and you will see The Anguish the Frustration Take An inhale The Deprived. You will see me Fight for my life and my Right To survive You will see Panteras Depresion and on the wourlds Disorder Vengeance is mine for the taking."*

Gale's letter in which he writes about "*Pantera*'s depression and on the world disorder" and that "vengeance is mine for the taking." Courtesy of Mary Clark.

Gale's mental decline is clearly demonstrated by his words. He had several notebooks that he used while in the Marines. After his discharge, he continued to use them but, instead of taking notes about fixing military vehicles, he used the pages to elucidate the turmoil in his mind. A writing entitled *"Black and Blue"* is typical of his prose:

"Voices in my head ringing in day and night
I can't stop the mind tracks
Shadows cast white flashes through my head
No excepting from the messages with in
I can't stop the mind tracks
Bruises in my mind that never go away
Hit me harder, I want to stay
Quit switching steps from a three diamond
Air trooper
Do you think it's wrong to be so head strong
Bruises in my mind that will never go away
Hit me harder, I won't stay."

The exact date Gale's lyrics and letters were written isn't clear. Based on the contents of his notebooks it would seem logical the vast majority of his known writing was done in the final year of his life.

Over the next eight months, Nathan Gale continued to live his reclusive lifestyle. Gale tried out for an offensive lineman position on the Lima Thunder in April, and was notified that he had made the team as a backup player. Thunder players did not receive any pay for participating, but were enticed by the opportunity to "try out" for the Arena Football League. In June, he quit his job at Minit Lube so he could devote time to playing football with the semi-professional team.[15] He drove from Marysville to attend practices in Lima on Wednesdays, and again on Saturdays for games. He wore number 65 and eventually started several games in the 2004 season as a guard. As far as Coach Green was concerned, there was nothing special or unusual about Gale. He was a quiet guy who appeared shy and kept to himself. As for his playing ability, Thunder Coach Green felt that Gale was an "okay" player who possessed average football skills.

Again without a job or steady income, Gale would often eat with his mom and borrow money from her. One of the things that Gale borrowed money for was ammunition for his Beretta 9mm. Several times per month, Gale would purchase 50 to 100 rounds of 9mm ammunition and visit a local shooting range. He seemed to really enjoy "target practice." While pistol shooting and target practice are legitimate pastimes for millions of Americans, Gale's intentions were sinister.

While it's not clear what Gale's actions were at the shooting range, it can be surmised, based on his choice of reading material, that he was preparing himself for "a mission." As far as can be ascertained, he only owned three books. The first was "*Zodiac*," a non-fiction book about a serial killer who operated in the San Francisco area in the 1960s. He also owned a book called "*Guerrilla Strategies: An Historical Anthology from the Long March to Afghanistan.*" This book is viewed as a primer for learning strategy and small-unit tactics. The third book in Gale's modest library was "*On Killing,*" written by Lt. Col. Dave Grossman.

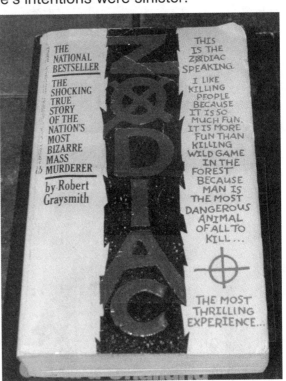

Gale's copy of the book, written by Robert Graysmith. Zodiac the movie was released in March 2007, directed by David Fincher.

Of the three books, Grossman's work "*On Killing*" is perhaps the most noteworthy. The book explores the psychological effects on human beings of killing other human beings. It takes a hard look at the efforts of government, the

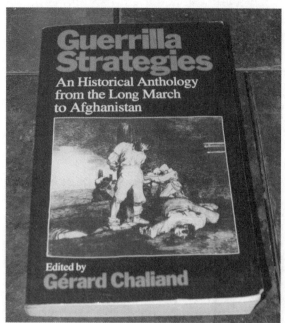

1. Gale's copy of "Guerrilla Strategies," cover depicting torture and executions. 2. Gale's well read copy of "On Killing" by Lt. Col. Dave Grossman. Courtesy of Mary Clark.

military and law enforcement agencies to train and prepare an individual to take a person's life. It details, through gripping interviews with military personnel and police officers, the psychological impact experienced when faced with a violent encounter, and the conditioned response of an individual who is put in a position of having to kill. Far from glorifying the act of killing, the book clearly articulates the argument that human beings are repulsed by the idea of killing another of their own species. For example, Grossman's research indicated that, in WWII, only 15 percent of U.S. personnel in combat actually aimed and *tried* to kill the enemy. By the time of the Vietnam conflict, that percentage rose to nearly 90 percent of U.S. combatants. The key to the jump in lethality by U.S. forces from WWII to Vietnam was directly tied to training, conditioning and desensitization.

The book has certainly helped thousands of military members and police officers understand the emotions they felt after being involved in a lethal incident. Typically, people who read "*On Killing*" close its final page with a profound respect for its content, yet shudder at the book's pessimistic message about the desensitization of young people via modern entertainment media and interactive video games. The author's grim outlook for the future theorizes that violent content in movies, music, television and especially video games is creating a generation of people completely desensitized to the true ramifications of killing.

How Nathan Gale came to own or purchase the book is speculation. However, while he was in the Marine Corps, "*On Killing*" was on the Corps' list of "suggested reading." Gale's copy was well-used, its dirty cover and dog-eared pages providing ample evidence that the book didn't just sit on his bookshelf. Gale read the book, but rather than digest its true meaning, he "reverse-engineered" its message. Why else would he read it? For a normal person, there is nothing in the book that would motivate you to want to kill. Instead of recognizing the revulsion and horror felt by those who were forced to kill, he used the information in an attempt to insulate himself from those feelings as he prepared for his murderous rampage. Tucked inside the pages of Gale's copy of "On Killing" was a handwritten list of approximately 50 words. Words on the list included *desensitization, atrocity, brutality, euphoria* and *contemptuous*. Also on this page of text, written in Gale's hand, is what appear to be lyrics or a sonnet called, "We are victims of our own brutality."[9]

With insight from his military training about "shot placement," coupled with his semi-monthly range visits, Gale practiced to become a lethal predator. From "getting his mind in the right place" to quickly reloading and changing magazines in his Beretta 9mm, he actively rehearsed the "skills" he would need to accomplish his mission of carnage. He wanted to be able to act without thinking. He wanted "The Beast" to be a cold, calculating killing machine.

---

[9] Read Lt. Col. Dave Grossman's insightful contribution on page 313.

Q-tips, a rag and Beretta lubricating oil on Gale's night stand, photographed Dec. 9, 2004. Columbus Police Department, evidence photo.

On December 8, 2004 Gale slept in. That evening Dimebag Darrell Abbott and his brother, Vinnie Paul Abbott, would be performing at the Alrosa Villa. How and when Gale learned of the show isn't known. He apparently didn't purchase a ticket but he recognized this as his best opportunity to do harm to the two men. As he normally did, he ate lunch at Maggie's and loitered around town. In the afternoon, he returned to his apartment and prepared for his evening. He cleaned and lubricated his gun and made certain he had loaded magazines and spare ammunition. At about 6:30 that night, he crossed Fifth Street and walked into the Bear's Den. He grabbed a seat on the sofa and began flipping through a tattoo magazine. Tattoo artist Bo Toller was minding the shop. Toller observed that Gale seemed agitated and hyped-up. Gale tried to engage him in conversation, asking Toller if he could purchase tattoo equipment. Occupied with a customer, Toller wasn't particularly interested in talking to him, so he told him that, to buy tattoo machines, he would have to be a "certified" artist. Apparently satisfied, Gale returned to the sofa and continued to read.

Suddenly, Gale stood up and threw the magazine onto the glass-topped coffee table in the shop.

"Hey, man," said Gale to Toller, "that's bullsh*t. This magazine sells tattoo equipment to anyone. You're a liar!"

He stormed out of the building, leaving Toller somewhat irked, as Gale was normally quiet and non-confrontational. Later that evening, when Lucas Bender arrived at the shop, Toller told him about the encounter. Bender told him not to sweat it and related how, three or four days earlier, Gale had been in the shop hanging out. After he left, a group of Bender's friends asked, "Man, what's wrong with that dude?" He replied that Gale was a guy they should stay away from. Referring to the perpetrators of the Columbine High School killings, he said Nathan Gale was like "those Columbine kids." Bender concluded by saying, "You never know when he might snap and go postal."

He had no idea how prophetic his words would prove to be.

Sometime in the final months before December 8, 2004, perhaps late at night as he contemplated his demons, Nathan Gale penned what might be the closest thing to his confession. It reads:

"I Apologize for what I done But I've tried to tell you but noone would listen there is a Band using my Name the Bands Name is pantera. I've Enclosed the CD which he uses my Name Quite Frequently. They've talked about me and laughed at me and told other people about my ideas. So I would think about committing suicide - What happed because of this I was forced into a severe depresion that I couldn't get over. I've tried to get a lawyer But there is Noone to take my case. Please Hear me it will Be the last time."

I Apoligize for what I Done
But I've tried to tell you But Noone
would ltsen there is A Band using my
nene the Bands Name is pentere
I've Enclosed the cd which he ~~used~~ uses my Name
Quite Requently. They're talked about me and
laughed at me and told other people about
my Idees. So I would think About committing
suicide — whet happed Because of this I was forced Into
The ~~story goes Back to when I was~~
~~Born at it.~~
they turned me into the Trumen show By Doing
this only ~~it instead~~ of ~~cameras~~ its just people
a severe ~~it~~ depresion ~~#~~ that I couldnt get over.
I've tried ~~to get~~ ~~date~~ a lawyer But there is
Noone to take my case. Plse Hear me it call
Be the last time.

Nathan Gale's "confession" in his own handwriting. Courtesy of Mary Clark.

Around 8 pm, Gale climbed into his car. Underneath his shirt, he concealed his loaded Beretta. In his pockets was another loaded ten-round magazine, along with an additional thirty rounds of ammunition. He plugged in his Walkman CD player and slipped the headphones into his ears.

As he drove to the Alrosa Villa, he listened to *Damageplan*.

Gale's portable CD player and the only disc in his vehicle; "New Found Power" by *Damageplan*. Columbus Police Department, evidence photo.

Dime Time

I saw *Pantera* in Albany, N.Y., on Vinnie's birthday in 1992 or 1993. When the show was over, I followed them to a local bar called "Saratoga Winners." The only people in the place were my friend Joe, *Pantera*, a few local bands, and me. Phil Anselmo came out for only a minute, signed a few autographs and left. He looked hungover as all hell. Vinnie was wearing cowboy attire and was sitting at a small bar talking to some ladies. Rex was walking around talking to everyone. It was loud in there, so conversation was limited to "hell yeahs" and "yeehaws."

I specifically remember Dime literally bouncing off the walls. He'd bounce off a door, into a fridge, then into me, then back to the door. He had a lot of energy. With the music blaring, every time Joe would ask him something he couldn't hear, he'd say, "shut up and drink." We all got each other drinks and at the time it seemed like the best night of my life. Dime was a man I truly admired for his playing and here he was, not only hanging with me, but also getting me beers. From time to time he'd climb on stage with the locals and play *Metallica* and *Slayer*. Then he'd come back and hang with us again!

To me he was truly the ultimate "rock star." The only negative that night was that later I found out Joe had a camera but he never took it out. He said he didn't want to seem like a pushy, cheesy fan. Little did I know at the time what a shutterbug Dime really was! We didn't even ask for autos or anything. But a lot of friends saw me that night smiling ear to ear. I turned a lot of people on to *Pantera* and it was so cool that I got to meet them. It's a great memory.

– John (no last name given), fan

Dimebag decorates a fan's face with *Kiss* makeup, July 1, 2004. Milwaukee, WI. Photo courtesy of Chad Lee, Rockconcertfotos.com

Chapter 8

Mayhem

"You just be nice until you can't be nice anymore."

-Keith "Shadow" Huddleston

Malcolm "Mayhem" MacGregor was born in September 1500. He was the son of no one who kept him as his mother died during his birth and his father shortly there after. He was raised by the village since it took more than one family to feed the lad. His strength and size were intimidating. He could beat up most men…and he often did. He was inducted into the military at a young age and moved up the ranks quickly. He grieved for and drank to the memories of his fallen comrades and outlived them all. He was the best at what he did and he could prove it. He grew up in Loch Awe spending his days working for anyone in the village that paid. Some paid with ale, hence his penchant for booze. Love and his word were his only loyalty. Money played a part as well but he could not be bought. Fiercely loyal to his king and queen, his main duties were as the commander of the Royal Scottish armies and purveyor of the highland games.

-Jeffery "Mayhem" Thompson

Fort Benning, Georgia, has been and remains one of the most important military installations supporting America's armed forces. Home of the U.S. Army Infantry, the base has hosted some of America's iconic soldiers, including generals George Patton, Omar Bradley, and Dwight Eisenhower. Previously stationed at Fort Devens, Massachusetts, with the Army Security Agency, Army Specialist Fourth Class Frank Thompson and his wife Christine joined the alumni who called Fort Benning home. In

Opposite page: The gentle giant, Jeffery "Mayhem" Thompson. Always up for a good laugh, Jeff models his new headgear. Photo courtesy of Randy & Sharon Wothke. Above: Frank Thompson, U.S. Army. Photo courtesy of the Thompson family.

Christine Thompson. Photo courtesy of the Thompson family.

1963 Thompson was changing duty specialties; departing the hush-hush world of the Army Security Agency, he returned to his armor roots[1] via a transfer to Fort Benning, where he was assigned to an armor squad of the 7th Cavalry, a subordinate unit of the Second Infantry Division.

Since the early 1960s, it seemed clear that the U.S. army would soon be drawn into combat operations in Vietnam. Fort Benning became a key installation for training units that would be deploying to the Southeast Asia Theater of Operations. Specialist Thompson and his brothers in arms in the 7th Cavalry assumed the role of "aggressors" or opposition force members in military exercises. These exercises were designed to acclimate air cavalry units to the tactics and mindset of the communist Viet Cong. Frank enjoyed the duty; when not employed in mock combat operations, he served as a Jeep driver, transporting officers around the installation and acting as a unit messenger.

On September 21, 1964, Frank and his attractive young bride Christine welcomed a son, Jeffery Allan Thompson, into the family. The following year, Frank was honorably discharged from the Army and moved with his family to Newport,

---

[1] Chapter 8 footnotes begin on page 308.

Arkansas, the Thompsons' family hometown. As they departed Georgia, Frank was optimistic about the future as he had been accepted for a position on the Newport Police Department. However, his hopes and plans for his family hit a snag.

Christine had been born and raised in and around Columbus, Georgia. It didn't take long for her to discover she desperately missed her friends and family. The product of a single-parent family, she had grown up with several sisters and was the prototypical "country girl." As a youth, she had rarely left the county and had no worldly experience outside of Columbus.

Frank, on the other hand, relished new experiences and enjoyed diverse places and challenges. He was nearly an exact opposite of Christine, who longed for the status quo of her life back in Georgia. Such conflicting traits caused problems for the couple, and soon the marriage disintegrated into resentment, anger, frustration, and vocal disagreements. Although the couple worked hard to make the marriage work, Christine's yearnings to return to her family in Georgia only intensified. As much as each grasped for a workable compromise, the reality of the situation became clear: The marriage wasn't going to survive. One summer day, Frank returned home from work to discover

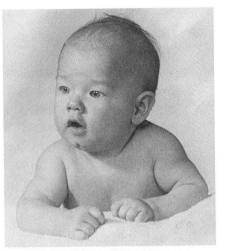

1. Jeffery Allan Thompson, born Sept. 21, 1964. 2. Jeff and his mother. 3. At about four years old Jeff correctly spells XIGOA. Photo courtesy of the Thompson family.

Christine had packed up and moved back to Georgia. After nearly seven tumultuous years of marriage, Frank filed for divorce.

With the marriage over, six-year-old Jeff found himself living in Georgia with his mother. Jeff and Christine were very close, and she loved her boy dearly. Having custody of her son, Christine sought to focus on career and educational ambitions. As a single parent, she wanted to improve her employment opportunities and viewed higher education as the catalyst to help her accomplish that objective. Throughout her life, Christine often felt she was an outsider, struggling to gain acceptance from others. She hoped that education would give her the knowledge and confidence to be more comfortable in her own skin.

Meanwhile, Jeff felt the effects of the divorce most acutely. As a young boy bouncing back and forth from his mother's home in Georgia to his dad's place in Arkansas, the circumstances surrounding his parents' marital split troubled Jeff, who wanted to understand what role—if any—he had played in the turmoil between his mother and father. Jeff's frustration was typical of children whose parents divorce; he felt excluded from consideration and, of course, was saddened by the love lost between his mom and dad. Throughout his life, Jeff never truly reconciled the fact that, even with smiles on their faces, animosity lingered just beneath the surface in both his parents. Jeff often contemplated what he might have done to help keep his parents together, but the fact is that Jeff had nothing to do with his parents' split. On the contrary, his parents tried to find a solution to their marital woes to keep the family together for their son's sake.

Jeff attended elementary school in Georgia while living with his mother. During holiday periods and parts of the summer, he would travel to Arkansas to visit and live with his father. Eventually, Christine's focus on her educational and career goals forced her to make a decision. As Christine became increasingly stretched thin for both time and money, Jeff became a "latchkey" child. He routinely returned home from school to an empty home because his mom hadn't yet finished her day. With time on his hands and limited supervision, 10-year-old Jeff occasionally pushed the behavioral envelope with his mother, and the two would butt heads over issues of discipline and responsibility. Wanting to do the right thing for herself and her child, Christine called Frank and together they decided that Jeff would relocate to Arkansas and reside full-time with his father.

Unlike Christine, Frank set down straightforward guidelines and expectations for Jeff's behavior and responsibilities as a member of the household. Frank, who had moved on from the police department and was now working as a floral designer, resided in an apartment inside the flower shop where he worked. He was pleased to have his boy home and had great hopes for his son's future, encouraging Jeff to apply himself in school and study hard.

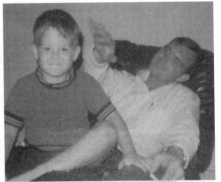

Jeff's life as a youngster was typical of boys growing up in the early 1970s. He put in a reasonable effort in school and garnered respectable grades. Looking back on his days in school, Frank still believes that Jeff's academic performance may have been better had he not brooded and fretted so much about the divorce of his parents. His mom may have been out of sight, but she wasn't out of mind; she remained in contact with Jeff through letters and telephone calls.

Jeff soon joined the Boy Scouts of America. Frank took his son to J. C. Penny's in Newport, the local retailer of scouting uniforms and accouterments, and helped Jeff pick

1. Jeff and his father around 1970. 2. Christine's happy little boy, Jeff, at age 7. Photos courtesy of the Thompson family.

Jeff at around 10 years old. Photo courtesy of the Thompson family.

out his uniform items and assorted gear. Stepping out of the dressing room, Jeff looked sharp in his green and khaki scouting attire; his pride at being a part of something bigger than himself was obvious. He wasn't simply Jeff Thompson, he was now a scout. He truly enjoyed his participation in the organization; scouting gave Jeff an outlet to be creative and escape the occasional doldrums of home and school life. Scouting also gave him the opportunity to experience the outdoors, introduced him to regimentation, and provided him a sense of teamwork while interacting with other youths his age. Throughout his life, Jeff kept many sentimental belongings, one of which was his Boy Scout cap.

Shortly after Frank divorced, he met a local Newport teacher named Marilyn. The two hit it off and became close friends. Over the next several years their friendship blossomed into love and in 1977 they were married. Marilyn worked hard to develop a bond with her stepson, going out of her way to help him in any way she could. She was very interested in Jeff's well-being and often tried to expose him to new experiences.

Marilyn enrolled Jeff in a summer camp in Georgia where he learned to swim. The camp experience demonstrated that, although Jeff was self-sufficient and individually skilled, his team and interpersonal relationship skills left much to be desired. It wasn't that Jeff wasn't a team player; it was simply that he had no desire to participate in many of the organized events available at camp. Jeff liked to do what Jeff liked to do. If he wasn't interested in something, he either didn't do it or simply went through the motions.

As Jeff reached puberty, the genes he inherited from his tall mother kicked in and the boy began to grow like a weed. In the blink of an eye, Jeff exceeded six feet tall, although he was only 13 or 14 years old. He became self-conscious of his height in comparison to that of his friends and peers and unconsciously altered his posture when he stood and walked, rolling his shoulders slightly forward and tilting his head to the side in an exaggerated and unconvincing effort to appear smaller. Like his mom, Jeff sometimes felt as if he didn't quite fit in.

In high school, his stature caught the attention of his school's athletic coaches, but Jeff wasn't really interested in sporting endeavors. However, in an effort to placate his father's urging, he tried out for his high school football program on several occasions. His attempts were half-hearted, and it was apparent that his staunch individualism ran contrary to the "team" philosophy. For several seasons he tried out for the team, but the result was always the same. The school's athletic

1. Jeff's step mom Marilyn. 2. At around 14 years old, Jeff was well in excess of six feet tall. Photo courtesy of the Thompson family.

The reluctant athlete. Photo courtesy of the Thompson family.

director would call Jeff's dad and let him know that, as much as they appreciated his efforts, his heart wasn't in it. Instead of sports, Jeff's skill and passion were better served working on engines and other pieces of mechanical equipment, an area in which Jeff excelled. He had a natural knack for understanding the complexities of the combustion engine.

In 1981, Frank and Marilyn became the parents of triplet boys. Jeff's new half-brothers were named Martin, Micah, and Seth. Jeff loved interacting with the triplets and he adored his role as "big brother." He loved their innocence and was fascinated by how small they were. He often stretched out on the floor with the babies, entertaining them as they crawled over and around his huge frame. The birth of the triplets brought with them new challenges. Baby Martin was born with heart complications and required extensive medial treatment and a great deal of care and attention.

In Jeff's eyes, the arrival of his baby brothers shifted the family focus. No longer the sole "kid" of the family, he now had to share affections with his three brothers. The babies were the priority and 17-year-old Jeff, while keenly aware of the immediate needs of his new brothers, fell victim to his own insecurities. His emotions ran the gamut from jealousy to abandonment, and at times he felt like an outcast within his own family.

Meanwhile, Jeff's academics were suffering. His performance in school had begun to slip early in his teen years—a result of his disinterest in much of the course content. With a combination of pride and frustration, Frank would often say that "Jeff marched to the beat of a different drummer." High school made that statement perfectly clear to all who knew him. His sense of individualism and ambivalence towards conformity were reflections of his mother. He barely squeaked through his final two years of high school. The boy seemed directionless and unmotivated and his future far from assured. His dad became increasingly concerned. Frank's frustration with Jeff's apathy and lack of drive gnawed at him. He recognized his son's malaise and made it clear that he was not about to permit Jeff to let the world pass him by. It seemed that his post-high school routine was hiding out in his room watching TV and spending time with his dog Reddy.

1. Jeff with his triplet brothers, Seth, Micah and Martin. 2. Jeff's senior photo from Newport High School, AR. Photos courtesy of the Thompson family.

Frank tried to encourage Jeff by discussing post-high school options such as serving in the U.S. military or attending college or technical school. Jeff initially seemed disinterested. Frank, however, wasn't about to give up on helping his son move forward and continually tried to stimulate Jeff's interest in taking the next step in his life. As time passed, the tones of the conversations between the two men became edgier. Frank's frustration was starting to wear thin, and the two men exchanged words more often. Over time, these frustrated exchanges escalated in volume, sometimes cascading out of control into all-out verbal jousts. As much as he despised what he saw happening, Frank felt it needed to be done.

Little by little, Frank's "tough love" efforts appeared to be paying off. Jeff finally enrolled in a local trade school, where he could academically demonstrate his skills with engines and other mechanical devices. Jeff clearly had the aptitude and the ability to learn. He went on to complete a vocational degree as a diesel mechanic. At nearly 20 years old and finished with trade school, instead of seeking employment, he reverted into his kickback routine, which drove his father crazy. Frank was "old school" when it came to work; he simply couldn't comprehend that Jeff wasn't taking advantage of his degree.

In the fall of 1983 the tension between father and son came to a head. It started innocently enough when Frank asked Jeff to rake some leaves. Unmotivated and disinterested in the chore Jeff slacked off and procrastinated while Frank peered out the kitchen window, fuming. He could take it no more and confronted his son. Jeff tossed the rake to the ground and the dark clouds of confrontation loomed. Both men exchanged harsh, cruel words. As the altercation apparently reached its peak, the situation erupted into a physical confrontation between father and son. Both men quickly realized that a boundary had been crossed and the struggle ended almost as soon as it began. However, the emotional scars of this brief, climactic conflict would linger, tormenting both men in the form of regret and guilt for years.

Frank, angry from the fight, temporarily banished Jeff to his grandmother's nearby home. He made it clear to his son not to return until he cooled down and was prepared to accept the rules, boundaries, and responsibilities of the household. Angrily, Jeff packed his belongings and headed to his grandmother's home. Without so much as uttering a goodbye, he slammed the door as he left. Frank, who was left hurt and frustrated by the situation, relied on his eternal optimism as he hoped Jeff's departure would prove to be an opportunity for each of them to reflect on and contemplate the situation. As much as it hurt him to see his son bitterly stomp away from home, he was sure that Jeff would recognize his role and return home.

Unfortunately, an immediate reconciliation wasn't in the cards. Within four days of leaving his dad's home, Jeff's grandmother, feeling sympathy for her grandson, supplied him with a beat-up old pickup truck and $200. Her good intentions instead created a situation that permitted Jeff to evade his culpability at home rather than work out his differences with his

This would be the last time that Jeff's hair would ever be this short! Photo courtesy of the Thompson family.

father. Still angry, but now with money in his pocket, Jeff fired up the old pickup and headed southwest on U.S. 67 out of Newport. Rather than return home and patch things up, he unexpectedly moved to Dallas.

On his lonely drive to Texas, Jeff pondered the altercation with his father. His regret was somewhat tempered by his stubbornness. He contemplated his life, knowing he had inherited his physical stature and occasional bouts of insecurities from his mom. What, however, had he learned or assimilated from his father? The two men seemed so different, so separate, and so far apart from each other in many ways. On the surface, there appeared to be a world of differences. Frank was a former cop and pillar in the business community while his son was an unemployed, intimidating, huge man who was seemingly prepared to live a nomadic lifestyle. Could any two men be more different? For all their perceived differences, there was one trait that father and son shared: stubbornness. In fact, this trait led to nearly eight years of silence between them—an estrangement that affected both men deeply.

After arriving in Dallas, Jeff found a full-time job working the night shift at Martin Engineering. The job was perfect for Jeff as he could put to use the skills he learned in vocational trade school while working at night, his preferred time for work. For eight years Jeff worked and lived in Dallas without communicating with his father. When it came to material things, Jeff wasn't particularly big on accumulating "stuff." He saved letters, photos, and small mementos, but he wasn't interested in owning big-ticket items. He had his pickup and a place to stay and was making friends—beyond that, as far as he was concerned, he simply needed to make enough money to make ends meet.

Then, in 1991, Jeff's mom flew to Texas to visit her son. The year before, Christine had been diagnosed with breast cancer; her prognosis was grim. Realizing her situation, she was determined to see her son one final time before she died. Jeff and his mother spent several days together. He showed her around metropolitan Dallas as they talked and caught up with each other. Before either realized it, it was over and she departed for her home in Georgia. Soon after departing Texas, Christine's health began to fail as she struggled with the cancer. Realizing that she could lose her battle at any time, Jeff traveled to Georgia one final time to be with his mom. A few weeks later she passed away.

The death of his mother affected Jeff deeply as he dealt with the reality that he would never see or speak with her again. Consequently, his thoughts turned to his father. Recognizing that the passing of his mother was a wake-up call, he realized that, after too many years of anger punctuated by silence, it was time to make amends with his father. It was time to try to reconnect. He hoped it wasn't too late for them. A few months later, Jeff picked up the phone and called his dad. It was a short, somewhat awkward call, but it was a start.

For his part, Frank had never given up on the hope that his eldest son would one day return home or at least reconnect with his family. While Jeff may have been silent over those eight long years, his father was not. Each year on Jeff's birthday and at Christmas, Frank sent his boy a card with a check for $100 as a gesture—a signal—that he was keeping the door open. Jeff had finally responded.

In early 1992, Jeff stopped at a small convenience store on the outskirts of the Texas town of Waxahachie. He passed on a friendly greeting to the clerk as he stepped up to the counter to buy a pack of smokes. A flyer on the counter caught his eye, and he picked it up and scanned it. It was promoting Waxahachie's upcoming Scarborough Renaissance Festival.

"Will you be going to the festival?" asked the woman behind the counter.

With a smile on his face, Jeff shyly replied that he'd never heard of it—nor was he exactly certain what a renaissance festival was. As it turned out, the woman worked at the festival each season, and she enthusiastically told Jeff about the events and reenactments that took place during the six-week long extravaganza.

"You know, you'd probably really enjoy it. In fact, you should try out for a part. They are always looking for people." Something—perhaps the thought of knights jousting or gallons of ale flowing—propelled him to heed her advice and he headed towards the festival grounds.

As he arrived at the festival gates Jeff felt as if he had stepped back in time. No longer was he in 20th century Texas; instead, he had been transported to 16th century medieval England. Unknown to Jeff, the festival wasn't open to the public yet. He had arrived a month early and stumbled upon dozens of performers in costume rehearsing their roles in preparation of the festival's debut the following month. Assuming the fair to be in progress, Jeff simply wandered in to have a look around the grounds. Soon he attracted the attention of several festival participants who asked him if he was new to the performing company. Jeff, as friendly as ever, explained that he was just poking around. They explained that the show wasn't open yet. Jeff, somewhat embarrassed, apologized for not realizing it. He asked several questions about the festival and before long found himself deep in conversation with the actors. They infected Jeff with their affection and enthusiasm for the renaissance festival experience. With just a little prodding, he was encouraged to apply for an acting position and was accepted.

Performing in a renaissance festival was more involved and more elaborate than Jeff imagined—it meant hours of study and preparation. Not only did he have to look the part, but he had to live the part when on the festival site, which meant an intensive indoctrination into "The King's English" with its formal pronunciations and somewhat laborious vocabulary for Jeff. For example, instead of saying "Have a nice day," an actor in character would say "Enjoy the day full well" or "God save thee." To look the part, Jeff scoured the Dallas metropolis in search of pawn and costume shops. He sought reproductions of medieval accouterments and clothing appropriate in color and textile for 16th century England.

Jeff Thompson in his guise as a 16th Century highlander. Photo courtesy of the Thompson family.

As the 1992 season of the Scarborough Renaissance Festival prepared to open, the actor portraying the king unexpectedly quit the show. With the opening just days away, the decision was made to move forward without a male monarch. Instead, the medieval landscape nestled into the Texas countryside would be ruled by the queen alone with a team of sentries devoted to the queen's protection, accompanying her in her journeys and protecting her honor. In his first year with the show, Jeff's intimidating size and clear enthusiasm for the festival led him to be invited to become a bodyguard to the queen.

In the role of her majesty, Queen Anne Boleyn of England, Marchioness of Pembroke, was Shannon Bradley. A vibrant woman of regal beauty, she portrayed the role of monarch with conviction and flair. Intelligent, articulate, and full of confidence, she found the huge "new guy" acting as her bodyguard and protector fascinating. He was charming, intelligent, exceptionally quick-witted, and an excellent actor. Yet, at times, he was modest to the point of shyness. She was

amazed that a man with his stature and diverse ability was so down to earth, so real, and so unassuming, as was his general behavior towards women. With Jeff, there were never catcalls or any inappropriate, unwanted innuendo. He was always respectful.[2] It didn't take long for Jeff and Shannon to bond, and soon he found himself sharing dinner and conversation with the captivating actress.

Jeff threw himself into the world of the renaissance and over the next year continued to develop and improve his portrayal. As he learned more about the history of the period, he decided to develop his own character. Rather than a 16th century Englishman, Jeff decided his character would be Scottish. In 1994 he unveiled Malcolm "Mayhem" MacGregor, a kilt-wearing, hard-drinking, medieval badass who was fiercely loyal to his king and queen. He had created a well-thought-out character, and Jeff fit the role to a tee. He jumped into

1. Shannon Bradley in her role as Queen Anne Boleyn with her protector. 2. The fierce persona of Malcolm "Mayhem" MacGregor. Photo courtesy of the Thompson family.

the role with enthusiasm, spending his money to festoon his attire with Scottish flair. Accentuating the exceptional life he had breathed into his Scottish guardsman persona, most of his Waxahachie friends soon were call him "Mayhem" instead of Jeff, even off the festival grounds. The nickname stuck. Before long, more and more people recognized him by Mayhem. However, Shannon, his friend and queen, never called him Mayhem; to her, he was always Jeff.

For Jeff, life in Dallas and around Waxahachie had become wonderful. He had found not only a vocation, but also a "home" filled with excitement and—more importantly—with people he could completely relate to.

With his knack for mechanics, Jeff became an increasingly valuable commodity in and around the festival complex. If a generator malfunctioned, Jeff could fix it. If a vehicle broke down, people would look to Jeff for help. Using a bit of savvy, he bartered a deal with the festival owner, swapping his mechanical skills for free room and board. He was hired on as a caretaker living on the festival grounds. He found his new home in a dilapidated workshop to be nearly unfit for human habitation, but soon fixed it up inside and out. According to Shannon, Jeff's home was one of the coolest bachelor pads ever, complete with a full bar. Mayhem's fridge was filled with Guinness, and the apartment well stocked with Crown Royal.

As word of his expertise in repairing vehicles spread, more and more of his renaissance colleagues and members of his "Texas family" sought his help. Incredibly generous with his abilities and his time, Jeff went above and beyond in his efforts to help his friends. Occasionally he required a tool or diagnostic device that he didn't own. To remedy this, he stopped in and spoke with Mike Settlemeyer and Rick Finley, owners of the Waxahachie Alternator and Starter on Howard Road. Located just down the road from the Scarborough festival grounds, Jeff explained his situation to the owners, who were impressed at the lengths he was willing to go to help his friends. They worked out a deal where Jeff could use the shop and its tools. In return, if the business was short-handed or needed assistance on a vehicle, Jeff agreed to step up and help out. It was a perfect arrangement for everyone. As with almost everyone he encountered, Jeff had made yet another friend. For the remainder of his life he could often be found shooting the breeze and working on engines at Waxahachie Alternator and Starter. To Jeff, the alternator shop was a place to escape and relax while lending a hand. Regarding Mayhem's mechanical abilities, Mike Settlemeyer said "Mayhem could fix darn near anything."

At the 1994 Scarborough Renaissance Festival, Jeff met the man who would in many ways be his closest friend and mentor in Texas. Keith Huddleston, better known as "Shadow," was a big man like Jeff and a professional in the security business. Standing in a line to refill their mugs with ale, the two men engaged in conversation and compared notes about their shared love of beer, motorcycles, and heavy metal music. It was one of those rare times when two people simply "click." Within minutes, Mayhem and Shadow felt as if they had known each other for years, as if they had been siblings

A typical photo of Jeff Thompson, a huge infectious smile that could light up a room or an entire festival. Photo courtesy of the Thompson family.

separated at birth. The friendship extended far beyond the renaissance festival; Mayhem and Shadow were as close as brothers for the rest of Jeff's life.

Each year Jeff's participation in the Scarborough Renaissance Festival seemed to spark a new friendship. This

Mayhem prepares to compete in the caber toss at the Highland games. Photo courtesy of the Thompson family.

was certainly the case in 1995, when Jeff met Linda McAlister, a newbie to the fair who filled the role of a costumed character. From the first moment she met the big man called Mayhem, she found herself charmed with the huge Highlander whose presence dominated any part of the fair he happened to be at. As was typical, Linda was initially intimidated by the gigantic man, but she soon discovered that his heart and demeanor were commensurate with his physical stature. To Linda, Jeff was the poster child for the old saying that "one can't judge a book by its cover." Sure he was big, and he certainly had the ability to cast an ominous shadow, but Jeff's true colors ran contrary to most people's first impressions. During the time she knew Jeff, Linda never saw him angry. He loved to laugh, he adored children and, like his character Mayhem, the free-spirited Jeff didn't simply play a protective role—he lived it. On the festival grounds, he not only stayed in character, but he also kept an eye out for the safety and well-being of his fellow performers as well as the patrons.

Yet Linda found herself fascinated with Jeff for another reason. She was the owner of a Dallas-based talent agency.

As she got to know Jeff, she discovered that he had landed a role as an extra on the TV show "Walker, Texas Ranger."[3] However, at only $75 per day, he made less acting than he did running machinery at Martin Engineering. Now, working at the festival grounds and with more flexibility, Jeff became one of Linda's part-time actors. Jeff responded very well to the arrangement, and Linda consistently found opportunities for him to audition for roles. When a studio needed "a big guy," there were few local actors who could compete with him. While he never obtained any major speaking roles, he also never lacked for work and was often seen in local Dallas television commercials. Jeff also appeared in several nationally broadcast commercials, including one for Ruffles Potato Chips in which he played a football player. He once played the role of a mean-looking biker hanging out with a bunch of elderly women for the convenience store chain 7-Eleven. In addition to commercials, he participated in several industrial and training videos.

The moment of truth as Mayhem launches a caber on the tournament field. Photo courtesy of the Thompson family.

Jeff Mayhem goofing off with Nelson Stewart of *The Rogues*. Photo courtesy of the Thompson family.

Mayhem's multiple talents made him a fixture and an incredibly important part of the renaissance community. At Scarborough, he and Keith "Shadow" Huddleston organized the "Highland Games," where men competed in feats of strength by throwing massive stones and tossing "cabers;" 100-pound logs resembling a telephone pole. Mayhem often competed and usually won the day. The fact was, few men—if any—had a chance against him. After several years of participating in the Highland Games, Jeff humbly dropped out of the contest to give other participants a shot at winning.

Following the competitions, Jeff wandered through the carnival looking at the various games of chance. It was here, among the contests of old, that he first met Michael "Mongo" Smith, struggling to throw an axe into a stump. Remaining in character, Jeff stepped up to Mongo and said, "Allow me to show you, sire." Taking the axe, Mayhem explained the proper technique and then, with a flip of the wrist, launched the double-bladed axe at the tree stump, embedding its steel head firmly into the wood. After the demonstration Mongo tried again, successfully sticking the axe. He never missed again. Another life-long friendship began.

The more Jeff learned about the renaissance era, the more he found he liked it, including the music of the period. Of all the Celtic bands that played the assorted renaissance festivals, his favorite was *The Rogues*, a foursome who played the pipes and drums. From the first time he saw them perform, Jeff loved *The Rogues* and was drawn to the stage whenever they played. Composed of Lars Sloan, Randy Wothke, Bryan Blaylock, and Jimmy Mitchell, *The Rogues* were a fixture at the Texas Renaissance Festival, where Jeff also participated. In 1996, *The Rogues* began performing at the Scarborough Festival as well. He eventually befriended the band and was taken in to an extent that many assumed he was a member of the troupe. Nelson Stewart, who replaced departing member Bryan Blaylock in 2001, remembered the day he met Jeff. Not long after joining the band, Stewart was preparing to perform in Waxahachie. He had heard

Nelson Stewart in the grasp of his friend Jeff Thompson. Photo courtesy of the Thompson family.

legendary stories from his fellow musicians about a giant of a man, a colossus whose chariot was a Honda Gold Wing and who spoke with the voice of God. He was both eager and a little afraid to meet this giant...afraid that perhaps Mayhem wouldn't take to him. As he was contemplating this eventual meeting, the sun became obscured and Stewart found himself peering upwards into the eyes of a titan. Mayhem was as massive as anyone who had played in the NFL or fought in the world of professional wrestling.

"My name is Mayhem. How are you doing?" the big man rumbled.

Noting the flowers in his braided goatee, Stewart thought for a second before replying. "Oh, you're Mayhem. I've been looking forward to meeting you. I was thinking, if you're

Mayhem jams with Bryan Blaylock of *The Rogues*. After Jeff's death, Bryan would start a new band called "*Scottish Mayhem*" in honor of his friend. Photo courtesy of the Thompson family.

Mayhem, do you think I could maybe be Apocalypse or Armageddon?"

"Are you making fun of my name?" Jeff replied.

Before the word "maybe" could escape Stewart's lips, Mayhem picked him up. "Okay, looks like were going to have to have a tickle fight," Mayhem said, and he proceeded to tickle Stewart until he couldn't breathe.[4]

Jeff's passion for *The Rogues* was appreciated and respected by the group's members. At performances, Jeff would introduce the band and occasionally sat in with them after learning how to play the *bodhran;* an ancient frame drum, traditionally made with a wooden body and a goatskin head. It is played with a double-headed stick called a *cipín*, *tipper*, or *beater*. He became so skilled at the instrument that he would be called to "sit in" with the band on occasions when Stewart was unavailable to perform. In fact, Jeff once hopped aboard his beloved Gold Wing and rode all the way to Wisconsin to help *The Rogues* out. He also took it upon himself to help add to the coffers of the performers. Prior to the end of a show, he wandered through the audience with a tip container, encouraging contributions by saying, "Please tip the pipers or I will have to get my daytime job back as a school bus driver. Really! I can show you my license!"

Left: Mayhem encouraging the crowd to tip the pipers and drummers of *The Rogues*. Jeff was a skilled people person who knew how to play to the crowds. Top right: Jeff Thompson playing the bodhran with *The Rogues*. Photos courtesy of the Thompson family. Bottom right: Members of *The Rogues* and several cast members of the Scarborough Festival pose with Jeffery "Mayhem" Thompson. Sharon Wothke is seated in front. After Jeff's death she created a beautiful photo album for Jeff's family. Many of her photos grace the pages of this book.

In 2001, Jeff had a verbal confrontation with the new owner of the Scarborough Festival complex and was fired from his caretaker role, consequently losing his rent-free home. He found a new apartment in the basement of a dark, dingy warehouse used as a rehearsal hall for rock bands. As he had at the fair, Jeff worked out a deal with the building's owner, swapping his maintenance skills for a place to stay. From the accounts of his many friends in Texas, however, Jeff almost never stayed at the warehouse apartment as he always had a dinner invitation and a place to stay. With lodging taken care of, Jeff's immediate need was to find a way to make some money. After years of hearing Shadow's stories and experiences working in security, Jeff decided to try his hand at being a bouncer. Jeff's massive physique and tactful, diplomatic temperament had led Shadow to realize that Jeff was perfect for a position in security. Shadow's previous security experiences included providing basic security at clubs and bars all the way up to personal protective services for celebrities and business executives. When it came to mixing the dual role of protector and deflecting potential trouble, no one was better than Shadow.

At 6-foot, 8-inches tall and tipping the scales at more than 350 pounds, Jeff's physical stature and communicative ability opened doors for him in the Deep Ellum district of Dallas. A fashionable, hip, entertainment and arts district east of downtown Dallas, its interesting shops and nightclubs promise plenty of opportunities for those urbanites looking for a chance to shop or cut loose and party. It was here, in Deep Ellum, that Jeff's friend Michael "Mongo" Smith helped him find work at

Jeff Thompson certainly did see short people as his shirt so accurately states. Photo courtesy of the Thompson family.

establishments like Coyote Ugly.[5] Mongo ran the sound and mixing board at various local haunts. With his input and Shadow's guidance, Jeff learned that trust, discretion, and professionalism were the primary keys to working security. Shadow, a true security professional, understood that the real gauge of effectiveness wasn't how much "butt one could kick," but the ability to calmly diffuse a situation with words. Shadow promoted his belief that it was all about "being nice until you can't be nice anymore." He made certain that Mayhem understood exactly what he meant. If however, physical force was required, Shadow's advice was simple and succinct: approach the biggest guy causing problems, put him in a headlock, and show him the door. With Jeff's massive size, Shadow knew that, if the big one went, the smaller troublemakers would be sure to follow.

It was solid, sound advice. Mayhem, as Shadow predicted, became an exceptional bouncer who relied far more on his wits than his brawn to keep order. In fact, Shadow remembers only one occasion where Jeff was compelled to use force to calm a situation. Jeff's attributes made him a much appreciated and sought after commodity for clubs in Deep Ellum.

"Is there a problem?" Jeff Thompson puts on his working face in his role as a bouncer.

Working at the nightclubs opened the door for Jeff to take advantage of other opportunities. Radio stations occasionally set up and operated remotely from nightclubs where Jeff was working; his enormous persona and fun-loving nature made him a favorite among the disc jockeys. Realizing that Jeff's talents extended beyond providing security, soon the jocks at 97.1, The Eagle, began inviting Jeff to give his "two cents" about topics on the air.

It didn't take long for Jeff to land a part-time job as part of the promotional team for DJs Kramer and Twitch. For Jeff, the job was perfect; he loved the "cool factor" of occasionally being on the radio, and his deep, booming voice was perfect for the medium. His forte with the show was participating in on-air stunts and gags, in addition to working security for them at public promotional events.

Working at The Eagle gave Jeff the opportunity to show his versatility. It also put him in a position to meet rock stars and other celebrities. He'd occasionally use the station's Hummer to take his close friend, Shannon, out to dinner. Photo courtesy of the Thompson family.

While the pay wasn't that great, perks like concert tickets and opportunities to meet rock stars made the job fun. On the air at The Eagle plus visible and well known in Deep Ellum's clubs, Jeff became a minor celebrity in and around Dallas.

As a part of the radio station promotions department, Jeff shared the duties of firing up The Eagle listeners with Anthony Schnurr, who had joined the Eagle's promotional team in 2002 and, in the eyes of some of his co-workers, had only gotten the job because he was a friend of the station's unpopular promotions director. The 6-foot, 3-inch tall Schnurr remembers meeting Jeff for the first time and feeling intimidated by the hulk of a man. Jeff, like others at the station, wasn't initially keen on Schnurr. However, as the two men worked together on promotional projects, they got to know each other. One day Jeff turned to Schnurr with a wide grin growing on his face and said, "You know man, you're all right." Jeff and Anthony became friends, hanging out with each other after gigs or when not working at The Eagle. Jeff owned what

Schnurr called "a crappy old truck" that broke down so often that Schnurr was constantly driving Jeff home or to gigs.

Jeff may have been a big, intimidating man, but his time at The Eagle also showcased his enthusiasm for fun and willingness to participate in typical rock radio juvenile behavior. During one particular on-air event, the radio station invited fans to apply for "apprentice positions" at the station in an attempt to play off the popular TV show, "The Apprentice." Those who had the courage to apply for slots volunteered to participate in wacky stunts and a myriad of foolish behavior. When it came to sheer humiliation, no stunt could equal the hilarious gag entitled "Marshmallow Mayhem," thought up by Schnurr. For the contestant unlucky enough to be selected to participate, the gag consisted of eating marshmallows out

Jeff Thompson doing an off-site promotion for 97.1 The Eagle in Dallas. Photo courtesy of the Thompson family.

of Jeff's butt crack. Jeff altered a pair of boxer shorts, cutting a hole in the backside to expose his butt cheeks. As unappetizing as it sounds, contestants eager to become a part of The Eagle team chowed down on marshmallows crammed between Jeff's cheeks. For The Eagle, the hilarious stunt proved extremely popular, and Jeff became a legend in his own time—in addition to making an extra $100.

While money continued to be tight, Shadow's wise counsel on performing in a security role was paying off for Jeff. Working in Deep Ellum as well as the radio station not only helped pay his bills, it also put Jeff in the position of meeting musicians and aspiring new rock bands in the Dallas area. Around 1999, Jeff found himself becoming more involved in providing personal security to bands and occasionally working at concerts. One of the first bands with which he worked was a new band called *Drowning Pool*. Through the members of *Drowning Pool*, especially its lead singer Dave Williams,[6] Jeff was introduced to two brothers, Vinnie Paul and Darrell Abbott from the massively popular heavy metal band *Pantera*. His first "working" venture with the boys was acting as a chauffeur, driving them around the Dallas area. With his intimidating size and obvious intelligence, the Abbotts soon recognized that Jeff could be an asset. They sensed that Jeff possessed an ability to defuse problems with diplomacy. In addition, he was polite and courteous and relied more on his brain than his brawn. In a world where public relations could make or break a celebrity, Jeff's attributes were something special. He used polite phrases like "What can I do for you, sir?" Soon the Abbott brothers began to hire Jeff for various chores in addition to driving their limo. They knew that if they asked something of Mayhem, the reply would be a respectful, "coming right up!" More and more he was providing personal security to the two rock stars when they were out and about in the Dallas area.

When it came to working with rock bands, Jeff was very discreet and never betrayed the trust placed in him. When it came to *Pantera* and the Abbott brothers, as far as Jeff was concerned, what happened around the *Pantera* camp stayed at the *Pantera* camp. Even with his frequent brushes with various celebrities, Jeff remained down to earth and never used his relationships with stars to be self-promoting.

Throughout the years, Jeff continued to work for the Abbott brothers, and his relationship with the famous musicians became stronger. They implicitly trusted him and often, on jaunts to casinos or other such trips, it was Mayhem who carried the money, frequently amounting to thousands of dollars. For his part, Jeff was truly devoted to serving them in whatever capacity they desired—be it security, as a driver, or just as a companion. Jeff never forgot that he worked for the brothers, but his relationship transcended even that. Vinnie Paul and Dimebag Darrell had taken Jeff into their inner sanctum; he'd been to their home, met their families and business associates, and traveled with them. To the Abbotts, Mayhem wasn't just some employee—he was a trusted friend. As with any of his friends, Mayhem often expressed his love for the brothers, remarking with complete seriousness, "I'd take a bullet for ya."

On tour with *Damageplan*. During a gig in Dallas, Mayhem, with his beard dyed red, keeps an eye on things from behind Dime's amplifier stacks. Oct. 24, 2004. Photo courtesy of Chad Lee - www.rockconcertfotos.com

Yet, as much as he liked spending time with the Abbotts and working his various jobs, Jeff found his greatest respite with Shannon. In his security jobs he was compelled to carry himself as a larger-than-life, always prepared defender. Around the radio station, he helped provide amusement to listeners and staff. Only with Shannon could Jeff simply be himself. There was no role-playing, he wasn't at anyone's beck and call, and he didn't need to try to impress anyone.

Jeff separated his rock 'n' roll world from his normal day-to-day life. He even kept his close friend and festival queen Shannon Bradley at arm's length from his brushes with his famous friends. Occasionally Jeff pulled up outside Shannon's home with *Pantera*'s limousine to take her to dinner, but he never exposed her to the lifestyle of heavy metal royalty. Sometimes Jeff would text message Shannon from events or e-mail her photos of himself with the guys from whatever band with which he was working as the time. Jeff's work with *Pantera* was a part of his life he really didn't seem to want Shannon to see. Even as his relationship with *Pantera* and other bands grew, Jeff never took her to the parties or concerts they hosted. His relationship with Shannon remained platonic, but it was obvious that Jeff was smitten with the dark-haired beauty. His father Frank refers to Shannon as "the love of Jeff's life." To that end, Jeff wasn't about to risk tarnishing his reputation with Shannon or her family. He didn't permit her to see him "acting up" or sharing in the shenanigans that often was a part of parties thrown by rock bands.

Shannon was Jeff's outlet. He felt completely comfortable and free to be himself and say what he wanted. The two spent quiet time together at dinner and at Shannon's home. He arrived at her door almost weekly to take her out to dinner. His favorite haunt was Outback Steakhouse, where he would start his meal with a shot of Crown and Coke.[7] For dinner, he loved a well-done steak with mashed potatoes or steamed veggies. Jeff spent nearly every holiday with Shannon and her family. If neither had a date on any given Valentine's Day, they shared it together while pounding Guinness with dinner at a steakhouse. On Thanksgivings, he spent the majority of the day with Shannon before jumping on his motorcycle to ride to Austin, Texas, to spend time with Shadow's family. Jeff boasted to his friends that each year he had two Thanksgivings.

Opposite page: Jeff Thompson with the love of his life, Shannon Bradley. Above: Jeff relaxes with a glass of wine and a puppy dog! Photos courtesy of the Thompson family.

As much as Jeff loved his "Texas Family," the holiday season prompted his thoughts to move slightly northeast and he would speak of his "Arkansas Family." Few in Texas besides Shannon and Shadow knew much of Jeff's blood relatives in Arkansas. Both knew that Jeff and his father had experienced an acrimonious parting of the ways the year Jeff moved to Texas. However, over the years they had witnessed a softening of Jeff's frustration as it evolved into regret. Both Shadow and Shannon were pleased to witness Jeff reconnecting more and more with his father and family in Arkansas.

Jeff and his father put the eight years of silence behind them by establishing more frequent communication. What started out as phone calls soon graduated to Jeff returning home on trips to Arkansas to visit and reconnect. In 1999, the triplets, Micah, Martin, and Seth, expressed an interest in

Mayhem playing the bodhran at the Scarborough Renaissance Festival. Photo courtesy of Sharon Wothke.

attending a *Motley Crüe* concert in Little Rock. One of the boys mentioned this to Jeff during a phone call, and Jeff told his father that he'd like to take his brothers to the show. He'd drive up from Dallas, pick them up in Newport, drive down to Little Rock, and bring them home. Without hesitating, Frank said okay. He knew that the triplets would be in safe hands.

Frank was thankful to be back in touch with Jeff. During his visits, Jeff regaled his father with his many adventures in Dallas and in the world of the renaissance. On one occasion, he brought his *bodhran* home to Arkansas and proudly demonstrated his skills in playing the instrument to his father. He spoke of his acting opportunities and—most of all—he talked about his friends in Texas. On each visit, Jeff did his best to try to explain the joys of his wonderful lifestyle to his father. From acting to bodyguard work, Jeff excitedly told his dad about the many opportunities he saw for himself in Dallas. He also spoke of working for the heavy metal band *Pantera* and that he'd become friends with Dimebag Darrell and his brother Vinnie Paul Abbott.

When it came to the heavy metal side of things, Frank

didn't approve. Over the years, he'd felt the callings of the Lord and fully accepted his faith. After answering the call, he had become a preacher. For Frank, heavy metal and all its trappings were part of a lifestyle he simply couldn't fathom. The fact that his son lived in what Frank perceived as a dark, evil world of debauchery frustrated him. He knew his son was special and wanted him to be doing "better" than living what he felt was a Godless life. Frank, as always, spoke his mind to Jeff about his beliefs and convictions. Jeff chalked much of what his father was saying up to "bible thumping."

Despite occasional disagreements, one thing was clear. Father and son had reestablished. "You know Dad, I'm so glad you taught me to work." Those few words filled Frank with pride as he recognized the thoughtfulness of his son's words. While Frank would never be comfortable with Jeff's lifestyle, he realized that his son was happy with his life in Texas.

Although Jeff rarely talked about his relationships with women, he told his father about one important girl in his life: Shannon. He told his dad that she was "the queen" at the festival and that he "laced her up" in her costume each day. Then he spent his day protecting her. Beyond

1. Jeff with Shannon Bradley. 2. At a friends wedding, the gigantic Jeff Thompson filled the role of "flower girl." With a sense of humor to match his size, laughter, jokes, pranks and an appreciation of juvenile humor were an important part of Mayhem's life. Photos courtesy of the Thompson family.

this, Frank knew little about Shannon, but he definitely sensed his son's strong affection for her.

Mayhem and a friend take a spin on his Honda Gold Wing. Courtesy of the Thompson family.

Despite their close connection and incredible friendship, the pragmatist in Jeff felt he wasn't a suitable "catch" for a woman like Shannon. A career professional, she was a senior officer and fire marshal in the Dallas Fire Department. Jeff, on the other hand, lived and worked like a gypsy, existing from paycheck to paycheck, staying out late, and brushing elbows with celebrities. His life was far from conservative, yet he adored her enough to refrain from trying to take the relationship to the next level. He wished only the best for her and knew that one day he would have to step aside when she found "Mr. Right." He was confident that, no matter what happened, he would never lose her as his friend or ever stop loving her.

In Shannon's company, Jeff occasionally expressed his concern about his longevity to her. He often confided to her that he felt he wouldn't live past the age of 40. It was just a feeling he had. Shannon chided him, reminding him that he had quit smoking, was exercising more, and was losing weight, yet even with these facts, Jeff simply shrugged his shoulders, unconvinced.

Throughout their friendship, despite the fact that they were in constant contact, nothing equaled the renaissance "season." They had created their own Scarborough Festival tradition—a tradition of friendship. Each looked forward to the bonding afforded by its innocent intimacy. For any woman, a renaissance gown is not something to simply "slip into"; the cumbersome, uncomfortable gowns laced up the back require a second set of hands. Each morning during the festival, Shannon parked next to Jeff's cabin on the Scarborough grounds. She brought a "firehouse" breakfast that the two enjoyed as they talked. After breakfast, Jeff—the enormous giant of a man—helped Shannon dress in her incredibly fragile and delicate renaissance costume. They then toasted the coming day with a shot of Vodka. It was a tradition that they had shared for more than a dozen years without fail. At the close of the show each day, they met up again so Jeff could help extract Shannon from her costume. Always the gentleman, he averted his eyes when required.

In the fall of 2001, Jeff became a player at the Texas Renaissance Festival in Houston. Allan Hopps, a fellow crew member, approached Jeff and told him he needed to talk about Shannon. When it came to Shannon and men, Jeff was extremely protective and suspicious. Most suitors who attempted to woo Shannon simply didn't cut the mustard and were run off by the woman herself, but Allan was different. Unlike the others, he hung around and seemed more persistent, perhaps more serious. Consequently, Jeff hovered near Shannon when possible, keeping an eye on his friend while wondering what mischief Allan was perpetrating. As Shannon and Allan became closer, she knew that one day she'd have to have "the talk" with Allan about Jeff. As far as Shannon was concerned, she seemed to sense that Allan would, on some level, have to gain Jeff's approval to date her or there would be no peace.[12] That day finally came, and Allan sought Jeff's "approval" to date Shannon. She had no idea about the conversation itself, but its results were revealed to her when she saw Jeff the following week.

"How's Allan doing?" he asked.

With that single question, she knew Allan had had "the talk." Before that day, Jeff had never used Allan's name. He had always been "that guy." When asked how she felt about Jeff's sense of over-protectiveness, Shannon wistfully replied, "how can you not love that?"

1. On tour with *Damageplan*, Jeff Thompson, aka, "Metal Elvis" occasionally rocked out on stage with Dimebag. Photo courtesy of Tracy Hill.

In July 2004, it was Shannon's turn to have a chat with Jeff. This time she broke the news that she and Allan were getting married. She would become Shannon Hopps. Jeff, with great kindness and sensitivity, unhesitatingly gave his approval and congratulated the bride-to-be. The wedding date was set for November 2004.

Meanwhile, from 2002 to 2004, Jeff was gaining greater exposure to the business of working with rock 'n' roll bands. His work with *Slow Roosevelt, Sevendust*, and *Drowning Pool* led him to realize that perhaps this was his calling. He began to express a desire to one day become a road manager for a touring rock band. Confident that it was something he would enjoy, he reasoned that, if he were going to make a "career move," he might as well take a management position. What Jeff lacked, however, was road time. To fill that square meant finding a band willing to give him a break and take him on tour in some capacity. He knew he'd never have the chance to be a road manager without real-world experience.

As summer turned into fall in 2004, life appeared routine for the man whose life was anything but routine. During the past eight months he'd worked the Scarborough Renaissance Festival, helped out *The Rogues* on a couple shows, and helped out part time with some new rock bands. In addition, he had filled some slots for several TV commercials and managed to keep his Honda Gold Wing out of hock. Financially, things were not the greatest, but this was nothing new for Jeff. Besides, he had friends who loved him and would help him if needed. He never lacked for a warm bed or a hot meal and rarely spent time at his dive of an apartment. Before he knew it, the holidays would be upon him and "his" Shannon would be getting married. Overall, for Jeff it hadn't been a bad year at all.

In the first week of October

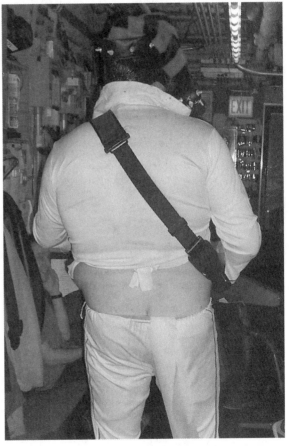

Shades of Marshmallow Mayhem. Backstage at the House of Blues in his "Metal Elvis" costume. Photos courtesy of Tracy Hill.

2004, Jeff's cell phone rang. It was Chris Paluska, the road manager for the Abbott brothers' new band, *Damageplan*. The band's chief of security had stepped down, and Dimebag Darrell and Vinnie Paul wanted to know if Jeff would be interested in taking over for the final leg of their 2004 North American tour. If he were to take the job, Mayhem would be on the road traveling the U.S. and Canada from October until the middle of December.[8] It was the job Jeff knew he needed if he truly wanted to take the next step to managing a band. Without hesitation, Jeff agreed to take the position. As he hung up he felt even better about the year!

Suddenly he realized what he had done. He immediately picked up the phone and dialed.

It was only six weeks before her wedding when Shannon's cell phone rang. It was Jeff. Softly he told her he'd just been offered the chance to go on the road with "the boys."

She knew this meant the Abbott brothers and their new band *Damageplan*. As excited as he was by this opportunity, he realized that if he took the job he would miss her wedding. Knowing that sharing the road with *Damageplan* was a great chance for Jeff to experience life on the road with a band, she downplayed the wedding and encouraged him to go.

"Hey, this is what you've dreamed of!" she told him without hesitation.

"But I'll miss your wedding," he moaned.

Mayhem encourages photographer Chad Lee to enthusiastically "flash metal." Oct. 24, 2004. Photo courtesy of Chad Lee - www.rockconcertfotos.com

"Go, go," she urged him. "This is your dream, and you know I'll see you when you get home." After all, her wedding would be a humble ceremony. He, on the other hand, had a chance to attain a dream and perhaps create an opportunity for a career. "You go or I'll push you on that bus myself," Shannon growled.

Jeff was thrilled and relieved that she supported him and "would let him go." His next call was to his father to tell him that he would be on the road with *Damageplan*. He explained that he'd be a bodyguard and a gopher for the band on the fall leg of their tour. His father congratulated him on the job and was confident that Jeff would be successful.

Jeff then called Shadow and excitedly told him about going on tour with the Abbotts. Shadow congratulated Jeff and offered him some serious advice. "Hey man, if you're going to be on the road, you need to carry. I mean you've got to think about the worst-case scenario." Shadow encouraged his friend to get a concealed handgun permit, but he never knew if Jeff took his advice or not.

Mayhem extricates Damageplan vocalist Pat Lachman from the grasp of the audience. Photo courtesy of Tracy Hill.

Allen and Shannon were married while Jeff was on the road with *Damageplan*. Although Jeff couldn't break free to attend the wedding, he did send his congratulations via text message.

On Thanksgiving Day 2004 while on tour with *Damageplan*, Jeff called his father from Washington, D.C. "Hey Dad, how's it going?" he asked. "I'm finishing up my laundry and figured I'd give you a call and wish everyone a Happy Thanksgiving."

It was the last time they would ever speak to each other.

While on the road, Mayhem was a jack of all trades. From security to photographer, Jeff could be counted on to make things happen. Here he takes some "creative" film of his friend Dimebag during a *Damageplan* performance. Photo courtesy of Tracy Hill.

Mayhem and Dimebag share a drink on Dec. 7, 2004. Less than 24 hours later both men would be dead. Photo courtesy of the Thompson family.

Have a drink on me. Dimebag's skills with the guitar extended far beyond playing! July 24, 2004, Madison, WI. Photo courtesy of Chad Lee - www.rockconcertfotos.com

Dime Time

The first time I ever saw Dime was on MTV's "Headbangers Ball" in 1990. I was just 16 years old. I loved metal and bands like *Metallica, Slayer*, and *Sepultura*. I was learning to play all that stuff on my guitar. I remember sitting on my couch with a smuggled beer, late at night, watching videos. All of a sudden, a new band called *Pantera* popped up on the screen. The song was called "Cemetery Gates." I heard the singer with his crazy vocal range and saw a long-haired guitarist playing through Randall amps. He was belting out some of the most blazing chops and his creative shrills and bellows fit the song so perfectly. After the video, the host did an interview with Dime and Phil. They seemed very down-to-earth and funny as hell. They were obviously very talented but didn't seem to have the arrogance of your typical rocker.

The next day, I made my way to the music store because I was so stoked about these dudes, I had to have the album and hear more! I shelled out my 13 bucks for the tape, and listened to that thing over and over and over. I was hooked, and in a major way. I told everyone I knew about Pantera.

About two weeks later, I discovered that Pantera was playing Flash Gordon's, a local heavy metal club in my hometown of Cleveland. "Flashes" was a small club and that night there couldn't have been 100 people there. We walked in and saw all the band members sitting at the bar pounding booze and talking. Unfortunately, we decided not to bother them, so we didn't even say hello.

When they played, from the first chord to the last drumbeat, they tore the s**t out of that place—so much so that they didn't want to stop playing and the owners finally shut the power off. It was 3 am. The highlight of the evening was when Dime broke the "Dean from Hell's" headstock off for the very first time. That was the guitar you see on the *Cowboys* album cover and Dime's first true love! So right in the middle of one of the songs, Dime jumps backwards and spins off the riser, accidentally cracking some kid over the back of the head with the headstock of the guitar. Dimes eyes got about as big as melons when it happened, but I'll tell you what, he never missed a note and finished the song with the headstock dangling as it broke behind the locking nut.

After the show, my friend and I ignored the people telling us to leave and went up by the stage to say hello. Dime was crouched over with his guitar tech talking about the headstock saying, "How we gonna fix this man? You know that's my love right there." He looked up at us standing there and said, "Hey guys! What's up?" He had just seriously damaged his favorite guitar yet he stopped and took time to say hello. He came over to us and we made small talk about the show! He was more than happy to talk to us and he spoke from the heart.

I explained how I loved his tone, and at that time, had a Randall RM100 that I used as my main amp. Again, his face lit up and he asked us if we wanted to see his setup. Now our eyes were like those melons. Both of us climbed up on stage and Dime took us through each piece of equipment he had. I told him I was struggling to find the right sound. His words to me were: "Just hang in there, man. Try everything and you'll find your sound. It took me forever to come up with this, but it's crushing, isn't it?"

Some more small talk and then the question, "Would you sign my album cover?"

"Hell yeah, man, no problem," he said.

I told him I felt honored and he gave me a look and said, "No man, I'm honored."

A few years later, I was in Baltimore, bar-hopping with some co-workers. We walked into this bar and I spotted two long-haired dudes. One of them had a bright red beard. Sure enough, it was Dime and Vinnie. They had just played a venue down the street. I walked over and said hello to them. Dime cocked his head to the side and gave me a squinty-eyed stare. I asked if he had ever managed to get the lightning-bolt Dean fixed after he broke the headstock in Cleveland a few years back. His face lit up and he said, "Holy s**t! I thought you looked familiar," and he gave me a big hug. To this day, those two times live on as if they happened yesterday.

Jeff "Stinger" Brown at the stage door to the
Alrosa Villa, November 2006. Photo by Chris A.

I remember waking up on the morning of December 9, 2004, and getting myself ready for work. As I headed to work, I had the local radio station on and was surprised to hear "Cemetery Gates" playing at 8 am. After the song was done, there was a long pause and the D.J. said that was a small tribute to the late great Dimebag. He then explained what happened in Columbus. I was in traffic and had to pull over. I said to myself, "this has to be a sick joke, no way"...I listened as they gave out the only details that were available and my soul sank, and I began to cry. I was frozen, horrified by the thoughts of what had happened. Doubly haunting that the same song that drew me to Dime was the same song I had to say goodbye to him with. Shocked, upset, and horrified, I called off work and returned home.

I sat miserably by the computer trying to gain some shred of proof that this wasn't a bad report that leaked out. That never came, and the truth haunts me to this day. In early 2006, I took a business trip to Texas. I rented a car and drove from San Antonio to Dallas. I met up with some friends and they showed me around the area. We went to Dime's favorite spots and visited his grave. I spent about two or three hours with Dime, crying. I told him stories of my life and how he changed me. I passed along hellos and a few goodbyes from other acquaintances of ours. It for me was closure to something that I still didn't want to believe...losing an idol, a hero, a brother. His radiating smile and endless humor still live on. In his honor, we make sure that his stories never die. His legacy continues in all of us. I love you, Dime. I'll see you soon, my Black Label brother. GETCHA PULL!

– Jeff "Stinger" Brown, Dime fan and friend of the author

Chapter 9

F'n Hostile

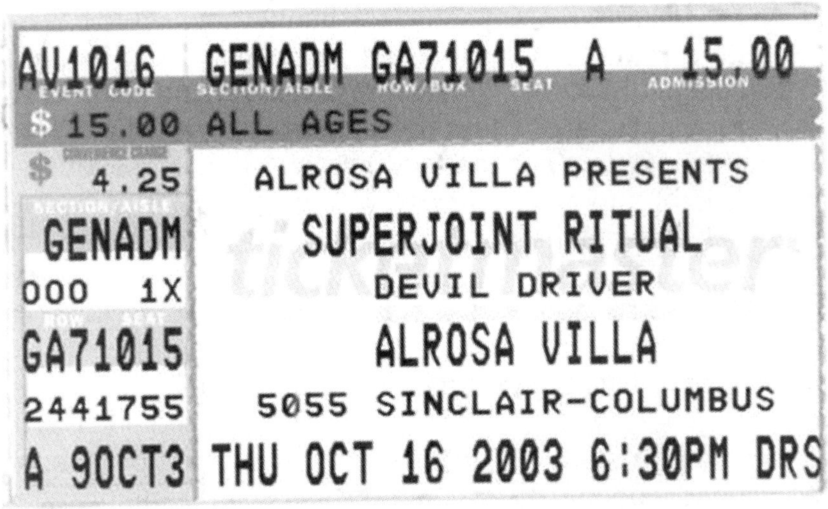

```
AV1016  GENADM  GA71015  A    15.00
EVENT CODE  SECTION/AISLE  ROW/BOX  SEAT  ADMISSION
$ 15.00  ALL AGES
$    4.25   ALROSA VILLA PRESENTS
CONVENIENCE CHARGE
SECTION/AISLE
GENADM      SUPERJOINT RITUAL
000    1X    DEVIL DRIVER
ROW    SEAT
GA71015     ALROSA VILLA
2441755   5055 SINCLAIR-COLUMBUS
A 9OCT3 THU OCT 16 2003 6:30PM DRS
```

"If you could see yourself
You put you on a shelf
Your verbal masturbate
Promise to nauseate."

F**king Hostile
Vulgar Display of Power
-Pantera

On October 16, 2003, former *Pantera* lead singer Phil Anselmo rolled into Columbus, Ohio, to perform with his new band, *Superjoint Ritual*. The venue was a small roadhouse called the Alrosa Villa.

From the moment *Superjoint Ritual* appeared on stage, there was an uncomfortable vibe in the venue. During his last few years in *Pantera* and with his first solo-project, *Down*, Anselmo's attitude toward his audience had become hostile and confrontational. He seemed to take pleasure in provoking his audiences.

On this night, many of the security personnel working at the Alrosa Villa were black. Anselmo couldn't help but observe the racial makeup of the security personnel working at the front of the stage. Throughout his career, Anselmo had been plagued by accusations that he was a racist. A case in point was a 1995 *Pantera* concert in Montreal, where Anselmo had made several comments that were interpreted as inappropriate and racist. Many of these concert ramblings were captured on film and posted on the Internet.

According to concert attendee Kevin McMeans,[1] Anselmo badgered the Alrosa Villa's audience and encouraged "stage dives," telling the audience; *"Our stage is your stage, you get up here and jump off!"* While the facts are somewhat questionable, apparently the volatile vocalist was told someone had allegedly gone through their possessions in the dressing room. Anselmo apparently became irate, and shouted into the microphone, *"That's something a nig*er would do."* Rick Cautela, owner of the Alrosa Villa was horrified by Anselmo's venomous outburst. And, in response, Alrosa's security men calmly shut down the *Superjoint Ritual* merchandise table, hitting Anselmo where it would hurt the most, his wallet. They then turned their attention toward Anselmo.

The venue's lights were turned up and a palpable concern spread throughout the audience. At the side of the stage, Phil Anselmo was confronted by half a dozen of the venue's security staff. They made it emphatically clear that

[1] Chapter 9 footnotes begin on page 309.

racist comments would not be tolerated at the Alrosa Villa. Anselmo sheepishly returned to center stage and offered a backhanded apology to the crowd, saying he was sorry for his poor choice of words. He concluded by saying, *"Hey, we're white trash and that's no better."*

The show was permitted to continue but *Superjoint Ritual* would never again see the inside of the Alrosa Villa. Cautela made a mental note never to hire Phil Anselmo again.

Thirteen months later, in November 2004, the British heavy metal magazine *Metal Hammer* conducted a telephone interview with Phil Anselmo. The primary objective of the interview was Anselmo's explanations and thoughts on the breakup of *Pantera*. The *Metal Hammer* journalist called from London to speak with the singer at his Louisiana home.

It was clear from the interview that Anselmo carried a huge chip on his shoulder. The interview was a rambling lecture of rationalizations and finger pointing. Anselmo was bellicose as he assigned responsibility for the breakup of *Pantera* to everyone but himself. It didn't take long for the interview to transition into a disjointed speech. Anselmo, seeming to lack cohesive thoughts, shifted gears. One minute he dictated his thoughts in the first person, the next in a pretentious and often confusing attempt to speak in the third person. His poor vocabulary, coupled with his self-absorbed arrogance, produced malicious quotes in a botched attempt to appear articulate and thoughtful.

As the interview progressed, Anselmo was asked about his various solo projects, including his other band, *Down*. Anselmo responded that it would take much soul-searching and compromises with his bandmates for him to consider taking the act back on the road.

As Anselmo continued on the topic of *Down*, his aggressive nature reared its ugly head again.

Anselmo: *"It hurt as well when Electra records s**t all over us. I guess they are feeling the karma of that now and what comes around obviously goes around, and that is definitely something that is a very powerful force in my life."*

Phil Anselmo. Photo by Frank White Photography and Photo Agency (973) 384-9133

The interviewer asked Anselmo what point he was trying to make, and said rhetorically: *"Things move in cycles?"*

Anselmo's answer was ominous. *"Beyond cycles. Cycles on top of cycles. Revenge on top of revenge. I suggest no one do me wrong."*

The interviewer was taken aback by Anselmo's less than veiled threat. Again, he tried to clarify exactly what Anselmo was alluding to and asked; *"Because people tend to get like revenged against when things happen to you? I don't mean that in a violent way, I mean things people get paid back?"*

Anselmo: *"Things don't go so well for them."*

Interviewer: *"I see."*

Anselmo: *"And I lift not a finger."*

Interviewer: *"Okay, I see."*

The interview continued with the journalist asking what created the distance between he (Anselmo), Vinnie Paul, and Dimebag. His answer was acerbic and ominous.

Anselmo: *"He (Dimebag) would attack me vocally, and just knowing that he was so much smaller than me I could kill him like a f**king piece of vapor. You know, he would turn into vapor. His chin would, at least, if I f**king smacked it. He knows that and the world should know that and so, physically of course, he deserves to be beaten severely. But of course that's criminal and I won't do such a thing."*

As outrageous as the statement was on its own, Anselmo's incendiary words continued as he stroked his own ego.

Anselmo: *"I proved clearly to everyone what I was. And what I was, was a unique, unbelievably magnetic front man that had not been around since the days of Robert Plant and Ozzy Osbourne. I am one in a million because I have staying power. I have a devoted following that would do anything for me, anything that I say."[2]*

His remarks were typical Anselmo bravado yet they were reprehensible as he seemingly tried to send a less than subliminal message. His own statement made it shockingly clear he recognized the power and influence his words conveyed to an element of his fan base.

"I have a devoted following that would do anything for me, anything that I say."

Metal Hammer magazine published the incendiary Anselmo interview in December 2004. The music media immediately recognized the sensationalism of his inflammatory and egotistical comments. The online, heavy-metal Website Blabbermouth.net posted several extracts of the provocative interview on December 1, 2004.

Nathan Gale was known to use the library, in addition to his mother's home computer, to access the Internet. Did Gale read the *Metal Hammer* interview or excerpts of it posted on-line? Perhaps someone told him about it. Factually, it's a question that will remain unanswered. No one truly knows if Gale was influenced by Anselmo's comment that Dimebag deserved to be beaten severely or that he could be killed *"like a f**king piece of vapor."*

What was beyond dispute was the fact that Dimebag and Damageplan would be playing a gig in Columbus in seven days and Nathan Gale would also be there.[3]

Skulls by Bob Tyrrell, done in pencil. Photo courtesy
of Bob Tyrrell, Night Gallery - www.bobtyrrell.com

Dime Time

Dimebag and his "brother" Zakk Wylde of Black Label Society hang out on the side stage as Kerry King and *Slayer* perform in Houston, TX. August 8, 2004. Photo courtesy of Chad Lee - www.rockconcertfotos.com

When I was growing up, there were four thrash bands that dominated heavy metal: *Metallica, Anthrax, Megadeth*, and *Slayer*. I think back to the metal information media available to me in the 1980s. No Internet, no YouTube, no MySpace, no message boards, and no e-mail. All I had were magazines like *Kerrang!* and *Metal Hammer*.

I also took a regular Friday night jaunt to the Rock Night at Bonnies, a club in Lower Sydenham, South London. Those Fridays were absolutely crucial to me in forming my musical appreciation. I can remember loving all the bands the D.J. was playing, asking him for a copy of his play lists.

A vivid recollection is of the dance floor filling up when the opening bars of *Metallica's* "Master of Puppets" came blasting out of the speakers. It was certainly the biggest and quickest floor-filler of the time. *Metallica* became my favorite band, after I'd been weaned on *Iron Maiden, AC/DC,* and *Black Sabbath*. Then I discovered *Megadeth*. *Megadeth* turned out to be arty and political in comparison to *Metallica's* chugging doom-filled riffs. Soon after, the manic *Anthrax* turned up and turned heads with their comedy routines, great entertainment, and mad moshing. *Slayer* had the devil on their side. They reigned in blood in my room for months. I also experimented with *Celtic Frost, Metal Church,* and the like. *Metallica's Black Album* was nearly upon us, and the end was nigh.

But still something was missing. I couldn't put my finger on it. However, the answer came from *Pantera* and the answer was...GROOVE! A single-guitar outfit that played an extreme sound vibe, but with a groove: a clean guitar busting through. Groove! Groove! Groove! I had been up close and personal with a few brutal bands, but *Pantera* was on another level, and they single-handedly reignited a decaying power-metal scene.

And once they had reignited it, they f**king burnt the house down. F**king hostile by name and f**king hostile by nature, they f**king spat out "grunge"—and kept us all sanely insane in between times! From *Cowboys* to *Vulgar*, they got all points in between—and carried on throughout their recording career. Throughout the decade, they continued to uphold the heavy end of things while all manners of strange music came and went.

Of course, to me, they were a band first and foremost. Phil scared the f**k out of me with his lyrics, drug-taking lunacy, and insane facial acrobatics. Rex was Mr. Cool and Vinnie was the beat master. And then there was Dimebag Darrell. He created the "groove guitar" sound.

Sounds funny now, but I remember Dime being the first guitarist to ever have a massive influence to me in terms of how a particular band sounded. I was convinced that without Dime there would be no *Pantera*. I am still convinced of that to this day. He was that individual; he was the nuts and bolts of the *Pantera* machine. Utterly irreplaceable, he made his guitar "the singer" of the band, while Anselmo merely carried out vocal duties. Make no mistake; Dime was the frontman of *Pantera*. People were paying money to see him play guitar.

I finally got to see them headline Ozzfest's second stage at Milton Keynes, England, in June 1998. They stole the day for me. *Pantera* and *Slayer* (who were on criminally early on the main stage) both blew everyone else away, including *Ozzy* and *Sabbath* themselves. I remember reading some reviews of the gig saying that *Pantera* would have played all day if they'd been given half a chance. They loved it up there.

Well, even to *this* day, Dime *does* still play on—in my heart and mind, anyway. The man completed my metal mission and he made it whole. He remains the king of metal groove in an odyssey of madness. He may be gone, but his music is immortal. Getcha Pull!

– Ross Irwin, fan

Chapter 10

The Alrosa Villa

"You're like a "rock 'n' roll reverend."

-Jo Robinson DJ, Q- FM-96 to Rick Cautela

Located on Sinclair Road, just off I-71, the Satoa Lounge was barley surviving. It was 1973, and the owners were struggling to meet the venue's financial obligations. The

Satoa was a "Top 40" bar, catering to soft, mellow folksy-rock, and business wasn't very good. Eventually, Albert Cautela, a Columbus businessman who owned the building, was forced to evict the owners of the Satoa Lounge after they defaulted on their lease.

As a businessman, Al Cautela soon realized that he had a vacant property that wasn't generating income. His 20-year-old son, Rick, an avid rock music fan, was working as an analyst for Western Electric. In a moment of inspiration, the senior Cautela asked his son and son-in-law Bill Colasante, if they would be interested in taking over the property and managing a business there. The younger Cautela and his brother-in-law, Colasante,

agreed to take on the project.

Their first priority was to pay off the debts and obligations left behind by the previous Lounge owners. Food and alcohol vendors were finally paid, as were the utility companies. Now that the venue was debt free and the new proprietors had restored the trust of the vendors who were vital to keeping the facility stocked with food and drinks, Cautela and Colasante sought a new identity for the bar. The 'Satoa Lounge' name would have to go. Initially, Rick wanted to call the venue "King Richard's," but his sister, Diane, who also had a stake

Preceding page: The south and east side of Alrosa Villa. Top. The front bar of the Alrosa Villa. Photos by Chris A. Above: Rick Cautela, the public face of the Alrosa Villa. Photo courtesy of Rick Cautela.

in the club, over-ruled him. Rick and Bill compromised and decided to call the venue, "The Alrosa Villa." The name was chosen to honor Rick's parent's, Al and Rosa Cautela. After all, Rick's father had given him the opportunity to operate the venture, and naming it for him and his wife would be a fitting tribute.

Neither Rick nor Bill had ever run a club before, but to Rick that didn't matter. He had a passion for music and was confident he could make the Alrosa successful while providing Columbus residents a place to rock.

While the building was being refurbished, Cautela toured the city's vibrant night spots in search of bands and musicians. He spent his evenings and weekends scouting local talent and gathering creative ideas from competing venues. As the grand opening for the Alrosa Villa drew near, Cautela was adamant that the first band to play at the Alrosa Villa be memorable. His research convinced him to hire the band *Freshwater*. Their reviews were good, and they always seemed to draw a houseful of people. The Alrosa Villa had a capacity of just 141 people, and with *Freshwater*, Cautela was confident that he would be able to pack the venue on opening night.

As anticipated, grand opening night turned out to be a memorable one for Cautela, but for all the wrong reasons. Rick's "dream" opening was a nightmare. Booked for two consecutive weekends, *Freshwater* was a heavy, loud rock band for 1973. Guests who attended the grand opening were not prepared for their volume or their style. Many in the audience were upset by the music and expressed their displeasure to Cautela as they left the venue on its debut weekend.

Mother Nature also conspired against the new venture by dumping four inches of rain on opening night, turning the parking lot into a quagmire. This was one facet of the property Cautela had neglected to improve. The new owners had worked feverishly to prepare the building, but they overlooked much-needed improvements for the parking lot. It was an omission that would come back to haunt them. Many patrons discovered that in order to leave the lounge, they would have

The namesakes of the Alrosa Villa, Al and Rosa Cautela. Photo courtesy of Rick Cautela.

to be towed out of the thick, sticky mud, formerly disguised as a parking lot. When the last guest left, the Alrosa Villa's Grand Opening was an official disaster.

Facing dim prospects, Rick and Bill were prompted to rethink their strategy. As much as Rick wanted the Alrosa to be a rock 'n' roll venue, even he had doubts it would be successful after that night. After listening to angry patrons complaining all night about the band, the two men decided that *Freshwater* was more of a liability than a draw. Cautela telephoned the band and fired them.

With a fresh start, the new club owners quickly shifted gears and started hiring soft rock artists. Typical acts included local Columbus musician George Westermeyer, who shared the stage with a female partner. The vocalists dressed formally and sang soft, pop rock emulating the popular 70's act, *The Captain and Tennille.* Cautela and Colasante maintained the sappy format for the next few weeks. However, these lounge-style acts were too mundane and drew small audiences. The Alrosa Villa found it was competing for the same audience as upscale Columbus venues like Valentines and The Silver Dollar and they weren't competing well at all.

Rick was frustrated. His vision for the Alrosa Villa was quickly drifting off course. He wanted his venue to rock. Instead, after one failed attempt at rock 'n' roll, the Alrosa Villa was playing it safe, relying on laconic lounge acts and mellow rock to keep afloat. A month had passed since the disastrous grand opening and their rapid course change, yet the Alrosa Villa was still sinking.

Suddenly, the normally quiet phone at the Alrosa Villa began to ring off its hook. Hard rock fans heard about *Freshwater*'s, loud, boisterous music and were calling to find out when the band would be back. The ever-hopeful Cautela took the interest as a sign that perhaps he'd been too hasty in writing off rock 'n' roll at his club. However, the Alrosa Villa would continue to wallow with its light musical fare for three more years.

In 1978, a frustrated Rick met with his partner Bill Colasante, his sister Diane, and his parents. He told them he was tired of lackluster profits. He was confident they hadn't yet tapped the true potential of the rock marketplace. He proposed his idea to transform the venue into "the place" for rock 'n' roll in central Ohio. Rather than cater to soft rock, he wanted edgier, heavier music. His family quickly disagreed. They didn't believe that rock could provide the club with a steady income stream. Realizing that his convictions were not making headway, Cautela did what many businessmen do when faced with adversity. He went berserk and threw a temper tantrum. The tactic shocked the family, but it worked. They agreed to let Rick take the reigns and try things his way. After all, the Alrosa Villa was just barely squeaking by financially anyway.

Over the next six months, with renewed vigor, Cautela immersed himself, head-first, into

1. The south and west end of the Alrosa Villa. This west end is where *Damageplan*'s bus would be parked. The door on the corner is the entrance to the rear of the stage. Photo by Chris A. 2. Diane Colasante, Rick Cautela's sister and part owner of the Alrosa Villa. Photo courtesy of Rick Cautela.

the rock culture. He voraciously read every trade publication and evaluated clubs and bars frequented by rock fans. He also began to hang out with the bands and musicians. Rick quickly befriended band members with his easy-going manner and honest enthusiasm for their music. Rick made his club and his home available to many of the local bands for equipment storage and rehearsal space. He realized that many of the guys in the bands had limited incomes and he wanted to help. His head-first dive soon proved to be a precarious double-edged sword. Without realizing it, he fell victim to the debilitating, addictive world of rock 'n' roll's notorious drug culture. Rick loved to hang out with the long-haired, leather wearing bands. He felt at home with them. He adored their music and he loved to party. Rick's downfall started with marijuana and alcohol, but quickly escalated to experimenting with much harder drugs.

With momentum gathering behind the vision for his club, Rick made the decision to fire the booking agent the Alrosa had relied upon for years. Instead of paying someone, he decided to do the booking himself. This decision raised some eyebrows in the Cautela family, but Rick was confident that he could do it, and be successful at it.

Soon after, the Alrosa Villa began to hire hard rock bands- bands influenced by groups like *Led Zeppelin, AC/DC* and *Black Sabbath*. One of the first heavy bands Rick Cautela hired was a biker band called *Black Leather Touch*. Motivated by his urge to assuage the doubts of his family, Rick decided that he would personally tout his club's new direction and vision. He took his convictions to the airways and booked several radio spots to promote the club and its new, edgier format. On the radio, Cautela was a natural. His passion and enthusiasm for his venue were apparent as he announced the *Black Leather Touch* gig. He ended his spot by challenging those listening; *"If you don't like what we're doing at the Alrosa Villa, then you can disco to hell."* His pot shot at the current musical rage struck a chord with listeners. When the Alrosa Villa eventually opened its doors for the *Black Leather Touch* show, the house was packed.

Cautela continued to groom his radio presentations as his primary means of promotion. Soon, the Alrosa was doing better than ever. In fact, the Alrosa Villa's success came almost too quickly, bringing with it some unanticipated challenges. With a legal maximum capacity of 141, the club soon discovered it was packing upwards of 300 people for each show. While great for the bottom line, these large crowds were a serious concern for the Columbus Fire Marshall's office. Cautela cooperated with the authorities to resolve the overcrowding issue, but by 1980, the small capacity of the Alrosa Villa was having a negative impact on sales. Popular local bands, such as *Spitting Image* and *The Muff Brothers* started drifting away from the venue as it became too small for their fan base.

In 1981, supported by his brother and sister, Rick expanded the Alrosa Villa. He envisioned taking the

Opposite page: Rick Cautela "flashes metal" from the behind the stage barrier in the pit of the Alrosa Villa.
Top of page: Sebastian Bach, one of the many rockers who has played the Alrosa Villa. Photo courtesy of Rick Cautela.
Above: Rick's brother and part owner, John Cautela. Photo by Chris A.

club to the next level, with hopes of attracting national acts in addition to the big-name local bands that were already packing the place. Within a year, Rick's modifications were completed. The Alrosa Villa could now host upwards of 600 patrons.

As the club's commercial success grew, so did Cautela's continued abuse and reliance on drugs. Alcohol was also taking its toll. He was no longer able to disguise his dependence from others. In 1984, with the help and support of his family and friends, Rick sought treatment and began working with Narcotics' Anonymous and Alcoholic's Anonymous to clean up. Over a six-month period, he weaned himself off his mind and spirit-altering crutches. With his sobriety came a renewed interest in business at the Alrosa Villa, and a new outlook on life. To this day, Rick takes great pride in his assertions that he has remained clean and sober.

Now clear-headed, Rick's conversion to sobriety found its way into his business dealings. One afternoon, while preparing to record a radio promotion at Q-FM 96, "*The Rock Station*" serving Columbus Ohio and surrounding Franklin

County, Rick bared his soul. He had a heart to heart talk with one of the station's most popular DJs, Jo Robinson. He gushed over the many virtues of a drug and alcohol free lifestyle. He encouraged the disc jockey to let others know his story. As far as Rick was concerned, if he could escape the grasp of drugs and alcohol, anyone could.

DJ Robinson was impressed by her friend's newfound convictions and genuine atonement for his past weaknesses. She casually remarked that he now sounded like a "rock 'n' roll reverend." The title struck a chord with Cautela, who soon adopted it as his moniker.

The "Rock 'n' Roll" Reverend. Photo courtesy of Rick Cautela.

Rick's transformation was contagious. Not only had he escaped drug dependence, but he had transformed a mediocre club into a viable, profitable business.

As "The Rock 'n' Roll Reverend," Rick sought to add to his congregation as he extolled the merits of hard rock. His club continued to prosper; and its successes led to the Rock 'n' Roll Reverend becoming a local celebrity as the voice of the Alrosa Villa- something he continues to do to this day.

With a larger venue and a fresh outlook on business, Cautela began to fulfill the dream he first had in the 1970s. He was able to bring national acts to his venue. Over the years, the list of artists who played the Alrosa Villa grew to include *Johnny and Edgar Winter, Steppenwolf, David Lee Roth, Ronnie James Dio, Jackyl*, and *Pantera*. All had played and packed the Alrosa, as did many other acts. In addition to its successes with national acts, The Alrosa Villa also continued to support local, up-and-coming bands. Rick Cautela's venue was a friend to all. He facilitated many newer national and local bands by providing them with opportunities to open for his headliners and to show their stuff to enthusiastic audiences.

Cautela and his family knew that they alone were not responsible for success at the Alrosa Villa. From the day he opened the club, it was accepted by the local community. Rick never took his patrons for granted. Over the years, he and

1. As the Alrosa Villa grew in size and reputation, Cautela began to bring recognized national acts to the club including Ace Frehley, one of Dimebag's idols. 2. Jackyl vocalist Jesse James Dupree during a performance at the Alrosa Villa. Photos courtesy of Rick Cautela.

his staff returned the love by supporting Columbus causes and charities. For example, Rick Cautela estimates that the Alrosa

Villa has raised nearly $20,000 for the Jerry Lewis Telethon.

But, in addition to wild success at the Alrosa, another important change occurred during the time Rick was escaping his dependencies. Ohio voters changed the drinking age from 18 to 21. For many venues that sold alcohol, this was a major blow, as most of their revenue was tied to alcohol sales. This was a concern for Cautela as well. As a rock venue, the Alrosa catered to younger audiences. The change in the state's minimum drinking age meant many of the club's patrons were no longer able to purchase alcohol and that it would have to target a slightly older audience. To address this issue, the Alrosa Villa changed its marketing strategy. To offset an expected reduction in alcohol sales, the venue began hosting "all ages" shows, generating revenue with increased ticket sales to events without relying on alcohol revenue. As a result, the club continued to flourish.

Such was the state of affairs at the Alrosa Villa by early November 2004, when a booking agent telephoned Cautela. The agent asked, "Would you be interested in booking a new band called "*Damageplan*," featuring Dimebag

1. Vince Neil plays the Alrosa Villa while on hiatus from *Motley Crue*. 2. The Alrosa Villa has been operated by the same family for over 30 years and has provided entertainment to thousands of people. Photos courtesy of the Rick Cautela. 3. Rick Cautela shows off one of his Muscular Dystrophy Association plaques. Photo by Chris A.

Darrell Abbott and Vinnie Paul Abbott, ex-members of *Pantera*?" Cautela thought back to the early 1990s when Dimebag and Vinnie Paul played

the Alrosa during *Pantera*'s breakout tour, *"Cowboys From Hell."* That was a great show. Rick loved the spirit of the young "wanna-be" rock stars. Plus, the Abbott brothers did bring out a large crowd. "How much to book them?" Cautela replied. The answer was a stunningly low $1,000.00. Rick immediately jumped at the offer and booked *Damageplan* to perform at the Alrosa Villa on December 8, 2004.

Cautela had a month to promote the show and to hire opening acts. As he always did, Rick used local talent for openers. He contacted local Columbus bands, *"12 Gauge," "Position Six"* and *"Volume Dealer,"* offering them the opportunity to open for *Damageplan*. The bands jumped at the chance to open for the legendary Dimebag Darrell.

In order to play at the Alrosa, each band was required to sell a specific number of tickets for the gig. Rick's rules were simple: sell enough tickets and you're on the bill. Cautela consulted *Damageplan*'s booking agent regarding any special requirements for the show. The only item mentioned was that the band requested a stage barrier. In his office, Cautela calculated the expenses, including staffing and costs of the barrier. Based on his

1. A ticket for the Dec. 8, 2004 *Damageplan* show. There are several variations of the ticket. Each band that was selling them was listed as opener on their batch of tickets. The black slash obscures the name of the band *Cross Thread* who pulled out of the show. Photo by Chris A. 2. An original handout for the *Damageplan* show. Courtesy of Dean Reimund 3. Columbus band, *Volume Dealer*. Photo courtesy of *Volume Dealer* - www.volumedealer.net

figures, Cautela determined that the ticket price for the show would be $8.00. Cautela then recorded his radio spots to promote the event.[1]

Initial ticket sales for the show were slow, but that didn't dampen Cautela's enthusiasm. His radio spots touted *Damageplan*'s *Pantera* roots and urged the audience to purchase tickets quickly because, "this show will sell out." As the show approached, ticket sales continued to lag.

Around 2 pm on December 8th, 2004, the *Damageplan* tour bus and equipment trailer pulled into the Alrosa Villa parking lot. The bus pulled directly to the rear of the venue and parked. For the past 45 days, *Damageplan* had been on the road. The tour had taken the band on a trek across the United States. They had traveled thousands of miles, playing gigs in all four corners of the country, and everywhere in between. They even ventured into Canada. It had been a long, grueling tour, and everyone in the *Damageplan* family was tired.

In addition to Dimebag, Vinnie Paul, Bobzilla and vocalist Lachman, the *Damageplan* road team consisted of: Manager Chris Paluska, Chief of Security Jeff "Mayhem" Thompson, Drum Tech John "Kat" Brooks, Guitar Tech John Graham and Sound Engineer Aaron "Wires" Barnes.

The Alrosa Villa gig wasn't even listed on the official tour itinerary; it was an "added" date. By all indications, *Damageplan*'s tour budget was tight and the band was barely making ends meet. Columbus was simply a pit stop on the tour, an effort to make a few extra dollars as the band journeyed back to Texas for Christmas.

---

[1] Chapter 10 footnotes begin on page 310.

As he had done for nearly 30 years, Rick Cautela, "The Rock 'n' Roll Reverend," was already waiting at the venue to meet the band when the tour bus pulled in. He was at the rear

Opposite page: The rear of *Damageplan*'s bus and the equipment trailer parked behind the west end of the Alrosa Villa. The open door is the stage door. Dec. 8, 2004. Columbus Police Department, evidence photo. Above: The Alrosa Villa's sign promoting *Damageplan*'s show. Photo courtesy of Kevin McMeans.

stage door as Dimebag Darrell Abbott stepped from the bus. With a grin on his face, Cautela gave Dimebag a hug and a friendly tug on his scarlet beard. Dime returned the hug and shook his hand. Cautela asked Dime if he remembered playing the venue back in the early 1990s. Dimebag said he

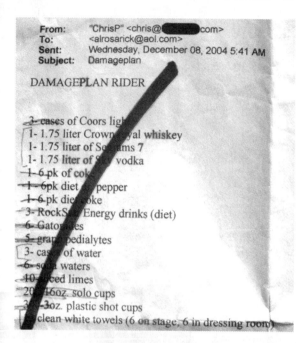

From: "ChrisP" <chris@████████com>
To: <alrosarick@aol.com>
Sent: Wednesday, December 08, 2004 5:41 AM
Subject: Damageplan

DAMAGEPLAN RIDER

3 cases of Coors light
1- 1.75 liter Crown Royal whiskey
1- 1.75 liter of Seagrams 7
1- 1.75 liter of █████ vodka
1- 6 pk of col█
1- 6pk diet ██ pepper
1- 6 pk diet ██ coke
3- RockS███ Energy drinks (diet)
6- Gator███es
5- grap██ pedialytes
3- cas██ of water
6- so██ waters
10- ██ced limes
20 ██6oz. solo cups
3██-3oz. plastic shot cups
clean white towels (6 on stage, 6 in dressing room)

remembered both the venue and Rick. After a few moments of friendly banter, Cautela introduced the catering staff and went back to work preparing the venue for the evening's event.

Cautela sought out the band's manager, Chris Paluska, to ensure that all the provisions of the bands contract and rider had been met. Paluska was apparently satisfied, as no issues were brought to Rick's attention. Cautela then focused on the next issue of business; security. According to Cautela, he asked Paluska if the band wanted to participate in a "security meeting" with venue security staff members. Paluska reportedly declined the meeting, expressing confidence that the band's security manager, Jeff Thompson, was more than capable of dealing with any security issue that might arise.

When Cautela later met Thompson, he understood exactly why Paluska had such confidence. The *Damageplan* chief of security was huge. Certainly his impressive stature was considered a great deterrent to any "typical," non-lethal threat. However, it is now clear that neither *Damageplan* nor Cautela had any inkling of the determined violence that would be brought to bear against the victims later that evening. When the issue of pat downs or patron searches was broached, Cautela contends that Paluska simply advised him to do what the venue normally would.[2]

Typically, fans attending a show at the Alrosa, featuring a band like *Damageplan* would not be searched. As with many venues, the Alrosa Villa was flexible in its approach to security. Cautela tailored the venue's security posture to both the requests of the band and past experiences with similar acts. Cautela was unaware of any potential threats to the band. If Paluska had any concerns regarding security, he failed to voice them beforehand. No one in the *Damageplan* entourage warned or advised Cautela about Nathan Gale's incursion on the band in Cincinnati.

Cautela, when interviewed, stated that he did remember the *Damageplan* crew discussing Phil Anselmo but he was unaware of the context. At no time prior to the shooting had anyone in the *Damageplan* crew told Cautela about Anselmo's incendiary comments having incited violence towards Dimebag.

Opposite page: E-mail from road manager Chris Paluska, titled "*Damageplan* Rider" lists beverages, food and supplies requested from the band. Above. Concert attendee Kevin McMeans snaps a photo with Vinnie Paul Abbott behind the Alrosa Villa. Dec. 8, 2004. Photo courtesy of Kevin McMeans.

As Cautela and Paluska discussed pre-show details, Erin Halk and the Alrosa roadies were assisting *Damageplan*'s crew to unload the band's gear. The winter sky was a bright, clear blue, and the temperatures were chilly. For most of the afternoon and early evening, the band rested on the bus. Pat Lachman slipped into the venue on occasion to grab a drink or to use the bathroom, but for the most part he sought the comfort of the bus so he could talk to his girlfriend on his cell phone.

Inside the Alrosa Villa, members of the local band *Volume Dealer* were dragging in their gear. Formed just six months earlier, the band was thrilled to be opening for *Damageplan*. Suddenly, Dimebag, looking as if he had just woken from a nap, walked in the back door and onto the stage to do a sound check. For *Volume Dealer*, it was a remarkable

moment. Here they were, this small upstart band, sharing the bill with a legend. They watched and listened as Dime plugged in and began to effortlessly shred away on his trademark Dean guitar. As always, his playing was incredible and the members of *Volume Dealer* were left stunned and impressed by his abilities.

Occasionally, Vinnie Paul and Bob Kakaha would wander through the parking lot and into the venue. Outside, they would chat with fans, sign autographs and pose for photos. Dimebag also made a few appearances in the parking lot to hang out with the diehard fans that came early with hope of meeting the band. In typical Dimebag fashion, he appeared in a hilarious outfit, consisting of a black t-shirt under a bright orange shirt that was buttoned up incorrectly. Over the shirt, he sported a faux leopard fur coat that looked as if it belonged in his grandmother's closet. All of his clothing was new, with the price tags still dangling. He topped off his ensemble with a shiny pullover cap that resembled tinsel. As Dime had always done throughout his career, he took time to chat with his fans. Lucky fans like Kevin McMeans, were there to collect autographs, pose for photos and shake hands with their hero, Dime.

Brian Fielder was also fortunate to spend some time with his friend, Dimebag. Fielder, who worked in the music business, was on the guest list and planned only to attend the after-show "meet and greet." Something, however, drew him to the Alrosa Villa early. He changed his plans and decided to head directly to the venue after work. Brian Fielder would be forever grateful he had altered his plans on December 8, 2004, and that he was able to share some "Dime Time." Brian and

Dimebag hadn't seen each other in nearly 10-years prior to the show at Alrosa Villa.

When Dimebag snuck up on his old acquaintance, he said "What the hell's going on here!?" Brian whipped around and found himself face to face with his buddy, Dime. Brian and Dimebag had first met in 1995, while Brian was working the VIP area at several venues. Now, at the Alrosa, the two old friends talked for about 15 minutes, reminiscing and joking with one another. Brian asked Dime about life on the road. Dime told Brian that the road was beating him down, but admitted, "It paid the rent." They ended their reunion by talking about the upcoming holiday season.

Fielder recalled how Dime's eyes lit up as he looked forward to the holiday.

Opposite page: Smiling, Dimebag takes a moment to pose with fan Kevin McMeans behind the Alrosa Villa. Dec. 8, 2004. Photo courtesy of Kevin McMeans. 2. With the price tags still dangling, Dimebag Darrell Abbott shows off his new clothing. Dec. 8, 2004. Photo courtesy of Brian Fielder.

"Brian, I can't wait for Christmas, man. I'll get some cool stuff and it's always the greatest time." Brian snapped a couple of photos with Dime and hugged him before leaving. Fielder then headed home to clean up and eat before returning to the Alrosa Villa later that night for the *Damageplan* show.

As the evening approached, *Damageplan*'s crew, aided by Erin Halk and the venue's other loaders, coordinated moving equipment with the opening acts and prepared for the show. Eventually, *Damageplan* conducted a cursory sound check to ensure instrument levels were appropriate and to make sure that their equipment was functioning properly.

Damageplan was scheduled to go on stage at 10:30 pm, but the Alrosa doors opened at 6:30. While the show wasn't a sell out, there was still a large crowd, brimming with considerable excitement in anticipation of seeing Dimebag and Vinnie Paul's new band.

By 9:30 pm, the band members had changed into their heavy metal attire and were ready to rock. As "show time" approached, each band member went through the ritual of stashing wallets, cell phones and other valuables into their cubbyholes on the tour bus before entering the club. Chris Paluska, Jeff Thompson, John Brooks, John Graham and Aaron Barnes finished last minute checks as the gear from the final opening band was being hauled from the stage. The band

members ambled off the bus and passed through the graffiti-decorated stage door and onto the Alrosa Villa stage.

Unbeknownst to all, it would be *Damageplan*'s final show.

Opposite page: Brian Fielder and Dimebag Darrell "back in the day." Above: Brian Fielder reconnects with his old friend. This would be one of the last photographs taken of Dimebag. Dec. 8, 2004. Photos courtesy of Brian Fielder.

Rehearsal at Dimebag's home. Oct. 23, 2004. Photo
courtesy of Chad Lee - www.rockconcertfotos.com

Dime Time

Once on tour with *Pantera*, Godsmack guitarist Tony Rambola remembered many good times with Dimebag. Besides Dime pushing "shots," Tony remembered a special time with Dime. On tour, Godsmack loved to jam and often set up a "jam room" near the dressing room. There was a drum set and a few amps so the guys could play and work on new material if the urge struck. Sharing the road with *Pantera*, Tony remembers Dime walking into the jam room. He climbed behind the drum kit and started pounding away. Tony reached for a guitar and soon the two men were improvising and jamming to some heavy riffs. Tony recalls that they didn't really come up with anything but he clearly remembered Dime digging the experience and flashing a huge smile as he "tore it up on the drums." Tony will always remember that special 10 minutes of his life when he shared some music with Dimebag.

"Dimebag was such a great guitarist, such an incredible player. He could just shred."

– Tony Rambola, Godsmack. Interview with the author.

Godsmack guitarist Tony Rambola. Oct. 31, 2006, Hara Arena, Dayton, OH. Photo by Chris A.

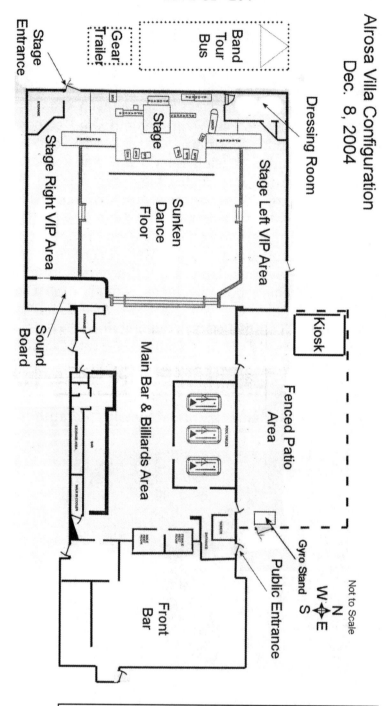

1. The layout of the Alrosa Villa on Dec. 8, 2004. Diagram by Chris A.

Chapter 11

By Demons Be Driven

"By demons be driven
Beckon the call."

By Demons Be Driven
Vulgar Display of Power
-Pantera

At about 9:30 pm, Dimebag Darrell Abbott, Vinnie Paul Abbott, Patrick Lachman, and Bob "Zilla" Kakaha slipped into the venue via the back door that was being monitored by Erin Halk. The band members discreetly moved behind the backline amplifiers and the drum kit as they crossed the stage and headed to the dressing room.

The room was an austere space with black walls plastered with stickers and defaced by the graffiti of 30 years worth of bands; it contained an old plaid sofa, some black plastic chairs, a few end tables and the entrance to a small bathroom in the rear right corner. Several flight case covers, used to protect Dimebag's guitars, also were stashed in the room.

The band members relaxed in the room, waiting their turn to step beneath the stage lights to rock the rowdy crowd. On several occasions, Dimebag slipped to the side of the stage to watch local Columbus band *Volume Dealer* play to their home crowd. Between songs, metal fan and guitarist Josh Drake

1. Taken from stage right, by the rear door of the Alrosa Villa. The band would have crept along the left wall, behind the drum riser, to get to the dressing room. The door is open and the word "ROCK" can be seen on the wall inside the room. Photo by Chris A. 2. The dressing room at the northwest corner of the Alrosa Villa. Note one of Dime's guitars on the sofa. The door at the right rear is to a small bathroom. Dec. 8, 2004, Columbus Police Department, evidence photo.

shouted a greeting to Dime, catching his attention. Dimebag cocked his head slightly backward and to the side, stroked his beard, flashed a grin, and pointed a finger at Josh, returning the greeting. During *Volume Dealer's* final song, *Gut Check*, Dime stood on the side stage pumping his fist, jamming to the tune and showing his support for the local boys. Moments later, he disappeared into the dressing room.

At approximately 9:50 pm, *Volume Dealer*, the third opening band of the evening, completed its set. Halk and other venue crew members took center stage as they helped the members of *Volume Dealer* move out their gear to clear the stage for the evening's headline band, *Damageplan*.

The audience was pumped up and ready. Many fans had been at the venue for four hours, rocking and partying hard in anticipation of what was certain to be a great show featuring one of heavy metal's greatest guitarists, Dimebag Darrell Abbott.

As *Volume Dealer's* gear was moved from the stage, Halk switched roles from roadie to security member. He was working at the Alrosa Villa as a "loader," making about $75 per day. But he wasn't a typical roadie at the Alrosa Villa. He had worked several shows at the venue over the past six months and had caught the eye of owner Rick Cautela. As Cautela got to know Erin, he learned the young man had been in the Marines. Considering Erin's age, demeanor, and his prior military experience, Cautela

The rear door of the Alrosa Villa on the night of the murders. Erin Halk's security role was to make certain unauthorized people didn't slip into the venue via this door. Erin's coat lies against the back wall. Dec. 8, 2004. Columbus Police Department, evidence photo.

felt that he'd be an asset to the Villa's security. He asked Halk if he wanted to make a few extra bucks working security between loading. Erin didn't object to earning a few extra dollars since he would have to stick around at the venue anyway to help load out after the show. For tonight's show, Halk's security role was to monitor the backstage door. It was an easy task and it afforded him an excellent view of the concert.

In the audience, Nathan Bray was having a great time. He and Jason Jewett had arrived early and both had been partying hard while enjoying the opening bands. As the stage was prepared for *Damageplan*, Bray and Jewett pushed their way through the crowd in an attempt to get closer to the stage. The two avid rockers worked themselves toward the front row on the right side of the stage; there were only a few people and the steel barrier between them and the band.[1]

John Graham tuning Dime's black Dean guitar before the start of the show. Dec. 8, 2004. Columbus Police Department, evidence photo.

With the stage prepared for the band, *Damageplan*'s crew began their preshow ritual. Behind the three stacks of Dimebag's Krank Amplifier rigs on stage left, Dimebag's guitar tech, John Graham, was tuning up a black Dean guitar that Dimebag would use to open the show. Venue sound and light technicians tested microphones and the lighting racks to make certain that the infrastructure for the sound and visual effects were ready to go.

As the band prepared to go on, Jeff "Mayhem" Thompson activated a small personal video camera and was panning around the backstage area. Apparently the camera belonged to Dimebag. Mayhem strode across the stage,

---

[1] Chapter 11 footnotes begin on page 311.

pointing the video camera at the audience. Seeing the big man with the camera, the audience erupted into cheers and began to chant "*Damageplan, Damageplan, Damageplan!*"

Jeff, his long hair tied back in a pony tail, was wearing his typical rock 'n' roll garb that evening: camouflage shorts and tennis shoes, complemented by a dark button-up shirt with the sleeves cut off, accentuating his massive size. The shirt had two small patches sewn above the left breast pocket. One had the word "Mayhem" on it; the other was a skull and crossbones.

He crossed the stage, walked over to a flight case next to bass player Kakaha's amplifiers, and placed the camera on it. The camera's view was a limited angle encompassing the front left of the stage and about one-third of the audience. The front of one of Vinnie Paul's kick drums also could be seen through the viewfinder.

As he positioned the camera, an Alrosa crew member reminded him to give a clear signal for dropping the house lights. Jeff replied, "Don't worry, you'll hear me." He then

Dimebag's video camera was placed on top of a flight case, next to Kakaha's amp setup by Jeff Thompson. The camera ran for over two hours. Dec. 8, 2004, Columbus Police Department, evidence photo.

moved to the center of the stage, scanning the audience while pacing back and forth, double-checking every detail. He waited for the signal that the band was ready. There was a slight delay because two vehicles were parked in an unauthorized location near the rear entrance. They were blocking the area used for "loading out" the equipment from the opening acts. An announcement was made over the public address system for the owners to move them immediately. The vehicles were moved without incident. Contrary to rumors, neither vehicle belonged to Nathan Gale.

Rick Cautela, "The Rock 'n' Roll Reverend," made several announcements over the public address system. He reminded the audience that there would be no fist swinging, kicking, or any violent moshing permitted. In addition, there would be no "*Wall of Death:*" an activity in which fans lock elbows and ram other fans into the front of the stage. Then he informed the crowd that tickets were on sale for *Hatebreed* and several other bands scheduled to appear at future shows.

As *Damageplan* prepared to start its show, the Alrosa's security staff was positioned around the building. There were at least three security personnel posted in front of the stage. Halk was at his post at the right rear of the stage, by the back door. According to Rick Cautela, ten security personnel were on duty at the Alrosa Villa. .

Fans stood In front of the stage, continuously chanting "*Damageplan.*" Fists were pumped into the air. There was no doubt that the crowd was ready for Dimebag and the boys to start the show.

Outside the venue, The Beast lurked. He smoked cigarettes and paced aimlessly in the parking lot, in no apparent hurry to enter the building. He was biding his time and, with the exception of fiddling with his cigarette, he kept his hands in his pockets.

He had pulled into the venue parking lot at approximately 9:15 pm in his red 1995 Pontiac Grand Am. Initially, he tried to park his car near the main lot, next to one of the entrances to the Alrosa Villa. Mitch Carpenter, the parking lot attendant, advised him the area was for employees. He then moved his car next to the Alrosa's large sign, but again Carpenter told him that area was reserved. Gale apparently waved and said "okay." He then crossed Sinclair Road and parked across the street.

He wore a black and blue "*Under Armour*" baseball cap, black tennis shoes, blue jeans, a belt with a Harley-Davidson buckle, and his favorite garment, his Columbus Blue Jackets hockey jersey, over a gray hooded sweatshirt. He also carried his concealed, loaded Beretta 92F 9mm handgun, a spare magazine and 30 additional rounds of ammunition. Both 10-round magazines were fully loaded. The other 30 rounds were still in the box.

He walked across the street and through the Alrosa's parking lot, then positioned himself near the public entrance, but made no attempt to step inside. He briefly wandered around the exterior of the building, but spent most of the next hour standing next to the fenced-in patio used as a smoking area for concert patrons.

Inside the patio enclosure, there were two doors to enter the Alrosa Villa. The doors were propped open and the pre-show announcements were clearly audible to the people on the patio and in the adjacent parking lot. Blocking the gate to the patio was a food vendor selling gyros.

The predator waited in the dark of the cool December night. He was quiet while listening for the signal to unleash his rage.

1. Gale's 1995 Pontiac parked across Sinclair Road from the Alrosa Villa. Dec. 8, 2004, Columbus Police Department, evidence photo. 2. The public entrance to the Alrosa Villa on the North side of the building, next to the patio privacy fence. Photo by Chris A.

Around 9:45 pm, parking lot attendant Carpenter strode past the hulking man and asked him if he had a ticket. Gale calmly responded that he did have a ticket, but that he had no interest in the local opening acts. He was waiting for the headliner. Carpenter would later state that Gale was suspicious in that he was pacing back and forth smoking cigarettes, but that he had seen that behavior at every show he'd worked.

Inside the venue, the show was about to start. Cold bottles of water dripping with condensation were pre-positioned around the stage to quench the performers' thirst. The crowd was fired up. Realizing the show was about to begin, renewed chants of "*Damageplan, Damageplan, Damageplan*" echoed through the hall as Bobzilla and Dimebag Darrell readied their instruments for the coming barrage of heavy metal. As the band nonchalantly prepared to take the stage, the massive figure of Jeffery "Mayhem" Thompson took center stage. Like the director of an orchestra, Mayhem made certain the

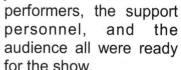

performers, the support personnel, and the audience all were ready for the show.

With a slashing move of his right hand in front of his throat, he gave the signal to cut the house lights. The darkness was greeted with a roar of approval by the crowd. Thompson stood with his back to the audience as he watched each member of *Damageplan* take up his pre-show position. The thick, heavy crunch of Dimebag's guitar, with its incredibly unique tone, launched the crowd into a pre-show frenzy as he quickly stroked the strings on his custom-made USA trans-black Dean guitar. When Thompson was certain the guys were ready to let it rip, he turned and walked to the microphone. He leaned forward to introduce the band, his huge body towering above the gleaming chrome microphone stand. He clutched it with both hands and he growled what were to be his final public words:

"For the love of God, are you ready to get this sh*t started?
From the land of God, here they are, Dam-age-plan."

...Drawing out the band's name as he let it trail from his lips. It was the cue that everyone was awaiting. As the stage exploded with the glare of colored lights, Thompson ambled off to stage left, and Vinnie Paul Abbott quickly struck his closed high-hat cymbal four times to set the timing and the opening for the band's first number, "Breathing New Life." The drums thundered, the bass and guitar roared, and the crowd erupted into a head-banging throng as Dimebag, Bobzilla,

Opposite page: "Mayhem" prepares the Alrosa Villa stage for *Damageplan*. Above: *Damageplan's* audience just minutes before the start of the show. Dec. 8, 2004. Columbus Police Department, evidence photo.

Vinnie Paul, and Pat Lachman cranked out the opening strains of what would be the final song *Damageplan* would ever perform.

Outside the venue, the introduction of the band and the opening chords of the song spurred The Beast, now turned predator, to strike. Unable to determine if patrons entering the Alrosa Villa were being searched, he made the decision to bypass the public entrance. He stepped behind the northeast corner of the six-foot high wooden privacy fence, grabbed the top of it, threw his legs over, and then dropped to the other side on to the patio.

His efforts to remain undetected and in the shadows failed when Mitch Carpenter, the parking lot attendant, saw Gale hop the fence. Carpenter immediately ran to the venue door to notify security personnel inside that a man had just climbed the fence and was attempting to enter the venue without a ticket.

The approximate location where the killer jumped the fence to gain access to the patio. Both doors to the venue were open. Once over the fence, he headed to the door directly in front of him. Photo by Chris A.

AVDOP -215-

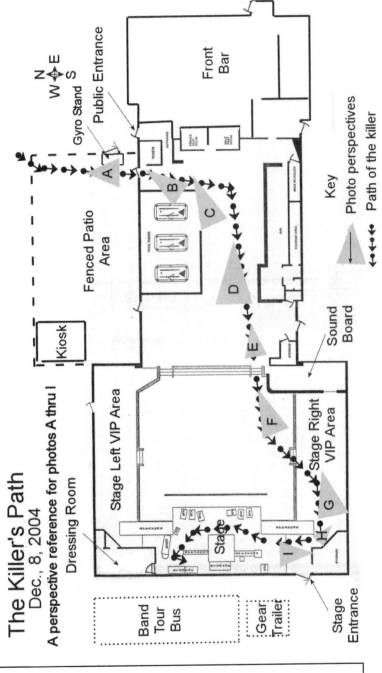

Diagram showing the path and viewpoint of the killer. Compare the shaded cones above with the following photos, A through I, to put Gale's path into perspective. Diagram by Chris A.

PHOTO A. Gale entered the venue through this door on the patio. Once inside, the ticket booth would be directly to his left. Photo by Chris A.

As Gale walked across the patio, an Alrosa Villa employee approached him and said, "Hey, no you don't, man." The 265-pound Gale reportedly responded by saying, "Hey, what's up?" and simply walked past the worker, then the gyro stand, and entered the club.

When Carpenter entered the front door from the parking lot, he saw Gale enter through one of the patio doors. Carpenter immediately began to follow him. He yelled at Gale to stop, but The Beast either chose to ignore the order or was unable to hear it over to the roar of the band.

As Gale moved inside the Alrosa Villa, *Damageplan* vocalist Patrick Lachman slowly sauntered onto the stage and began to sing.

"Can you feel it building?"
"Can you feel it building?"

PHOTO B. Now inside the venue, Gale strode past the ticket booth and looked to his right, in the direction of the stage. Photo by Chris A.

Now, The Beast was moving across the black and white checkerboard floor of the upper bar area heading toward the sunken main floor.

Lachman continued singing…

"Can you feel it building?
"Can you feel it building?

With Carpenter and several other security personnel a few steps behind him, the predator snaked his way through the audience. He maintained a steady pace as he focused on the stage and the target of his rage.

Lachman's prophetic lyrics continued:

"Can you feel it building?"

PHOTO C. Just about to turn the corner next to the pool tables, looking towards the stage.
PHOTO D. Moving between patrons, Gale headed towards the dance floor. Photos by Chris A.

Gale stepped from the upper bar area down to the main dance floor, threading his way around and between the throng of fans whose attention was captured by *Damageplan*.

PHOTO E. Approaching the steps to the dance floor. Photo by Chris A.

Lachman continued to growl the ominous lyrics of the song:

"Devastation is on the way, feel the hairs on the back of your neck, let the rush begin."

Gale approached the stairs to the elevated VIP section on the right of the stage with security still trailing just a few steps behind.

He quickly bounded up the stairs separating the VIP section from the main floor, bumping into several patrons and past security member Ronald Jenkins, who was unaware of the situation. The Beast then headed towards a gap between the public address system and the wall of the venue.

PHOTO F. Now crossing the dance floor, he heads towards the three steps that would put him on the stage right VIP section. PHOTO G. Gale is now on the stage right VIP section and is heading towards a gap between the PA and the south wall of the venue. Photo by Chris A.

When Carpenter reached the VIP stairway, he yelled at Jenkins to go after the intruder. Jenkins couldn't hear what Carpenter was telling him but realized something was happening and joined the pursuit.

Perhaps the final photo taken of Dimebag doing what he loved to do. He came to rock and he rocked like no other. Dec. 8, 2004. Photo courtesy of Steve Patrick.

Audience members Steve Patrick and his brother Scott were positioned on stage left of the dance floor. Both were college students, Eagle Scouts and big-time rock fans. Steve was discreetly taking a few photos of Dimebag with his small digital camera. Scott banged his head to the onslaught of heavy metal music that had begun just seconds earlier. Like most patrons, the Patrick brothers were unaware of the intruder breaching on stage right.

"You can't take it away, I earned this with sweat and blood, you can't take it away, take what's mine..."

The lyrics filled the venue and many in the crowd sang along and banged their heads to the song.

Thompson, who had been on stage left, jogged, head down, quickly across the stage behind Dimebag, Kakaha, and Lachman. He repositioned himself on stage right, unaware that a predator was stalking his friends. Only 86 seconds had elapsed since he had introduced the band. Four seconds after Thompson crossed the stage, the marauder burst from the side of the public address system via the VIP section on stage right.

For the first time since entering the building, Gale's brisk but calm stride changed into a run as he crossed behind the

PHOTO H. The predator is now between the PA speakers on stage right. Photos by Chris A. PHOTO I. The stage and Dimebag lie directly in front of the killer. Dec. 8, 2004. Columbus Police Department, evidence photo.

PA speakers and strode up the single step separating the side stage from the main stage. Now on the stage, Gale focused on his mission. He ignored bass player Kakaha and vocalist Lachman, who were near the front of the stage on the right side. Gale's prey, his target, was clearly Dimebag Darrell Abbott.

As he stepped into the full, bright lights on center stage, he lifted the Columbus Blue Jackets jersey with his left hand. He quickly produced the stainless steel Beretta that had been secured in the waistband of his jeans. Now, with both hands holding the gun, arms outstretched, he extended the firearm in the direction of Dimebag, who was totally unaware of Gale's presence. As he reached the center of the stage directly in front of the drum kit, his gait converted to a purposeful, steady march.

Nathan Gale, his weapon aimed, advances on Dimebag. Dec. 8, 2004, Columbus Police Department, evidence photo.

Behind his drum set, Vinnie Paul Abbott was flailing as he slammed away at his drums. At that moment, he looked up and saw a "blue blur" as Nathan Gale crossed the stage directly in front of him. Gale's weapon was pointed squarely at

Vinnie's brother. A moment earlier, Dimebag had grabbed a microphone stand and moved it from the front of stage left. He had his back turned to the audience as he placed the microphone stand off to the side of the stage. Suddenly, The Beast grabbed the guitarist by the hair with his left hand and yanked Dimebag's head toward him.

Thompson, on stage right, immediately ran at Gale upon seeing him on stage. He was literally one second behind the predator. As Gale grabbed Dimebag's hair, Thompson seized him by the shoulders and tried to pull him off his friend. As the three men struggled, Dimebag reached up with his right hand in an attempt to escape Gale's grasp. His hand was now between his head and the barrel of Gale's handgun as he grappled to escape the predator's clutches. But it was too late. With the barrel of the gun inches from Dimebag Darrell's head, Gale squeezed the trigger. The bullet struck Dimebag between the ring and middle finger, exiting just behind his thumb. It continued on its path and struck the guitarist in the side of his head. A gush of blood coated Gale's face, soaking his glasses and obscuring his vision.

Jeff Thompson has Gale in his grasp as Chris Paluska and John Brooks run onto the stage to try to subdue the intruder. Dec. 8, 2004, Columbus Police Department, evidence photo.

Simultaneously, Thompson employed all of his strength and threw the 265-pound ex-Marine to the stage floor in a frantic attempt to stop the attack. As he tackled the semi-pro football player, Thompson's hands raked across the gunman's face, ripping Gale's glasses off, and seriously degrading his vision. As he fell, Gale pulled Dimebag toward him and fired another point-blank round, striking Dime's right cheek.

The Beast's blood soaked glasses, knocked off his face by Jeff Thompson, lie on the stage next to a monitor. Dec. 8, 2004, Columbus Police Department, evidence photo.

As Dimebag and Gale fell to the worn, carpeted stage, The Beast lifted himself up with his left arm and placed his handgun directly on the back of his prey's head. For a third time he pulled the trigger, the round killing Dimebag instantly.

Darrell Abbott's life ended as he cascaded to the stage. His body came to rest on top of his guitar. Its mournful screams of feedback filled the Alrosa Villa with a haunting wail; a frightening, pitiful accompaniment to the macabre spectacle unfolding in front of 350 incredulous people.

Pushed to the stage floor, Gale was on his hands and knees next to Dimebag. Thompson stepped between the two prone men in a vain attempt to use his 6-foot-8-inch, 350-

pound body as a shield. He continued to try to overpower and disarm the killer.

Band manager Christopher Paluska, drum tech John "Kat" Brooks, and Alrosa Security member Ronald Jenkins burst from stage right, sprinting onto the stage to help Jeff Thompson and Dimebag. As the three men reached the point of the altercation, Paluska reached out to grab The Beast. The murderer, his contorted face soaked with Dimebag's blood, and unable to see clearly without his glasses, instinctively raised his gun. He fired one round, his fourth shot, at *Damageplan*'s manager. The round struck Paluska in the upper left side of his chest, exiting out his back. Seriously wounded and in great pain, Paluska grasped the side of his body and mustered up the strength to retreat to the right side of the stage to seek aid. Jenkins saw Gale fire at Paluska. He

Damageplan's road manager, Chris Paluska reacts to being shot. Dec. 8, 2004. Columbus Police Department, evidence photo.

could smell the gunpowder. In an act of self-preservation, he intuitively leaped off the left side of the stage to avoid the gunman's wrath.

While firing, Gale lunged at Thompson, pushing the big man backward, escaping his grasp as he moved towards the drum riser in search of his next target, Vinnie Paul Abbott.

Brooks dropped to his knees and quickly examined his friend, Dimebag Darrell. Brooks was horrified by the carnage. Shock and anger enveloped him as he realized that Dimebag was dead. He looked behind him and saw Thompson regaining his balance and fearlessly advancing on the killer. Thompson was committed to protecting his friends and the audience from the armed killer.

As Gale had unleashed his initial assault, drummer Vinnie Paul watched in horror as his brother was shot multiple

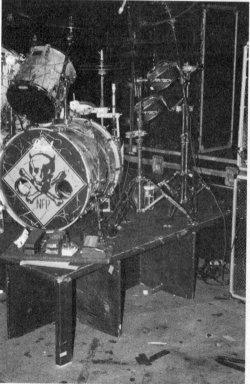

times. Hoping to intervene and somehow save Dime, Vinnie Paul leapt from his drum kit. Fortunately for Vinnie Paul, Dimebag's guitar technician, John Graham, immediately pounced on the drummer, pushed him to the floor and shielded his body with his own. Graham was concerned that Vinnie Paul also was one of Gale's prime targets. While he had no way of knowing it, he was certainly correct. As he held Vinnie down, Graham urged him to remain quiet and still. In the darkness behind Dime's amps, Graham watched as Gale extricated himself from the pile of bodies on the stage floor. Transfixed, Graham's eyes locked on the dull-silver glint of the killer's gun as he moved toward them.

Vinnie Paul's drum kit. Dec. 8, 2004, Columbus Police Department, evidence photo.

In the darkness, fear and desperation began to overtake him. His worst fears played out a vicious scenario of "what if" in his mind as he maintained his focus on the gun. Just when it seemed that Gale would find the two defenseless men, he suddenly and inexplicably turned away. What Graham didn't know was that Thompson had reengaged the killer. Taking advantage of the momentary respite, Graham prompted Vinnie Paul Abbott to flee, and both men quickly bolted from behind the drum riser. Graham moved to stage right and took cover behind "Bobzilla's" bass amps while Vinnie Paul escaped around the public address system, reversing the very path that Gale had used to access the stage.

It was in this small area in front and behind Dimebag's amps that Jeff Thompson battled the killer. Dec. 8, 2004, Columbus Police Department, evidence photo.

At this point, Thompson could have made the decision to take cover, but instead he chose to reengage Gale. Were it not for "Mayhem" Thompson's actions, Gale most certainly would have stumbled upon John Graham and Vinnie Paul Abbott, and killed them both.

As Graham and Vinnie Paul Abbott sought cover, Jeffery Thompson was now alone in his battle with the determined killer. The two men engaged in a life-and-death struggle. For a moment, it appeared that the loyal protector had the upper hand as he grabbed Gale from behind. Mayhem reached beneath Gale's arms and attempted to employ a full nelson in hopes of subduing the killer. Struggling to elude

Thompson's powerful grasp and acting out of desperation, Gale, the gun in his right hand, blindly and awkwardly pointed the 9mm over his right shoulder and fired the weapon. Gale's fifth round struck the fearless bodyguard in the right upper chest slicing through the skin, muscle, and bone before exiting out his back.

Thompson's body reacted immediately to the lead and copper projectile as it knifed through his body, causing him to involuntarily release his grip on Gale. Thompson's body twisted to the right and he staggered, seriously injured, toward the side of the stage, his back to "The Beast." The killer then turned around, stepped forward and in a supreme act of cowardice, aimed the Beretta at the wounded and defenseless Thompson. He again fired at the gentle giant known as "Mayhem." In a haunting way, the promise Jeff had made only a few weeks prior had come true: "I'll take a bullet for ya." It was a prophetic statement that Jeffery "Mayhem" Thompson had made to the Abbotts several times.

This sixth shot ripped into Thompson's back and severed the huge man's carotid artery. His body, suffering the traumatizing effects of multiple gunshot wounds and massive blood loss, could sustain him no more. He fell to the stage floor, unconscious and mortally wounded.

John "Kat" Brooks, his eyes wild and wide open in astonishment and horror, initially ran toward stage right, screaming "No!" His arms were outstretched, his body language clearly demonstrating shock from the carnage he had just witnessed. Suddenly, Brooks' fear and shock erupted into rage. In a split second, an eerie resolve coursed through him as he made an unconscious decision to attack the person who was shooting his friends. Damn his own personal safety, he was done watching his friends being slaughtered. He turned and vaulted over the body of Dimebag Darrell, launching himself at the monstrous killer, just as Gale had fired his sixth round, the second bullet into Jeff Thompson. Brooks grabbed Gale's gun and began to wrestle with the killer.

Opposite page: Nathan Gale's hat lies in the void between the stage and the steel barrier. Dec. 8, 2004. Columbus Police Department, evidence photo. Above: The area behind Dimebag's amps where The Beast struggled with hostage Brooks. A broken guitar and the contents of an ice cooler litter the area. Dec. 8, 2004. Columbus Police Department, evidence photo.

In the 20 seconds that had passed since Nathan Gale stepped on stage, the spectators were spellbound as they tried to decipher just exactly what was happening in front of them. Many concert acts, such as Alice Cooper and Metallica, make a living out of trying to shock audiences with bogus carnage. Perhaps for this reason, few at the Alrosa Villa immediately recognized the reality of what was unfolding. Dozens of audience members would later relay in police statements and through various media outlets that they thought it was "part of the show."

As Brooks was wrestling the armed beast, vocalist Patrick Lachman leapt from the stage while bass player Robert "Bobzilla" Kakaha fled via the rear door of the Alrosa Villa, not certain what was happening but realizing that someone was firing a gun. Lachman, with microphone in hand, screamed to the audience that this was not part of the act. He pleaded over the public address system to anyone who would listen, *"Call 911, somebody!"* The urgency in his voice was unmistakable as he again shouted in frustration; *"Someone f**king call 911!"* He then left the building and tried to provide aid to wounded tour manager Chris Paluska.

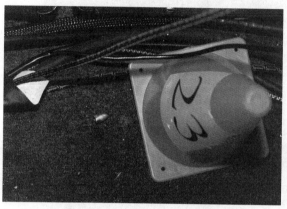

One of the 14 bullets fired by the killer. This round was found on the stage floor behind Dimebag's amp stack. Dec. 8, 2004. Columbus Police Department, evidence photo.

Brooks was engaged in an unimaginable battle with Gale as the two men lashed out at each other. Gale retreated behind the amplifiers and grabbed Brooks by the hair as he attempted to get control of the professional roadie. The fighters tripped over a cooler. Beer cans, water, and ice tumbled to the stage as both men fell behind Dimebag's amps. Gale violently stuck the gun directly to the side of Brooks's head. He screamed at Brooks to stop fighting and to shut up or he'd blow his brains out. Brooks was now a hostage.

The audience began to react to the situation and several Alrosa Villa security personnel, including Erin Halk, swung into action. Halk, seeking any kind of tool he could employ as a weapon, clutched a beer bottle and began to advance on Gale from the front of the stage. However, Halk's mind quickly reverted to the wisdom and training of his two years in the Marine Corps. He astutely determined that a direct frontal assault would be next to impossible. He retreated back to the right side of the stage, his mind whirring as he sought to put an end to the carnage. He pulled off his jacket and tossed it near the rear door of the venue as he focused on the gunman and considered what to do.

Meanwhile, Gale and his hostage remained on the stage behind Dimebag's three towering stacks of amplifiers. As soon as Gale was out of view, Alrosa Villa security personnel stationed in front of the stage, along with several audience members, clambered onto the blood-soaked platform to provide aid to the injured.

Erin Halk, clutching a beer bottle, creeps forward to see if he can engage the killer. Dec. 8, 2004, Columbus Police Department, evidence photo.

With the speaker cabinets separating him from the audience and venue security, Gale repeatedly ordered Brooks to stay still and not move. Brooks was not about to be pacified by the brazen murderer's threats. He resumed his attempt to disarm the thug by grabbing his gun. Though held tightly by Gale, Brooks suddenly jerked toward stage left, and both hostage and gunman appeared in the open between the amps and the closed dressing room door.

Frustrated by Brooks' continued efforts to resist him, Gale lashed out with more force. When Brooks placed his right hand over the end of the gun, Gale pulled the trigger for the seventh time. The 115-grain full metal-jacketed bullet passed through Brooks' hand, then struck the defiant roadie in the leg.

As the seventh shot reverberated in the venue, several members of Alrosa's security team advanced to confront Gale. After shooting Brooks, the murderer once again sought concealment behind the amp stacks. He then reappeared, moving to his left, and took up a position at the side of Dimebag's amps while holding his gun to Brooks' head.

Gale squinted as he tried to see without his glasses. The bright stage lights glared at him as he screamed for people to stay back. He blindly pointed his weapon towards the stage and erratically placed it to the head of his wounded hostage. Witness Brandon Thompson stated that Gale would occasionally place the barrel of the gun to his own head as if he were preparing to commit suicide.

Brooks, in great pain from the multiple injuries caused by the bullet, was genuinely concerned that he was going to be executed. He did his best to remain calm as events spiraled beyond his control. He continually questioned the gunman, asking him why he was shooting people and pleaded with him to stop his murderous rampage. Gale told Brooks to "shut the f**k up and quit being such a little bitch."

Venue security and audience members kept their distance, fearing any attempt to rush the gunman would be met with a hail of gunfire or the execution of the hostage. They felt increasingly frustrated despite repeated encouragement from audience members screaming for them to "kill the motherf**ker."

Fans offstage were now leaning over the barrier on the left side of the stage, reaching out and calling to Dimebag in hopes of a response. Others pointed at his motionless body on the stage and screamed for someone to help him. Posted behind the barrier, Alrosa Villa security member Charles Cochran pulled himself up to the stage and made his way around the front of Vinnie Paul's drum kit toward stage left. As he passed the body of Dimebag Darrell, he looked down and quickly recognized that the guitarist was dead. His fellow security personnel screamed at him not to approach the killer. They feared that he, too, would be shot and killed. Cochran ignored their warnings and moved forward to see if he could safely engage the shooter or rescue the hostage. A member of the audience soon joined him, but both retreated when the killer pointed his weapon at them.

In the audience, 23-year-old Nate Bray was stunned and confused as he tried to absorb the ghastly scene unfolding in front of his eyes. To Bray, Dimebag Darrell Abbott wasn't just a musician; he was a friend who had entertained and inspired him for years. The young man who idolized the guitarist decided he would not, could not, simply stand by as his hero's life slipped away alone on the stage floor, a dark pool of blood beneath him.

Bray began to try to climb the barrier separating the audience from the stage, screaming Dimebag's name all the while. On his fourth attempt, he pulled himself

Nathan Bray and his friend Jason Jewett were positioned slightly to the right of this photo. Dec. 8, 2004. Columbus Police Department, evidence photo.

over the barrier and placed a foot on the stage, but then he lost his balance. He fell to the floor in front of the stage, nearly pulling one of the stage speaker monitors down with him. Tenaciously, he continued to try to reach the stage, despite the attempts of Alrosa security member Dan Weitz, who on several occasions tried to hold him back. Bray persisted, and when Weitz was looking toward the rear corner of the platform, he grasped the side of two monitors and clambered onto the Alrosa Villa stage. The young man with short cropped blonde hair, wearing a white shirt, crawled on his hands and knees to try to aid the man he had such a burning desire to meet.

Wearing a white T shirt, Nathan Bray climbs onto the stage to aid Dimebag and Jeff Thompson. Dec. 8, 2004 Columbus Police Department, evidence photo.

As he made it to the stage, several others in the audience also leapt into action and converged on the prone, lifeless body of Dimebag Darrell Abbott. Unsure if he was alive or not, Bray and another member of the audience sought to give Dimebag any help they possibly could. They carefully rolled the guitarist over on his back, with his guitar continuing to moan and feedback as his body moved on its still functioning strings. Bray began CPR and gave Dimebag several chest compressions in a desperate attempt to sustain the guitarist's life. As Bray applied the pressure to Dimebag's chest, blood gushed out of the gaping wounds in his head.

Momentarily aghast, the audience member checking Dime's pulse leaned backward, his outstretched hands palms up in front of him, his mouth dropping open as he stared at the man who moments ago had been so full of life. Bray realized that his hero was gone and quickly scanned the stage. He relinquished his position over Dimebag's body to another member of the audience and moved toward Thompson, who was lying just a few feet away.

As more spectators and security personnel crept onto the stage, The Beast remained behind Dimebag's amplifiers. He continued to struggle to control Brooks, holding him in a headlock and menacing him by jamming the gun into the side of his head.

Bray now had some help as he tried to tend to Thompson's injuries. The men rolled Thompson onto his back and tried to determine what course of action to take. Suddenly, Bray looked up and saw Gale emerge from behind the bank of amplifiers. Gale, dragging his hostage with him, moved toward the dressing room door. As if by reflex, Bray stood up, his arms to his sides, his palms up, fingers spread in a gesture of great incredulity and screamed, *"Man, what are you doing?"* Simultaneously, he took a single step toward the dangerous killer.

Gale's response was cruel and terse. He raised his Beretta and fired a single round at the unarmed, married father just three feet away from him. The eighth bullet fired by The Beast slammed into the center of Bray's chest, exiting out his back. It continued on its path, into the leg of Jeff Thompson. Bray clutched his wound as his forward momentum carried him past Gale. He crashed into the black door of the dressing room and fell inside. He then managed to kick the door shut. Gasping for breath

Nathan Bray was directly in front of the mixing board when he was shot by Gale. He staggered past the gunman and ended up in the dressing room. Photo by Chris A.

and fighting to survive, he looked around and realized he was trapped in the room. Nathan Bray moved away from the door and leaned against the side wall, slipping into unconsciousness. Little more than two minutes had passed since The Beast violated the stage, and five people had been shot.

It was 10:18 pm. Audience members and employees at the Alrosa Villa were telephoning the Columbus Police Department via 911. Most of the calls were lucid, descriptive, and clearly understandable to the professional dispatchers tasked with fielding the notifications. The dispatchers clearly and concisely questioned 911 callers and very quickly disseminated the subject's description and his location to responding officers. They activated the department's alert tone, signaling officers that a serious emergency was unfolding. Just two minutes into the attack, the Columbus Police Department was scrambling its units to respond. The dispatchers remained calm and professional as they routed the calls to the appropriate agencies and dispatched police and paramedic crews. The clarity and demeanor of the dispatchers resulted in exceptional coordination of responding units.

Back on stage at the Alrosa Villa, the carnage continued. When Gale fired at Bray, his weapon "stovepiped:" a malfunction that occurs when the weapon's slide locks to the rear as it catches on an empty magazine, or in this case, a partially ejected casing. Several people on the stage saw this, and some began to scream, "He's out of ammo." In reality, the fired casing was stuck in the ejection port, holding the slide back. For that moment, Gale's weapon was ineffective. His hours of shooting practice and firearms training in the U.S. Marines were pivotal as he quickly assessed the situation. He immediately jerked back on the slide twice, which cleared the jammed casing and also ejected a live round. He quickly dropped the slide and returned the weapon to its operational state before would-be rescuers could get to him.

This live 9mm round was ejected from Gale's weapon when it jammed. It was the only live round found on the stage. Dec. 8, 2004. Columbus Police Department, evidence photo.

There were still hundreds of people in the audience; most were unable to see the threat. Gale's position at the rear of the stage wasn't visible to the vast majority of the patrons, especially those on the left of the venue. As the reality of the situation filtered through the crowd, patrons began to evacuate the building.

Contrary to the "hysterical chaos" described by the media, the evacuation was orderly, with people helping each other and pointing out exits. Instead of widespread panic, there was a sense of "we are in this together." The vast majority of people at the Alrosa Villa conducted themselves with honor, comforting each other and performing their civic duties.

In the 1990s, William Weaver performed at the Alrosa Villa with his band *Bloody Mary*. Tonight, he was in the audience. Weaver, now a corrections officer, aided by tattoo artist James Vanfossen, teamed up to perform CPR on the victims even as Alrosa Security personnel were urging everyone to exit the building. Weaver and Vanfossen realized that the killer lurked just a few feet away, in the dark void behind the speaker cabinets. They could smell the lingering, acrid odor of burned gunpowder, but they ignored

Taken from just left of center stage from the dance floor. This photo demonstrates that most of the audience were unable to see the predator as he lurked in the far right corner of the stage. Photo by Chris A.

the potential peril and focused on trying to keep the wounded alive. At the time, both men believed they were working on Dimebag. Dime and Mayhem were wearing very similar clothing. Adding to the confusion was the fact that Mayhem also had dyed part of his beard red.

Gale, with his hostage, John Brooks, remained in the dark back corner of stage left, primarily staying behind and to the side of Dimebag's amp stacks. From the audience, Jeffery Greene stood next to the towering public address speakers on stage left and pleaded with the killer to stop his rampage.

"What do you want, man?"

Gale aimed his gun at Greene and growled back, "I want my f**king glasses, where are they?"

Greene quickly scanned the stage and spotted Gale's blood covered glasses next to one of the monitor wedges. He pointed at them and said to Gale, "They are right over there." Gale squinted and ordered Greene to retrieve them, but

Greene wisely chose to ignore the killer, instead taking cover behind the PA system.

The killers view of the crowd from his lair by Dime's amplifiers. Due to the speaker cabinets, bright lights and PA speakers, Gale had a limited view of the venue. Taken five minutes before the start of the *Damageplan* show at the Alrosa VIlla. Dec. 8, 2004 Columbus Police Department, evidence photo.

Meanwhile, on stage right, roadie and Alrosa security member Erin Halk made the decision to act. If the gunman made a mistake or provided an opening, he would try to subdue him. John Graham, Dimebag's guitar tech, repeatedly encouraged Halk to be cautious and not to take any risks. Realizing the danger, Halk took cover, but he waited for an opportunity to strike out at the killer. He understood that there was a very real possibility that the big man in the corner with the gun had the intent and the capability to kill or injure more people.

As Halk contemplated his options, Brooks began to believe his time was running out. He looked to the audience for help but soon realized that he was on his own with the armed madman. Once again, in a desperate attempt to break free of Gale's grip, he grabbed the gun and tried to yank it out of the killer's hands. As he grabbed it, his hand struck the weapon's magazine release button and the magazine dropped from the handgrip of the gun to the floor.

Gale, who may or may not have been aware that he'd lost his magazine, jerked the gun away from Brooks and again pulled the trigger. His ninth round struck Brooks below his arm in the right side of his body. As he fired the round, his weapon's slide locked to the rear again. Without the magazine, the weapon was out of ammunition. The men on stage erupted into a chorus:

"He's out! He's out of ammo! He's out of bullets!" they screamed.

The 10 round magazine that fell from Gale's weapon when Brooks grabbed the gun. Dec. 8, 2004, Columbus Police Department, evidence photo.

Sensing an opening, Halk rushed the armed intruder. He maneuvered around the storage cases behind the drum kit, hoping to overpower the kneeling killer. Gale remained calm and reached into his pocket, producing a loaded magazine. Squinting, he never took his eyes off Halk as the roadie/Alrosa security member attacked. Without dropping his gaze, the killing machine slapped the magazine into the weapon and thrust it toward Erin Halk, the slide dropping as he extended the gun.

He quickly fired two rounds. Both struck Halk as he moved toward the predator. The tenth bullet fired by Gale struck Halk in the left hand, passed through it and struck him in the left thigh, breaking his femur. The second bullet, the eleventh fired, penetrated the left side of his chest. Halk fell to the stage floor behind the amplifier backline, just a few feet from the gunman and the hostage. The beast callously aimed

his weapon at Halk's prone body and quickly fired three more rounds, each finding their mark. Gale had now fired fourteen rounds, all of which struck their targets.

In other areas of the venue, members of the audience, aided by Alrosa Villa security personnel, pulled the body of Dimebag from the stage. Jason Jewett, friend and companion of Nathan Bray, removed Dimebag's guitar from the stage. He stood in front of the public address system on stage left, clutching and protecting his hero's bloody guitar, which he later gave to a *Damageplan* crew member for safekeeping. Patrons and Alrosa staff moved Dimebag to the left side of the sunken dance floor and carefully placed him on the dingy red and white tiled floor. People immediately surrounded his lifeless body and tried to give him first aid. Others shouted encouragement or said silent

prayers. Despite the potential perils of the gunman on stage, people stayed, holding the guitarist's hand, some kneeling in an ever-growing pool of crimson. Mindy Reese, a nurse who had been at the show, used a shirt to apply pressure over the gaping wounds at the side of Dimebag's head in a desperate but vain effort to stem the massive blood loss.

1. Corrections officer William Weaver stands outside the Alrosa Villa after trying to save the life of Jeff Thompson. Dec. 8, 2004, Columbus Police Department, evidence photo. 2. The 18th Precinct, about two miles away from the Alrosa Villa. The vast majority of patrol officers who responded to the shooting were from the 18th. Photo by Chris A.

With Dimebag off the stage, audience members turned their attention to Jeff Thompson and attempted to remove him from the platform. William Weaver and James Vanfossen pushed and pulled the big man around a flight case toward the edge of the stage. Several people in the crowd grasped the huge man by his legs in an effort to pull him to safety.

By now, most patrons had escaped the confines of the building and were in the parking lot milling around, some hiding behind vehicles, unsure of what would happen next. Would the killer exit the building with a hostage? Would he continue to shoot more people? In the background, the screams of dozens of sirens could be heard as Columbus police officers began converging on the scene.

Inside the Alrosa Villa, Nathan Gale, The Beast, the predator, realized he was trapped. He pulled his hostage toward the dressing room door, opened it, and quickly scanned the inside. He saw Nathan Bray leaning against the side wall of the room and discovered there was no exit. As the realization of his situation began to sink in, he again alternated between pointing the gun at the head of his hostage and at his own head as he attempted to keep the audience, security, and stage crew members at bay. "Don't do it, man!" people screamed at the gunman as they looked into the frightened eyes of John "Kat" Brooks. Brooks, bleeding and frightened was still held in a

1. Columbus Police Officer James Niggemeyer. 2. Unit 185, the police car operated by Officer James Niggemeyer on the night of the shooting. Photos by Chris A.

headlock. The barrel of the now bloody gun was pressed firmly to the side of his head.

Officer James Niggemeyer had been a Columbus cop for almost five years and was just starting his normal 10 pm shift. He was a member of the 18th precinct and was assigned to police cruiser #185. As he was leaving the precinct lot, his radio squawked with the garish alert tone from dispatch. It was followed by an announcement of a "43," the code for a shooting in progress at the Alrosa Villa on Sinclair Road. Niggemeyer had worked in the area many times but had never been inside the venue. He flipped on his emergency lights and siren and headed west on Morse Road mashing the gas pedal of car #185. He monitored the radio dispatchers intently as they continued to provide details gleaned from the 911 calls pouring into the station. Niggemeyer keyed his radio microphone and advised dispatch that he was armed with a shotgun. He shut off his siren as he accelerated down Sinclair Road toward the Alrosa Villa. His vehicle turned sharply, the tires squealing as he barreled into the southeast entrance to the parking lot. He quickly positioned his police car near the southeast entrance of the building and grabbed his shotgun as he dismounted the car.

People in the parking lot immediately screamed to him, "He's still inside! He's still shooting at people! This is for real!" Niggemeyer's mind was reeling. There was so much to take in, so much happening, so many people in the parking lot screaming at him. It was overwhelming. Outwardly, he remained calm and focused. Inwardly, his heart was pounding out of his chest. A man in a white shirt and long hair ran towards him.

"Officer, come this way, the guy is reloading and still shooting at people."

Niggemeyer quickly scanned the crowd to determine if any of the people in the parking lot posed a threat. Satisfied that they did not, he moved quickly down the south side of the Alrosa Villa to the open door at the side entrance. Niggemeyer chambered a round into his shotgun, a police-issue, 12 gauge Remington 870. He looked cautiously inside the building. It was dark but he could see people scurrying about. As he was about to enter, he heard shouts ring out from the southwest exterior corner of the Alrosa Villa.

"No, no, come back here; go in through the back door," the people at the corner of the building screamed.

Niggemeyer wisely retreated from the side entrance and made his way to the back door as other Columbus Police vehicles pulled into the parking lot of the Alrosa Villa. At the rear door, Niggemeyer queried the patrons and tried to assess the situation inside the building. He wanted to know how many shooters there were and what they were wearing. The breathless crowd told him there was only one shooter; he was at the left rear of the stage; and he was wearing a Blue Jackets hockey jersey. As the lone officer peered into the open rear door of the Alrosa Villa, he saw another group of men taking cover behind amps and sound equipment. They were focused on the opposite side of the stage. When they saw the officer, the men began pointing at the suspect, who was crouched down, his knees digging into the back of his hostage, Brooks.

Most audience members either had taken cover, aided the injured, or evacuated the building. Approximately six people leaned against the stage barrier for the majority of the incident, watching as the situation unfolded. They all were lucky not to have been injured or killed.

Patron Tim Bryant met Niggemeyer at the door and said, "He's right there, he's got a gun!" Bryant gestured and pointed toward Gale. Niggemeyer made his way inside the venue, urging the people to get out of his way as he looked toward the area being pointed out by the men. Once inside, he was able to get a waist-up view of the gunman illuminated

The stage of the Alrosa Villa as seen from the rear door. In the left rear corner of the photo is the dressing room door. It was near this door that Gale crept, holding a gun to the head of John Brooks. Photo by Chris A.

by the stage lights. His right hand grasped the stainless steel 9mm pistol; his left arm was wrapped around the neck of his hostage. Up to this point, Niggemeyer had absolutely no idea that Gale was holding Brooks at gunpoint. As he watched, he saw the gunman point the weapon toward the front of the stage, over his hostage's right shoulder.

Niggemeyer felt an intense wave of fear engulf him; it was unlike anything he had ever felt before. Later, he would not be able to articulate how intense the sensation was. He couldn't believe what he found himself in the middle of. Not only was the shooter still armed and menacing, he also was holding a hostage. Niggemeyer noted the faces of the people around him: the fans, the roadies, the security people. He was struck by the realization that they were all looking to him to act. At that moment, James Niggemeyer never felt so alone. He knew he would have to take action and he had no one to look to for help. Trying to remain focused, Niggemeyer quickly evaluated the situation and determined that the gunman had not seen him. This might be credited to the fact that Jeff Thompson ripped Gale's glasses off at the beginning of the assault. He decided to move toward the suspect from behind the bass amp cabinets and the drum riser, using the speaker cabinets as cover. As he advanced, Tim Bryant and several other men at stage right started screaming at the officer.

"Shoot him! Shoot him! Shoot that motherf**ker!"

The screams to shoot the assailant were incessant and demanding. Niggemeyer tried to block them out as he continued to move forward, concentrating on the suspect. When he reached the amp cabinet next to the drum riser, the officer was approximately 20 feet from the suspect. Breathing deeply and feeling the fear and stress rising inside of him, Niggemeyer realized his worst fear: he might have to employ deadly force. Recognizing that the shooter could at any time rush forward toward the remaining spectators or execute his hostage, Niggemeyer decided to ready himself to fire at the shooter if it became necessary. As far as Niggemeyer knew, he was the only officer in the building. He cautiously rose up from behind the speaker box and leveled the Remington 870 at the subject's head. To Niggemeyer, time slowed to a crawl as every millisecond seemed to drag. He was acutely aware that the ammunition he carried was double-aught (00) buckshot. Each of the shotgun rounds contained nine lead pellets, each approximately the size of a pea. He knew that if the pellet pattern spread too much, or if he didn't place his shot correctly, he could accidentally kill or wound the hostage or a bystander.

In the few seconds he had to assess the entire situation, Niggemeyer not only had to deal with controlling his own fear, but he also had to use tactics, employ cover, consider the safety of the hostage, and ensure that a round would not inflict injury to bystanders. He also had to fully comply with his department's use of deadly force policy. If he acted incorrectly, he could lose his job or even face criminal charges. A police officer in this situation has to make a split-second decision, which all too often is picked apart by citizen review boards and media pundits who have no concept of the pressure associated with such a life-and-death decision.

Prepared to fire, Niggemeyer concentrated and silently hoped that his actions would be the right ones. He controlled his emotions and blocked out the distractions as dozens of people continued to scream at him to "shoot that motherf**ker!" His concern about accidentally wounding or killing the hostage due to an errant shotgun pellet nagged at him. He decided that if he had to shoot, he'd aim slightly high. Brooks's head was just below and in front of Gale's head. If he had to fire, it was going to be a tight shot.

As Niggemeyer was taking his position, Alrosa Security staff and stagehands distracted the gunman, yelling at him and waving their arms from the front of the stage, urging him to surrender. At the same time, five other officers had entered the Alrosa Villa from several side doors, guns drawn as they sought out the killer. Suddenly, Gale saw an officer by the front of the stage. This was most likely Officer Bryan Stumph, who advanced from stage right. What he did next forced Officer Niggemeyer's hand. As Niggemeyer concentrated, Gale placed his weapon to the side of his hostage's head and prepared to kill him. Brooks closed his eyes and prepared to die. Niggemeyer, sensing that Gale was about to kill Brooks, could hesitate no longer. He had to act now! Officer James Niggemeyer would later state, "I flat out felt that from what I had seen and what I was witnessing, there was no doubt in my mind that he was going to shoot the hostage." He gritted his teeth, took a deep breath, and squeezed the trigger of the shotgun, just as Gale turned his head in the officer's direction. Watching from stage right, guitar tech John Graham, who had helped save the life of Vinnie Paul Abbott, covered his ears and turned his head. He simply couldn't bear to watch another person die.

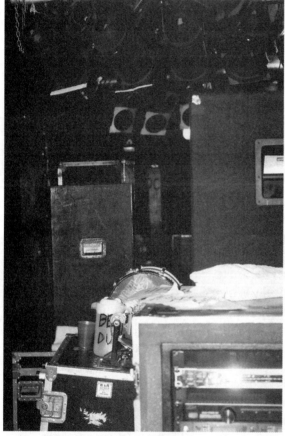

The shotgun blast erupted like a cannon inside the confines of the Alrosa Villa, startling everyone in the building. The round's impact was sudden, precise and devastating. A single pellet struck the mass murderer directly in the center of his forehead, while another pierced his shoulder. Another six pellets struck the killer in the face. Niggemeyer was so close that the plastic wadding inside the shell casing was embedded in the dead killer's right cheek.[2]

Unlike many of his

This is the view Officer James Niggemeyer had when he shot and killed The Beast on that fateful night. The area behind the drum riser was clogged with road cases and equipment. He could only see Gale from the waist up. In the background the dressing room door is open and the letters "OC" painted on the back wall of the room can be seen. Dec. 8, 2004. Columbus Police Department, evidence photo.

innocent victims, Nathan Gale was killed instantly. He collapsed backward, striking the black door to the dressing room. His head and torso fell into the room. A large pool of blood immediately formed beneath his bloody face and head. The lower half of his body remained on the stage.

As the round struck the killer, Brooks, for an instant, believed Gale had shot him. Suddenly, he was pulled backward; then the pressure around his neck ceased. He crawled away and jumped off the front of the stage, his life saved by the actions of Officer James Niggemeyer.

Immediately, Alrosa Security and band crew members rushed toward the body of the fallen killer. Some kicked and punched the dead man, cursing and spitting on his bloody corpse. From the moment Gale, the predator, The Beast, stepped onto the stage until the moment Officer Niggemeyer dispatched him with a single shotgun blast...

...4 minutes and 59 seconds had elapsed.

...The carnage had come to an end.

...The Beast was dead and his demons were silenced.

Nathan Gale, dead at the rear of the Alrosa Villa stage. He was struck by eight of the nine pellets fired from Niggemeyer's shotgun. It was from this very small area that he wreaked most of his havoc. Dec. 8, 2004, Columbus Police Department, evidence photo.

Dime Time

Dean Zelinsky hangs out with Dime. Milwaukee, WI. Nov. 20, 2004. Photo courtesy of Chad Lee - www.rockconcertfotos.com

Dean Zelinsky first met Dimebag Darrell when the guitarist was just 16 years old. At the time, Darrell had won a guitar, a Dean, in a talent competition. The young guitarist had heard that the man behind the guitars would be visiting a local music store, so he showed up in hopes of meeting him. The two hit it off, as Darrell expressed his love for his Dean guitar and Zelinsky was clearly impressed by the playing ability of the young man from Texas.

In 1991, Dean Zelinsky sold his guitar company. While the name would stay the same, the company discontinued

U.S. production and began to sell imported guitars. Over the next decade, Dimebag continued to play Dean guitars, but eventually *Pantera*'s fame exploded. It didn't take long for Dimebag's potential influence on young guitarists to catch the attention of several instrument manufacturers. With his first love, Dean Guitars, selling only imports, and with his friend Dean Zelinsky no longer running the company, Dimebag signed an endorsement deal with Washburn Guitars, a company whose instruments bear a striking resemblance to the Dean.

In 2000, Zelinsky returned to the Tampa, Florida-based company he founded. One of the key tasks that he hoped to accomplish was to develop a quality U.S.-made guitar for the company.

In 2004, Dimebag was on tour with his new band, *Damageplan*. He ran into a friend of Dean's, who invited the ex-*Pantera* guitarist to consider returning to Dean Guitars. Dime rattled off his number and soon Dean gave his old friend a call. The two men rekindled their friendship and, over the course of the conversation, Dimebag told Dean that his contract with Washburn was ending. He said that once his obligation was completed he'd take a serious look at the new line of Dean guitars. Even without a formal endorsement deal, the fact that Dimebag Darrell had played Dean guitars was huge for the company. When Dimebag used other brands, fans and guitarists realized that his influences and his greatest work were tied to Dean Guitars. In late 2004, Dimebag found his way back to Dean and even designed a guitar for the company. The guitar would be called "The Razorback."

No single artist had done more for the popularity of the Dean brand of guitars than Dimebag Darrell Abbott. He took Dean and heavy metal to a whole new level and showed rockers how the instrument was played.

Just two weeks before Dime's death, Dean was with him at a *Damageplan* show in Milwaukee, Wisconsin. Dean recounted, "Backstage, two kids were waiting at the stage door and refused to leave without first seeing Darrell. When he got wind of this, he insisted they be brought to him. These kids were in awe to meet their idol. Darrell rocked their world when

Tracy Hill Photo

Dean with Metal "Mayhem" Elvis.
Photo courtesy of Tracy Hill.

he put them on the VIP list for the Chicago show the very next day."

For Dean, those final months working with Darrell on new guitar designs and talking to him just about every day were some of the most invigorating times in his long career. Seeing Dime onstage with a Dean in his hands brought back feelings that the guitar designer thought were gone forever.

The day before his death, Dean had a final conversation with Dime. They spoke by phone discussing a photo shoot to introduce the new Razorback design.

Zelinsky clearly feels the loss of his friend and speaks reverently of him.

"Darrell was a living legend. He lived every day of his life to the fullest. I will always remember his smile onstage. He loved what he did and it showed. No matter how big the crowd, he could always find you and fling a guitar pick your way. We at Dean have lost a great artist but more importantly, a true friend. The world has lost a great human being."

– Dean Zelinsky, Dean Guitars

Chapter 12

Shattered

"It's storming broken glass, corpses left in piles
Ungracious bludgeonment that breaks the earth for miles
Nothing can stop it, the day has come, from below it's catastrophic"

Shattered
Cowboys From Hell
-Pantera

The gray haze of burned gunpowder from Niggemeyer's deadly accurate shotgun blast filled the air. Columbus police, firefighters, paramedics, ambulance crews, venue employees and fans were poised to hustle into action in an attempt to save lives. Immediately after Officer Niggemeyer fired, he wanted to approach the suspect to make certain he was incapacitated and unarmed. He found his path forward blocked by the drum riser and other equipment. He retraced his steps behind the bass amplifiers and crossed the front of the stage to advance on the killer.[1] As he made it to the side of the stage, he realized that he wasn't the only officer in the building. A huge wave of relief quickly came over him.

Now able to soak in the scene, Niggemeyer realized that several of his colleagues had converged on the predator from the front of the stage. Joining him inside the Alrosa Villa were Officers Bryon Stumph, Rick Crum, Kevin Ferencz, David Lares and Jeremy Landis. Crum was armed with a shotgun; the others, with handguns. Landis and Crum cautiously approached the body of the killer. They discovered the

---

[1] Chapter 12 footnotes begin on page 311.

suspect's weapon lying next to his right hand. Landis cautiously grabbed the weapon and placed it on a shelf in a guitar rack out of the killer's reach in case he was still alive or faking injury. Further inspection revealed devastating head injuries to the suspect. Officers Stumph and Ferencz were confident that the perpetrator was dead. They quickly scanned the club, including the area behind the stage. As soon as they were confident that the Alrosa Villa was secure, ambulance and fire crews were cleared to enter the cordoned area around the building.

Opposite page: 1. The empty 12 gauge hull fired by Niggemeyer at the predator. Dec. 8, 2004. Columbus Police Department, evidence photo. 2. Just a few of the heroes who put their own lives at risk to save others. From left to right, Officers, Crum, Landis, Ferencz, Stumph, Niggemeyer & Lares. For a list of all the officers and detectives who responded please visit the Appendix. Above: The Remington 870 shotgun carried that night by Officer Niggemeyer. Dec. 8, 2004 Columbus Police Department, evidence photo.

As dozens of Columbus police officers spread throughout the building, a visibly shaken Niggemeyer sought witnesses who could corroborate Gale's threatening gestures toward the hostage.

"You're my witness. I had to do it," he said to several people on stage.

Officer Crum quickly moved to Niggemeyer's side. He took the shotgun and escorted Niggemeyer out of the venue. The weapon was evidence. Earlier in his career, Crum had been involved in a police shooting and understood the required protocol. He drove Niggemeyer across Sinclair Road to remove him from the crime scene. They parked in the darkness behind a warehouse and waited for members of the Columbus Police Department Officer Support Team (OST) to arrive. Officer Rick Crum was a member of the OST, but since he was directly involved in the incident, he could not be assigned to James Niggemeyer. Crum kept Niggemeyer company and offered his assistance until a "neutral" officer

Dozens of police cars, vans and evidence trucks responded to the Alrosa Villa to assist. Dec. 8, 2004. Columbus Police Department, evidence photo.

arrived on the scene. Niggemeyer never made it to the location where the suspect's body lay. As he was whisked away, Niggemeyer was advised that his round had struck the suspect. Later, Commander Mary Mathias informed him that he had caused no injury to the hostage.

Back at the Alrosa Villa, the wail of sirens pierced the cold night air as ambulances proceeded to the venue. Firefighters and paramedics quickly unloaded their equipment, split into teams, and began to assess the status of the victims at the venue. Dozens of police, venue employees, crew members, and fans had already converged on the victims.

In the dressing room, Nathan Bray was found semi-conscious and seriously wounded. Fans and crew members performed first aid on Nathan and gave him encouragement while waiting for medical help. At the back of the stage, police officers and fans lifted the seemingly lifeless body of Erin Halk and placed him in front of the drum kit in the center of the stage. Just 10 feet away, fans and venue personnel were performing CPR on Jeff Thompson. In the parking lot, Chris Paluska, who had been shot in the chest, was being helped by his friends and *Damageplan* fans. Wounded hostage John Brooks, after jumping off the stage, found his way to *Damageplan*'s tour bus, where he sought aid.

On the side of the dance floor, at the base of the north side of the VIP stairs, remaining crew and audience members surrounded the body of Dimebag Darrell Abbott. Some attempted CPR, but the damage done by The Beast was fatal. Dimebag's life slipped away in the opening seconds of the assault. The guitarist was most likely dead before his body fell to the stage floor. John Graham, Dime's guitar tech, made his way to Dimebag and sat next to his friend's lifeless body. Graham held Darrell's hand and wept.

The buzz of the amplifiers and "hot" microphones echoed in the Alrosa Villa. At the front of the stage, police officers and fans urgently tended to Erin Halk. Unconscious and gravely wounded, Erin was in the care of brothers whom he had never met. Officer Jeremy Landis and patron Jeffery Greene urged Erin to fight for his life.

"C'mon man. Don't die, dude. It's not your time to die."

Greene continuously repeated this to Erin as he gently held his hand. Officer Landis cut open Halk's clothing to reveal his wounds in preparation of the arrival of paramedics. Another patron elevated Erin's legs to help ward off the effects of shock by inducing blood flow to his upper body. The man also urged Erin to fight for his life.

The same scenario was being played out around the venue as caring individuals tried to save the lives of people they had never met. Patty Zink, Erin's girlfriend, slowly approached the stage from the right. She cautiously stepped up onto the platform, her hands clasped and held to her face. She let out a painful wail as she realized that the man being treated was her boyfriend. Officer Landis firmly ordered her to stay away from the area and told her to wait outside. Over the public address system, an announcement ordered patrons to exit the building. Slowly, those who were not engaged in direct life-saving actions began to filter out into the parking lot.

As soon as the ambulance, fire department, and paramedic crews rushed into the building, a chorus of requests for help erupted from those who were aiding the victims. Remaining completely focused, rescue personnel from the Columbus Fire Department, Clinton Township, and the Worthington Fire Department worked hand in hand in an incredibly organized and professional effort to save lives.

Seventeen minutes after the shooting erupted, Jeff Thompson was placed onto a gurney and prepared for emergency transport to Riverside Hospital by Clinton Township Medic #61. He had been continually receiving CPR and was now intubated and wheeled out of the venue.[2] On the dance floor, Columbus Fire Department paramedics Bryan Coss and Mark Williams, assigned to Medic #24, quickly intubated the prone body of Dimebag Darrell. The monitoring system booted up and confirmed that he had no vital signs. Other indications "incompatible with life" prompted the medics to request an on-scene supervisor to "make the call." Dimebag was pronounced dead. Ambulance crews placed his body on a backboard and gently lifted him onto a gurney for transport. Police officers, upon hearing that Abbott was deceased, advised the ambulance crew that his body was part of the crime scene. The crew was ordered to place him back on the floor as they originally found him in order to maintain the integrity of the crime scene. The crew of Medic #24 quickly moved onto other patients.

From left to right, Worthington Fire Department. paramedics, Ty Stewart, Joe Pichert, and Chris Craig. Photo courtesy of Worthington Fire Department.

On the stage, Worthington Fire Department paramedics Ty Stewart, Chris Craig and Joe Pichert, who were assigned to Medic #101, instantly took over efforts to save Halk. The vital signs of the free spirited ex-Marine had quickly eroded. The multiple injuries caused by the five bullets fired into his body proved insurmountable. Without ever regaining consciousness, Erin passed away despite the best efforts of medics, police officers, and firefighters.

Paramedic Chris Craig then moved to the dressing room to assist in treating Nathan Bray, who had been receiving care from paramedics Ryan Bryzinski, Mark Williams, and Brian Coss of the Columbus Fire Department. His condition was critical. His vital signs indicated his body was failing in its fight to live. The paramedics worked hard to stabilize his status. It was apparent that he needed to be transported to the hospital immediately. The young husband and father was placed on a backboard and carefully lifted out of the dressing room. They carried him through the doorway and over the body of The Beast who had so callously shot him. Quickly placed on a gurney, Nathan was covered with a blanket and wheeled out of the Alrosa Villa to an ambulance headed for Riverside Hospital.

Almost unnoticed, Columbus Fire Department Lt. Rick Schoch knelt next to the body of the silenced Beast and declared him dead. He quickly moved on to assist other victims. Only 23 minutes had elapsed from the start of the shooting.

The local media described the scene as 23 minutes of pure, utter chaos and uncontrolled panic, but the reality was completely different. It was 23 minutes of sheer terror, punctuated by incredible courage and heroism. It was 23 minutes in which much of the audience melded into a caring, cooperative team of 350 souls, aiding and assisting cops and paramedics. They helped one another, comforted those in need, and shared jackets, smokes, and cell phones. Despite the cold and the fear from the

Hundreds of fans wandered the parking lot and waited in cars to provide statements to the police. Lead Detective Gillette was staggered by the reaction. He couldn't believe so many people wanted to help. Dec. 8, 2004. Columbus Police Department, evidence photo.

shocking scene that they had witnessed, most patrons remained to provide authorities with eye witness statements.

Above the fray, a Columbus Police helicopter illuminated the scene below, scanning the immediate area for any potential suspects who were outside of the venue. Using an infrared thermal imaging device, officers detected the heat signature of a person hiding in the bushes near the railroad tracks behind Alrosa. CPD officers Dilello and Heinzman approached the location, guns drawn. Under the helicopter lights, a man rose and held up his hands. Peter Voedisch was arrested but subsequently released after passing a gunshot residue test. He had simply heard the sirens and wanted to see what was happening.

As Medic #61 screamed into the parking lot of the Riverside Hospital Emergency Room, attendants were waiting. The crew flew out of the vehicle and removed Mayhem. Jeff Thompson's condition was grave as he was wheeled into the trauma room surrounded by paramedics, nurses and doctors. A final, frantic effort to save Thompson ensued. Sadly, the gentle giant could not be saved. At 10:50 pm, Doctor Marco Bonta pronounced him dead.

Inside the Columbus Fire Department ambulance, Medic #24, Nathan Bray's condition continued to decline; it became clear that he was very near death. Less than a mile away from the Alrosa Villa, cardiac monitors in the ambulance flat-lined. Nathan's strong heart stopped beating. The paramedics immediately began CPR and respiration in an attempt to keep him alive, pumping cardiac drugs into his system and shouting words of encouragement. By the time Medic #24 arrived at the emergency room, Nathan was gone. Ignoring the indications of the instruments, Medic #24's crew never gave up hope. They quickly moved their patient into a trauma room where doctors immediately opened Nathan's chest in an attempt to stem his bleeding and restart his heart. Unfortunately, the damage done by the bullet was too severe. Despite the heroic efforts of paramedics and doctors at Riverside Hospital, Nathan Bray died.

Back at the Alrosa Villa, Worthington Fire Department Paramedics, Ty Stewart and Eric Erhardt climbed aboard *Damageplan*'s tour bus to treat and transport gunshot victim John Brooks. Brooks, with adrenaline coursing through his body, initially refused to leave the scene. He wanted to thank the police officer whose courageous actions had saved his life. Stewart and Erhardt made it clear to Brooks that staying wasn't an option. They bundled the wounded man into Medic #101 for transport to Riverside. While en route, the paramedics assessed his injuries and noted gunshot wounds to Brook's hand, leg, and flank. His condition was satisfactory. He was one of the lucky ones who would survive. According to the medics, Brooks was incredibly "hyped up" and thrilled to be alive. He shouted over and over what a "bad motherf**ker" he was.

Meanwhile, Columbus Fire Department Medic #6 scooped up Chris Paluska, who had a gunshot wound to his chest. He, too, was transported to Riverside for treatment in serious condition. Like Brooks, Paluska would also survive.

Behind a warehouse across from the Alrosa, a Fraternal Order of Police Attorney and Officer Rob Vass, the OST member assigned to the case, met up with Crum and Niggemeyer. Officer Vass had been assigned to help Niggemeyer through the intricacies of the "police-involved shooting" process. Vass answered his "what happens next" questions and helped to reduce his stress level.

Upon the arrival of the Critical Incident Response Team (CIRT), an experienced group of officers, detectives, and technicians, conducted the on-scene investigation. After the Alrosa Villa had been totally secured by the CPD, Officer Crum was contacted by radio and advised to escort Niggemeyer back to the crime scene. Once inside, Niggemeyer was asked to reenact his movements and actions. He explained how he had moved to the rear door, his actions once inside, and what prompted him to use deadly force. The procedure only took a few minutes, and then Niggemeyer was whisked away to police headquarters.

Once at headquarters, detectives photographed Officer Niggemeyer and the clothing he was wearing as evidence. His handgun was checked to ensure that he had not fired any rounds. Niggemeyer was then asked to give an official statement. Following the advice of his FOP attorney, he declined comment, which is common for officers to do until they can review the facts of the incident with their lawyer. A few hours later, he returned home around 5:00 am in the hopes of getting a few fitful hours of sleep. He never did.

Locations Of Those Killed

1) Nathan Bray (transported)
2) Suspect
3) Jeff Thompson (transported)
4) Erin Halk
5) Darrell Abbott

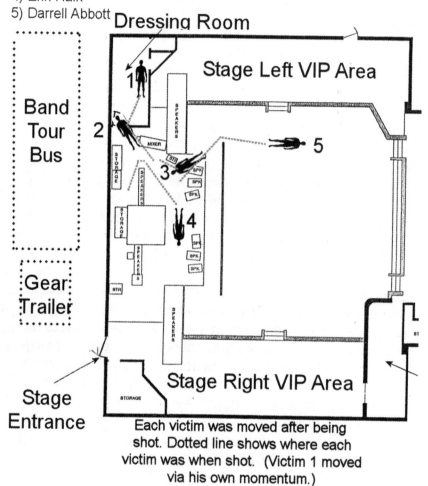

This diagram shows the location of those killed at the Alrosa. Jeff Thompson and Nate Bray were transported from the scene. Diagram by Chris A.

Officer Niggemeyer's movements as he engaged the killer.

X = Niggemeyer's location when he fired upon the suspect.

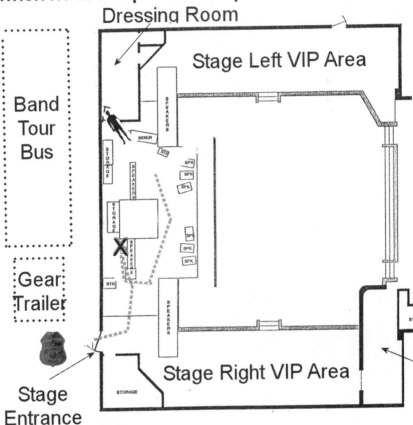

Officer Niggemeyer's movements inside the Alrosa Villa. Diagram by Chris A.

After escaping the carnage on stage, Vinnie Paul Abbott was ushered to safety behind the heavy door of the front lounge at the Alrosa Villa. Rick Cautela stayed with him, giving him a blanket to stave off the cool temperature in the previously unoccupied bar. Once the Alrosa Villa was secure, Vinnie Paul slipped out of the front bar. He slowly and cautiously wandered back into the main hall of the venue.

On the dance floor, he saw people kneeling around his prone brother. As he inched closer, they finally noticed him. Trying to protect Vinnie, they pleaded with him to get back and

1. Vinnie Paul Abbott and approximately 20 other people were placed into this front bar at the Alrosa Villa to provide statements. Photo by Chris A. 2. Overturned chairs and spilled drinks caused by the sudden departure of the patrons. Dec. 8, 2004. Columbus Police Department, evidence photo.

stay away. Horrified, Vinnie Paul retreated back to the lounge area. He asked Rick Cautela to check on Dimebag. Greeted by silence and disorder, Cautela walked back into his club and was appalled by the tragic scene before him: overturned tables and chairs, broken bottles, spilled drinks, and items abandoned by patrons stood as mute testimony to the urgency of those fleeing the bloodbath. On the main dance floor where, over time, thousands of people had partied and celebrated, a bloody sheet now covered a body. Slowly looking around, struggling to take in the horrific scene, Cautela recognized the body of Erin Halk and realized that he was dead.

Engulfed by a great sense of disbelief and overwhelmed by sadness, Cautela meekly asked one of the detectives about the status of Dimebag. The detective pointed at the body on the dance floor and confirmed that Dimebag was dead.

Cautela slowly returned to the lounge and gently broke the horrific news to Vinnie Paul. Vinnie Paul used a cell phone to call his brother's long-time girlfriend, Rita Haney. Together, they cried. Word of the murder quickly spread through the *Damageplan* and *Pantera* families. Moments later, the phone in the front bar rang. Cautela answered to hear the voice of ex-*Pantera* vocalist Phil Anselmo. Having already received news of the shooting. Anselmo asked to speak with Vinnie Paul. Cautela covered the receiver with his hand and asked Vinnie Paul if he wanted to speak with Anselmo. Vinnie Paul apparently growled that he had no interest in talking to "that son of a bitch." Cautela curtly passed on the message to Anselmo and hung up the phone.

By this time, Detective Christopher Rond had entered the front bar to interview Vinnie Paul. Sitting in one of the bar chairs, covered by a blanket and clutching the guitar that his brother had been playing at the time of his murder, a subdued Vinnie Paul gave his statement. As he was playing, he had seen the shooter advance across the stage. To Vinnie, he was just a blue blur, but because of his stance and how he held the gun, he believed that the shooter was either a cop or someone in the military.

Taking a statement from the shaken drummer, Rond asked, "Do you know who this guy is?"

"The shooter?" Vinnie replied "No. No earthly idea. My brother had not one enemy in this town, never had. The only thing that crosses my mind is that *Pantera* had a pretty nasty breakup and there have been a few things that have been said back and forth in magazines and recently the lead singer made a statement on the Internet and in a large print magazine that said 'Dimebag Darrell deserves to be severely beaten.' That is the exact f**king quote."

As he completed his interview, Detective Rond advised Vinnie Paul that he would have to take Dimebag's guitar as evidence. Vinnie Paul pleaded with him to let him keep the

Dimebag's guitar leans against the wall so detectives
could process it for evidence. Dec. 8, 2004.
Columbus Police Department, evidence photo.

guitar, as he was told that someone had already tried to steal it.[3] Rond assured him that he would get it back. Vinnie Paul also told Rond about the small video camera on stage that had been recording the show. For homicide detectives, the video would prove to be a valuable piece of evidence.

It was near the end of his shift when Detective William Gillette of the Columbus Homicide Department was dispatched to the scene. A country music fan, he'd never heard of Dimebag Darrell Abbott, *Pantera*, or *Damageplan*. As he arrived at Alrosa Villa, Gillette was stunned to see hundreds of patrons milling around, waiting their turn to provide statements to the police. Gillette was amazed by the cooperation of the patrons and the staff at the Alrosa Villa. Typically, homicide detectives are faced with little more than a body and silence. Though facing the worst homicide crime scene he had ever experienced, he also observed the remarkable support of heavy-metal fans. In nearly a decade of working homicide, he never had witnessed so much participation involving a murder.

Outside the venue, police had cordoned off the parking lot and blocked off Sinclair Road to secure the surrounding area. The landscape took on a surreal appearance. Dozens of police cars, ambulances, and fire trucks, nearly all with flashing lights and blaring sirens, created a strobe effect. Hundreds of shocked patrons wandered through the eerie scene while a police helicopter's spotlight danced from the black sky. The volume from its whirling blades made communication on the ground difficult. Police realized that the suspect's vehicle was probably somewhere in the parking lot. With the exception of official vehicles, no one was allowed in or out of the crime scene.

Police asked the patrons to be patient as they worked out a process for conducting witness interviews. With temperatures in the 40s, the Columbus Police contacted the Central Ohio Transit Authority (COTA) and requested the loan of a half-dozen busses. As the clock ticked past midnight, the COTA busses passed through the cordon and pulled into the parking lot. Cold fans climbed aboard, grabbed a seat, and waited their turn to be interviewed. For the next five hours, nearly 70 police officers and detectives from a variety of divisions within the Columbus Police Dep-artment interviewed, chronicled, and document-ed the observations of the Alrosa Villa witnesses.

Patrons Tiffany and Roger Caron were in total disbelief. Waves of deja vu splashed over them as they

1. Homicide Detective William Gillette would be tasked as the lead detective and responsible for investigating the dual homicide and police involved shooting. Photo by Chris A. 2. Central Ohio Transit Authority or COTA busses were brought to the Alrosa Villa to provide a place for witnesses to sit and escape the cold night air as they waited to be interviewed. Dec. 8, 2004. Columbus Police Department, evidence photo.

waited their turn to speak. How could it be that in less than a year they would witness a similar assault on the same band? They felt numb when they reflected back to eight months earlier at Bogarts in Cincinnati, when a large man had climbed onto the stage and appeared to be going after Dimebag Darrell. For the Carons, the similarities seemed beyond coincidence. When interviewed, they immediately told police about their experience at Bogarts; it was the first indication that perhaps Dimebag and *Damageplan* were being stalked. Days later, Columbus police followed up with the Cincinnati Police Department and were provided with a copy of the Bogarts incident report.

Inside the Alrosa Villa, Detective Gillette was informed that he would be the lead detective on the two-tiered investigation. The case would be labeled as a homicide and a police-involved shooting. Not only would Gillette be responsible for coordinating the investigation into the murders, but he would also gather and present evidence regarding the actions of Officer Niggemeyer.

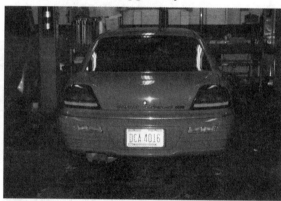

Nathan Gale's car at the Columbus Police Impound lot. Columbus Police Department, evidence photo.

Mitch Carpenter, the parking lot attendant, alerted police that the suspect's vehicle, a red 1995 Pontiac Grand Am, was parked across the street from the venue. The vehicle was cordoned off, and a license plate check revealed that it was registered to Nathan M. Gale. The vehicle was impounded, transported to the Franklin County Morgue, and placed in a secure garage; two days later it was searched, photographed, and processed for evidence. The only item found of evidentiary value was a yellow CD player that contained the *Damageplan* CD, *New Found Power*. The vehicle was subsequently transported to the Columbus Police

Department impound lot and eventually released to the suspect's mother; soon afterward, it was repossessed.

By 3:00 am, most of the witnesses, band members, and venue employees had been permitted to depart the Alrosa Villa. For the remainder of the night, only Rick Cautela remained, watching quietly as Detective Gillette and his colleagues processed the crime scene. Evidence was collected in the form of shell casings, bullet fragments, clothing, and blood swatches. Photographs and video images were taken inside and around the Alrosa Villa.

Between the hours of 6:30 am and 8:00 am on the morning of December 9, the bodies of Erin Halk, Darrell Abbott, and the suspect were transported one at a time from the crime scene to the Franklin County Coroner's office for autopsy.

Around 10:00 pm on December 8, Kerri Bray laid out her clothing for the next day and went to bed. She'd finished addressing the vast majority of her Christmas cards. About a half-hour later, her cell phone rang. She picked it up and saw that Nathan was calling. As she lifted the phone to her ear, she figured that Nathan needed a ride home or that he was simply going to hold his phone up to the stage so she could hear the music. Instead, it was Jason Jewett calling on Nate's phone. Nathan and Jason were concert pros; they never brought anything inside that they could drop or lose. On that evening, they had stashed their valuables in Nathan's car. A Columbus Police Officer had helped Jason gain entry to Nate's car to obtain the phone. Now on the line with Kerri, an obviously shaken Jason told her that Nathan had been shot. Kerri couldn't believe what she was hearing as she fought off the rising fear. Deep inside, as much as Kerri hoped for the best, she sensed that her sweet hippie boy was gone. Kerri fired off a barrage of questions, but Jason didn't have the answers. He was urged to hang up and board one of the COTA busses to wait his turn to provide a statement. As Jason hung up, fear gripped Kerri. She felt as if she were out of her mind.

Not familiar with that area of Columbus, Kerri had no idea to what hospital Nathan would have been taken. She quickly called Nathan's mother, who also had been informed of the tragic shooting and told Kerri that he had been taken to Riverside. Kerri called her father, who was working third shift at the post office. When he answered, all he heard was his little girl's tearful voice and a mournful cry of "Daddy!" Without any further conversation, he told her that he was on his way. Kerri tried to find Nate's father, Gene, but it was his pool night and she wasn't able to track him down.

Her phone rang again. This time it was Nathan's mother calling from the hospital. She told Kerri that she was in a special room but didn't have any more information. Frightened and frustrated, Kerri screamed at her mother-in-law to find out what was happening.

"They don't put you in a special room unless they are coming to give you bad news!" As those words left Kerri's mouth, a doctor entered the room.

"Hang on," said Nathan's mother. She held out the phone so Kerri could hear the conversation.

"Are you Mrs. Bray?" There was a pause, and then, "I regret to inform you..."

Kerri never heard the end of the sentence. The pain of anticipating those next words ripped the strength from her body. She cried, dropped to her knees, and buried her head in her hands. At 23 years of age, Kerri Bray was now a widow. Alone in the dark and mourning the loss of her husband and best friend, she wept as she tried to comprehend what she had just heard.

It was 4:00 am on December 9, when the phone rang in Dublin, Ohio. Rousing from a deep sleep, Margie Carvour mumbled, "Hello?" The call was from a police officer, who told her that he needed to speak with her about her son.

"Okay, what do you want to tell me?" she asked.

"Ma'am, I just can't tell you over the telephone."

"Well, which of my son's are you calling about?"

"Oh, its Erin."

Calmly, Margie gave him directions to her location. She was staying with her in-laws. The officer thanked her and said that he would be there immediately.

Margie's mouth was dry; her breathing was deep and deliberate as she fought the rising tide of panic. She quickly walked upstairs to her mother-in-law's room and woke her.

"Helen," she said painfully, "get up please, I know something horrible has happened to Erin."

Somehow, perhaps with a mother's sixth sense, Margie Carvour realized her baby boy was gone. She was certain Erin was dead. Two minutes later, the police officer arrived. He sat Margie down and told her that her son had been murdered. She remembered the officer as being kind, very kind, as he passed on his grim report. Margie, in a state of shock, asked what happened. The policeman explained that no one could be certain, but there were reports that perhaps some sort of Internet chatter may have driven the killer to his actions. Before he departed, he encouraged her to avoid televisions or newspapers for a while. To this day, Margie avoids all media reports about the murders.

In Newport, Arkansas, Frank Thompson's telephone rang at about 11:47 am on December 9. He was mystified to speak with a detective from Columbus, Ohio. Detective Larry Reese carefully and skillfully spoke with Frank; after he determined that he was not alone, he broke the terrible news that his eldest son, Jeffery, had been murdered. The call was professional but brief, as Reese wasn't in a position to answer Frank's questions. He provided Frank with the telephone numbers of the Franklin County Coroners Office and Detective Gillette.

In the early morning hours of December 9, Mary Clark was startled by a knock at her Marysville apartment door. When she opened it, she found herself faced with five grim-faced police officers. They identified themselves and asked if she was Mary Clark, the mother of Nathan Gale. She replied that she was and slowly backed away from the door to let them in. Waves of fear cascaded through her body. She could feel her heart racing, and her hands shook. Something had happened to Nathan. As gently as possible, Mary was told that her son was dead. The detectives explained that a Columbus

Police Officer had been forced to shoot her armed son after he stormed the stage at the Alrosa Villa. With tears streaming down her face, Mary asked if her son had injured any police officers. They assured her that he had not. She then asked if anyone else had been hurt. Her question was initially met with silence before she was told that her son had shot and killed four innocent people. Her sorrow was instantly replaced with hysteria as she felt the weight of guilt and shame.

"Oh my God. Those poor people. Why did he have to kill those people!"

It was a question being asked by millions around the world.

A postcard mailed to Nathan Gale's apartment a few weeks after the murders. Photo courtesy of Mary Clark.

By 8:30 am, the Alrosa Villa was nearly vacant, except for Rick Cautela and the volunteers who helped to remove *Damageplan*'s equipment from the stage. Eventually, Cautela was alone in his building. He let his mind wander for a moment, lifted his head and closed his eyes in the hopes that it was all just a bad dream.

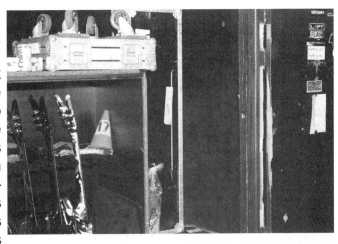

Dimebag's guitar rack. The murder weapon, placed in the rack by an officer, is just beneath the evidence marking cone. Columbus Police Department, evidence photo.

Cautela propped open the door at the rear of the stage and got to work. With his bare hands and tears streaming down his face, he ripped out the blood soaked carpeting that covered the Alrosa Villa's wooden stage. Exhausted from nearly 24 hours without sleep, Cautela threw himself into the task, desperate to erase any physical signs of the carnage. Rick removed the carpet from the stage and the dressing room. Next he was faced with the grim task of mopping up the blood that soaked the floor. Dark and coagulated, it took seven gallons of bleach and four hours to remove the stains. Cautela, overwhelmed by his gruesome chore, ran outside several times to vomit.

Rick Cautela completed his tasks around 1:00 pm. He locked up the Alrosa Villa and shuffled to his car. Before he made it to US-71 for his 15-minute drive home, he was assaulted by the thoughts, questions and fears he hoped to avoid earlier by keeping busy. He couldn't pretend it didn't happen, he couldn't ignore it. It was almost too much to bear.

Dime Time

I came to rock music relatively late. My first memory of Pantera is when I started to learn guitar. I can remember picking up a copy of Total Guitar magazine and being blown away by the riff, the solo—just the power of the song. Not only that, but by the picture of Dime they had next to it. I didn't know much about rock, but I knew there and then that this guy was some rocking guitarist!

I remember getting into Pantera more seriously some time later. One thing that really sticks in my mind is hearing "Cemetery Gates" for the first time the day after my Gran died. The clean guitar in the intro and the verse, and the lyrics, especially "and when she died, I should have cried," just seemed to strike a chord. I just thought it was incredible how a song could be so touching and so heavy, too.

Here was a guitar player who wasn't just playing chords, but putting his heart and soul into every note. Not just playing what people wanted to hear, but what felt right. But aside from the music, it didn't take long for me to realize what a great person Dime was.

I've suffered from problems with self-esteem and depression for many years, and not only does listening to positive music help me, but being part of such an amazing *scene and meeting so many great people has given me the confidence to not feel sorry for myself, to deal with things, and to live each day to the fullest.*

It doesn't matter about how you look or whether you fit in with the latest trends. All that matters is that you stay true to yourself and what you feel. That's the great thing about Dime.

Sadly, I never got to meet him, but somehow, I feel like I knew him. You don't need to have met him to feel his spirit and zest for life, you just know that he was first and foremost one of us. Just by thinking about Dime, listening to his music, or watching the Pantera home videos, I almost feel like some of that spirit rubs off on all of us. I know I'm certainly grateful for that. Dime lives on in my heart and my mind forever.

– James Daly, fan

I never heard a guitar player with so much heart. Dimebag influenced me in music and in life. He loved what he did. He loved to play the guitar and perhaps more than anything, he loved to make friends. That's how I plan to live my life, too.

– Erin Ludewig, *Sinaria*

Chapter 13

Cemetery Gates

"Sometimes when I'm alone
I wonder aloud
If you're watching over me"

Cemetery Gates
Cowboys From Hell
-Pantera

For the families of those killed at the Alrosa Villa, the holidays were filled with anything but joy. Instead of gathering for a holiday dinner, the families gathered together for funerals.

Nathan Bray was the first to be laid to rest. Nate's wife Kerri felt alone as she tried to make funeral arrangements and prepare an obituary in honor of her late husband. As she was escorted into the casket display room, she shuddered as she walked by the infant caskets. Reality struck hard. With Nathan's death tied to Dimebag, the media was telephoning for interviews. The American Red Cross inquired about organ

Photo courtesy of Mandy Drake.

donation. Kerri couldn't help but think about how quickly the "reality" of death had been replaced by the "business" of death.

Aided by her parents and Gene Bray's wife Theresa, Kerri drifted through the process of laying Nate to rest. She tried to involve everyone in helping to say goodbye to her Nathan, especially his friends. She asked them to contribute their thoughts for an appropriate song for the memorial program. Nate's friends decided upon "Angel's Son" by the band *Sevendust*. Over 200 people journeyed the 30 miles south of Columbus to Nathan's hometown of Circleville, OH for his funeral. At the memorial viewing, Nathan's friends and family left small tokens of their love inside Nathan's casket; Cincinnati Bengals souvenirs, a lock of his father's hair, letters, and an autographed photo of his favorite heavy metal band, *Pantera*.

It was less than 72-hours since Nathan had been killed. December 11 was an overcast, rainy, cold, gray day. The state police blocked off U.S. Highway 23 to accommodate the two-mile long funeral procession to the Floral Hills Memory Garden Cemetery. When the procession entered the cemetery grounds, Kerri stared in amazement; watching police officers stand at attention, saluting as the hearse rolled past in the rain.

After the funeral, she did her best to avoid the inquiring press. Kerri, along with friends and family, gathered at Josh and Jason Jewett's home to eat, reminisce and drink. They drank all night long. They talked, they laughed, and they tried to forget. It was the first time Kerri remembered laughing in a long time. Everything was done, the funeral was over, and it seemed as if a wave of relief had splashed over them. Eventually, Kerri's friends, relatives, neighbors and well wishers had to return to their own lives. Kerri found herself back at her apartment, just her and Anthony. Things would never be the same without Nathan.

A flat, bronze, memorial marker identifies Nathan's resting place at the cemetery. Those who visit his grave are greeted by the words *"The memory still remains"*- a refrain from the eerie *Pantera* composition, "Cemetery Gates," etched onto his grave marker.

Two days later, on December 13, Erin Alexander Halk was laid to rest. His funeral was held in Upper Arlington, OH, the day after the Catholic anniversary of The Feast of our Lady of Guadalupe. He was buried at the Resurrection Cemetery in Lewis Center, just north of Columbus.

Photo by Chris A.

Erin's mom, Margie, vowed to honor her son's legacy by trying to demonstrate an act of kindness each day.

A few months after his death, Erin received a posthumous honor when Roadie.net proclaimed Erin Alexander "Stoney" Halk, *"Roadie For Life."* The certificate, signed by Karl Kuenning, Roadie for Life President and Founder of *www.roadie.net* stated:

"Having exhibited all the true qualities of a Roadie For Life as witnessed and affirmed by his Roadie.net Crew. He is now or has been a Roadie in good standing at some incredible point in his life. He is NOT a complete ass nor does he insist on being called a "Technician." He has every intention of remaining a Roadie (at heart) the rest of his natural (or un-natural) life."

Erin Alexander Halk would have been proud.

Left: A prayer card from Erin's funeral. Courtesy of Dean Reimund.
Right: Behind the soundboard in the Alrosa Villa hangs this tribute to Erin "Stoney" Halk. It was erected by his fellow roadies. Photo by Chris A.

Dimebag. Cincinnati, OH. April 4, 2004. Photo courtesy
of Amir Marandi - www.Marandiproductions.com

The next day, some 1,600 miles away in Texas, family, friends and admirers of Dimebag Darrell Abbott filled the Arlington Convention Center to pay homage to the scarlet-bearded guitarist. The public memorial for Dime was part tribute and part concert, as rock gods, old and new, journeyed to Arlington to pay their respects. Luminaries, including Zakk Wylde, Eddie Van Halen, Jerry Cantrell, and others, spoke of their affection and love for Darrell Abbott.

Photo courtesy of Jeff "Stinger" Brown.

The crowd assembled at the convention center cheered as photos of Dime flashed on the screen and enthusiastically applauded the many eulogies. It was a memorial filled with booze, music, words, laughter and tears. It was a fitting tribute, and so very rock 'n' roll; just as Dimebag would have wanted. Before it ended, Vinnie Paul Abbott made certain that each and every person in attendance knew that his brother Dimebag had always given his all for his fans and had gone down doing what he loved.

Noticeably absent from the memorial was Phil Anselmo. Shocked by Dimebag's death, Phil flew to Arlington to attend his ex-band mate's funeral. Despite his pleas, he was told not to attend the funeral. He was not welcome.[1]

Earlier in the day, a private ceremony was held at the Moore Funeral Home in Arlington. The attendees were family and close friends, both famous and otherwise. Dimebag's swan song was as "metal" as it could get. Dime would be laid to rest inside of a Kiss Kasket; a hardcore Kiss fan as a boy, and even later when *Pantera* toured with them, he remained enamored with the band.[2]

He was dressed in his favorite garb: cut-off camouflage pants, a black t-shirt, flip-flops and his Black Label Society colors.[3] The rock stars attending the service spoke of Darrell Abbott jamming in heaven, with Jimi Hendrix, Randy Rhodes, John Bonham, Cliff Burton and other rock legends who had died too young. Mourners filled the casket with bottles of Dime's favorite whisky, "Crown Royal." Eddie Van Halen slipped a guitar he had built into the casket with Dime.[4] Dimebag was buried later that day at the Moore Memorial Gardens Cemetery next to his mother.

---

[1] Chapter 13 footnotes begin on page 311.

Two days later, on December 16, 2004, Jeff Thompson was laid to rest.

The sight of tour buses rolling into Newport, Arkansas was surreal. The surviving members of *Damageplan*, accompanied by Rita Haney, and several other bands, descended on the small community to pay homage to their friend and brother "Mayhem."

Jeff's friends and comrades from the renaissance community also journeyed to Newport to show their support and love for the gentle giant. Members of *The Rogues* made the trip and even performed at the funeral.[5]

At the viewing, a slide presentation displayed photographs of "Mayhem" in his many guises; renaissance actor, television actor, musician, bouncer, biker, friend, brother, and son. Jeff's casket was open from the waist up, the lower half covered by the Scottish St. Andrews flag. The big man's body was adorned in his beloved Scottish attire, complete with black shirt, jacket, and his favorite Macleod yellow kilt. His friends from Texas placed a broad sword inside the casket to accompany Mayhem on his final journey. Members of *The Rogues* and the pallbearers all wore yellow rose boutonnières, symbols of Texas, and of Mayhem's yellow and black kilt. At the funeral service, the left side of the church was reserved for Mayhem's Texas family, while the right side was filled with his Arkansas family.

Hilton Jackson gave the eulogy; his Shakespearian delivery was moving, his words overwhelming Jeff's father.

After the service, Mayhem's casket, covered by a sprig of red roses, was carefully placed into the hearse for a short ride to the Walnut Grove Cemetery. At the graveside, a lone piper, resplendent in his traditional Scottish garb, played "Going Home." The mournful melody echoed eerily in the chilly wind of the afternoon.

Sharon Wothke, whose husband, Randy, was a member of *The Rogues*, had crafted a beautiful memory book for Jeff's family. At the graveside, she saw a face in the crowd whom she recognized only from photographs. It was Vinnie Abbott, Dimebag's brother, surrounded by his friends. Sharon did not recognize any of them, but assumed they were with *Damageplan*, because of their black leather jackets and chains. Sharon observed that the normally tough-looking, heavy-metal rockers were deeply grieving. With their women holding them from behind, they looked fragile and in shock.[6]

Opposite page: Jeffery "Mayhem" Thompson wearing Dimebag's *Black Label Society* vest backstage in Chicago. Nov. 21, 2004. Photo courtesy of Chad Lee - www.rockconcertfotos.com
Above: Pipers play at Mayhem's funeral. Photo courtesy of the Thompson family.

Jeff's casket, covered by the blue and white St. Andrew's flag. Photo courtesy of the Thompson family.

Over the next few months, Frank Thompson tended his son's grave and erected an impressive plinth of black granite. It pointed to the sky, towering above the majority of the tombstones in the cemetery, its height equal to that of the man whose memory it commemorated. Even in death, Jeffery "Mayhem" Thompson's spirit and calling as a protector and guardian is evident. His gravestone stands vigilant and silent, a sentinel on watch.

In March 2005, Shannon Bradley Hobbs stood in the parking lot next to Jeff's old cabin. It was the first day of dress rehearsal for the Scarborough Renaissance Festival. The realization overcame her that Jeff would never again be there to dress her. The tradition was gone. Standing there, feeling lost and alone, she broke down. Overwhelmed by grief, Jeff's queen wept.

To this day, each and every morning of the Scarborough Faire, Shannon Hobbs, often in the shared company of others from the cast, opens the day with a thought of their departed friend.

Photo courtesy of the Thompson family.

In the quiet town of Marysville, Ohio, another memorial service was taking place. Unlike the other services, it was low-key, discreet and out of public view. Due to threats and security concerns, few even knew about it. Fewer still were invited to attend. With his mother, brothers and a few close family friends present, the small gathering struggled to make sense of the carnage and misery that the boy turned Beast had wrought upon so many. For the man ultimately responsible for the carnage at the Alrosa Villa, the fire of cremation would consume his body as certainly as Hell would consume his soul. There would be no monument, no headstone and no dedication to remind the world that he ever existed.

Memorials

Before completing "A Vulgar Display Of Power: Courage And Carnage At The Alrosa Villa," the families of the victims were invited to contribute to this memorial section. The following pages contain a loving devotion from the families of Jeffery "Mayhem" Thompson, Nathan Bray and Erin Halk.

The family of Dimebag Darrell Abbott declined to be interviewed for this book.

Dime Tattoos by Bob Tyrrell. Photo courtesy of Bob Tyrrell, Night Gallery - www.bobtyrrell.com

From Jeff Thompson's Family

Jeffery "Mayhem" Thompson. Photo courtesy of the Thompson family.

On the morning of December 9th, 2004, Detective Gillette of the Columbus, Ohio Police Department phoned to inform me of Jeffery's death. Life as I understood it vaporized. A gloom ensued like the sudden appearance of a summer thunderstorm darkens a humid day. How could this have happened to ordinary folk in the small city of Newport, Arkansas? The lilt of chatty conversations in the kitchen area turned into mutterings and endless questions. Souls became twisted into utter despair. No longer was I to hear the sound of his voice on the phone: "Hi Dad!" I called his cell number to hear his recorded message just to hear his voice once more. Since then, special days always pass with a painful throb. We will miss him, as will his dear friends who loved the big Texan from Dallas. "Oh Mayhem!" with a beautiful and loyal heart, you were deeply loved and you gratuitously loved back. "*I'll take a bullet for ya*," he often said. How ironic that his prophetic words would come true.

Grief is a timeless black hole where uncertainties and assaults pervade. A complete understanding may never reveal itself, but eventually grief turns tears to philosophy. We ask ourselves, "Why do so many younger people perish as they do?" Wise people know evil forces lurk in the shadows for opportunities to subvert the unwary and indiscriminate. So many of them suffer ill needlessly! Such was the premeditated carnage inside the now infamous Alrosa Villa.

I have asked for accuracy in the writing of Jeff's story. Jeff's life was rich in loyalty, close personal relationships, ridiculous antics, humor, and even severe hardship. Mayhem's gentle personality dissolved differences and molded friendships. Speaking for his "Texas family" and my family, we encourage the reader to absorb with all their emotions an accurate portrayal of the life of Jeffery Allan "Mayhem" Thompson. The author has assured my family that he will exert himself to the best of his abilities to this end.

In closing, my family and I extend to the families who grieve with us, a time of peace, a time to accept and forgive. We hope that their lives be without continued malice and fear, and a lasting time to care for others in need.

God be with you in your time of healing.
Sincerely,

E. Frank Thompson, for the Thompsons

Frank and Marilyn; Jeff's brothers, Seth, Martin, and Micah. Martin's wife and their young daughters, Davina and Taylor.

From Kerri, Nathan Bray's Wife

The thing I hate more than the fact that my Nathan was killed was that he was killed with a famous rock star.

Dimebag Darrell Abbott was like a superhero to so many people. He was the Michael Jordan or the Babe Ruth of the heavy metal world. Immediately after the murders, some people were calling it the "9/11" of metal, with memorials, benefits, concerts, and vigils popping up everywhere.

For me, while all of the publicity and madness was occurring, I felt just devastation and a terrible loss. This really was my "9/11." I felt as if there was a huge snowball rolling out of control and in the center of it was my little boy who had just lost his father.

Nate was my superhero and to me, he was larger than life. He was a guy whom I felt was also, in his own unique way, an invincible "rock star." Yet, somehow he was taken from me. Nathan was immensely important to so many people. He was a wonderful human being. He possessed a kind, generous spirit and was a wonderful father, son, and the best friend one could ever ask for. He was loyal, honest, patient, responsible, and very loving. He had a passion for everything he chose to do. He loved being a father. He loved the sports teams he supported. He loved being a respected employee. He loved being a competitor. And of course, he loved music.

I can remember him all but forcing me to watch the *Pantera* home videos in college. It's almost impossible for me to realize that Nathan's death will now forever be tied to all of that. I wasn't surprised that Nathan tried to be the rescuer. That was in his nature. I remember a white water rafting trip we took on the Alleghany River. He and his friends talked for weeks about their plans to dominate the rapids that had ejected them from their boat the previous summer. Sure enough, once again we were all bounced out of the boat—all of us except for Nathan. I watched him with pride as he fought the river trying to maneuver the boat to pick up his fallen comrades. Knowing Nathan as I did, I'm not shocked or surprised by his selfless behavior that evening. What does shock me, however, is that his death is so closely tied to people who seemed so far away and so untouchable in those videos we watched in college.

Ultimately, what I hope people will understand about this event is that it didn't just devastate the lives of "heavy metal royalty." It also changed ordinary people's lives. Nathan, Erin, and Jeff were unique men who had a special something inside of them that drove them to rise to the occasion. They did extraordinary things on an evening that many of us would not have had the strength or courage to do.

At the end of the day, I am a lucky girl. I am colossally lucky to have known Nathan, and even luckier to have a piece of him in Anthony. As proud as I am of Nate and his actions that fateful evening, I know he's more proud of Anthony, his little boy whom he loved so much.

- Kerri Bray

Donations in the memory of Nathan Bray can be sent to:

*Anthony M. Bray Scholarship Fund
c/o The Citizens Bank
120 S. Court St.
Circleville, OH 43113

*Memorial fund information was added by the author.

From Danielle Clark, Erin Halk's Sister

A little boy, the babe of the bunch, his head so filled with dreams.
An infectious smile, a gentle touch, he makes his sister gleam.
The stubborn boy, the hard road traveled this path he chose to take.
School reviled, attention wandered, but loved and consumed the written word.
He inspired my path, to teach those with less chance,
I will show the world his struggles were not in vain.
A family man, a gentle soul yet joined with the few and the proud.
Not the best of times, but struggle and fortitude exemplified.
His power blinds me, but I see clearly; don't get lost in one mistake.
A man of conviction, of life, and love, a mark on all he's sure to make.
A joy to his nephew, his family and friends.
This brings me to the end of his dearest crazy life,
Courage of a lion, yet sweet as a lamb, qualities evil can never understand
I yearn to slip deep into sleep, to see your face, to hear you speak.
Yet I know I'll awaken to the pain again.
We have our dreams and the music sweet brother.
As I wake I swallow my heart as I yearn for a final embrace.
Uncle Erin, you Go Bragh with your memory is my son.
The winds at my back. Rest with peace my brother and friend, for soon we'll play again.

-Danielle Clark

Erin Halk. Photo courtesy of the Halk family.

Contributions in the memory of Erin Halk may be sent to:

*St. Agatha School Fund
1880 Northam Road
Columbus, OH 43221

*Memorial fund information was added by the author.

Thanks for thinking of me for the book! I'm a huge fan Of Dime, and love him and miss him like everyone else.

-Bob Tyrrell, Night Gallery www.bobtyrrell.com

Dimebag Darrell with guitar pick in hand. Tattoo by Bob Tyrrell.
Photo courtesy of Bob Tyrrell, Night Gallery - www.bobtyrrell.com

For people wishing to make a donation in Dimebag's name, two memorial funds have been established. The Dimebag Darrell Memorial Fund has been set up to cover medical expenses for John "Kat" Brooks and Chris Paluska. It also contributes to bereavement expenses for Jeffery "Mayhem" Thompson. Please make checks payable to "The Dimebag Darrell Memorial Fund." Donations can be sent to the mail-only address:

*Dimebag Darrell Memorial Fund
110 SW Thomas
Burleson, TX 76028

Another fund has been set up through VH1's Save The Music Foundation. Save The Music purchases new musical instruments to restore and maintain music education programs that have been cut due to budget reductions in the past or to save programs at risk of elimination due to lack of instruments. The Foundation also conducts awareness campaigns, musical instrument drives and fund raising events. Checks can be mailed to:

*VH1 Save The Music Foundation
1515 Broadway, 20th Floor
New York, NY 10036

*Memorial fund information was added by the author.

Final Thoughts

What happened at the Alrosa Villa on the fateful night of December 8, 2004, was extraordinary. It was extraordinary in the sense that, like the events of September 11, 2001, what occurred was a calculated, unprecedented attack on innocent people. It wasn't foreseeable. It wasn't predictable. It wasn't expected, nor could a simple "security enhancement" have prevented it. What happened came from nowhere and no one other than the perpetrator contributed to it; it was truly an extraordinary crime.

However, more extraordinary were the acts of heroism, courage and selflessness demonstrated by so many, during the event and in its aftermath. Jeff Thompson instinctively acted when he perceived a threat to his friend. He knowingly placed himself in extreme peril as he struggled to disarm the assailant. His actions saved the lives of Vinnie Paul Abbott and guitar tech, John Graham.

From the audience, Nathan Bray, watched with shock and horror as the man he idolized was gunned down before his eyes. His determination and kind heart propelled him to climb onto the stage to try to save Dimebag Darrell Abbott. When he realized that his hero was gone, he immediately began to give aid and comfort to Jeff Thompson, a man he had never met, and whose name he did not know. One can only hope that Nate's final moments were filled with solace, knowing his son would be raised with love and goodness.

On the side stage, Alrosa Villa security member and professional roadie Erin Halk agonized as he watched the horror unfold in front of him. Cautiously, carefully, he analyzed the situation. When presented with what he believed was an opportunity to save the hostage and disarm the predator, he heroically acted, yet tragically, Erin died.

Courage and heroism wasn't isolated to those who paid the ultimate price at Alrosa Villa.

One can't help but be in awe of the bravery and selflessness shown by so many members of the Columbus Police Department on that night. Officer James Niggemeyer, when faced with an incredibly frightening, life-threatening situation, unhesitatingly entered the unknown when he slipped into the rear door of the Alrosa Villa. At incredible risk to his own life, he quickly, but carefully, took action. He effectively saved the hostage and ended the crisis.

In a turn of events largely ignored by the media, Niggemeyer is quick to acknowledge that he wasn't alone in the venue as he advanced toward the killer. Officers Crum, Landis, Ferencz, Stumph and Lares, also at grave risk to their own personal safety, entered the Alrosa Villa in the midst of confusion and danger with the intention of resolving the incident.

Before the police had even arrived, dozens of people in the Alrosa Villa had ignored the deadly peril and their own personal need to seek safety. They provided first aid to the injured or directed others towards exits. Once outside the venue, they assisted police and rescue personnel, while at the same time comforting each other. The conduct of the vast majority of Alrosa Villa survivors was extraordinary.

In the midst of great chaos and very tangible danger, the true spirit and compassion of humanity took center stage. While "metal heads" are often considered "outsiders," maligned by media pundits and do-gooders who have no concept of the metal music lifestyle, this "heavy-metal" audience effectively turned 30-years worth of stereotypes on its head. When one truly contemplates the carnage and courage at the Alrosa Villa, it's not the carnage of the killer that is memorable but the courage of so many regular people.

If it was the killers' intention to extract vengeance and to gain personal notoriety, albeit infamy, by killing Dimebag Darrell, he failed miserably. In death, Dimebag, the person, the guitarist, and the all around "good guy," has only been elevated in status. He is a true martyr of rock 'n' roll, respected by his peers and missed by his family, friends and fans, with little thought given to his killer.

It's a travesty that purveyors of evil such as Jeffrey Dahmer and John Wayne Gacy, are well known, yet few people can recall the name of even one of their victims. Left to the media, the memories of Nathan Bray, Erin Halk and Jeff

Thompson would surely suffer a similar fate. However, these heroes live on in the memories of those they assisted that fateful night, their families, friends and heavy-metal music fans. In this case, it is the killer who has been exorcized from memory; obscenities used in place of his name are spat like venom from the mouths of those who speak of him.

Fueled by a bloodthirsty, violence-loving, celebrity-mad media, it was the carnage and the violent death of a heavy-metal musician that dominated the "spin" of media reporting in the aftermath. With those blinders in place, even over time, many of the truly extraordinary elements of the evening were ignored, glossed over or simply never reported.

The media's first predictable gasp, or perhaps, knee jerk reaction, was to assign blame for the events of Alrosa Villa to the music itself. When simply stating the truth about an incident isn't politically correct, or sensational enough, rock 'n' roll music, especially metal, has become a convenient scapegoat.

Take for example, the Columbine shootings of 1999. In our politically correct world, pointing the finger of blame at heavy-metal music, or *Marilyn Manson*, is far easier than assigning responsibility to the parents of the two juvenile killers. When 15-year old boys can construct pipe bombs in their back yards and assemble an arsenal in their own homes; Mommy and Daddy aren't doing their job.

It was the same for the Alrosa Villa murders. The killer wasn't a true metal fan, and the music didn't speak to him or encourage him to kill. A mental defect in his brain and his failure to medicate himself for it are what drove the killer.

For metal fans, music is a passion. Certainly metal music often focuses on the dark side of life, but that's nothing new. One simply needs to read, watch or listen to some of the best works of Shakespeare, Spielberg, or Wagner to realize that angst, frustration, death and sorrow have always been a part of the human and artistic experience.

Factually and historically, heavy-metal fans live vicariously through their music. *They don't react to it with violence*. Rather, the volume and intensity of the music serves as an aggressive outlet as they bond with their fellow rockers and bang their heads to the music.

There were approximately 350 true metal fans at the Alrosa Villa that night. However, in the eyes of the media, the deeds of one madman trumped the innumerable acts of courage, kindness and compassion that were demonstrated by the majority of metal fans at the venue. That night, over 250 heavy-metal fans offered witness statements to the police. Compare that to the murders of "rappers" Tupac Shakur or the Notorious BIG. Both were gunned down in public areas, surrounded by their friends, yet no one "saw anything," and the murders remain unsolved.

The next predictable culprit was the venue itself. Almost immediately, the media called into question the viability of the Alrosa Villa's security force. It was denigrated in the press by well meaning, but factually uninformed rock musicians, such as Anthrax guitarist Scott Ian.[1]

Consider for a moment, The Who tragedy in Cincinnati in 1979, where eleven fans were crushed to death or the fire that killed 100 patrons at The Station Nightclub in Rhode Island in 2003. In both of these tragedies, the venue clearly contributed to the death of patrons. At The Who tragedy, people died due to poor crowd management when a huge throng of fans arrived before the venue was prepared to accept them. Building managers refused to open the doors early and people were literally crushed to death.

In the case of The Station Nightclub, pyrotechnic devices set off by the band ignited foam insulation in the building. With limited exits and the foam burning at a furious rate, 100 patrons were unable to escape the fire that ensued in time.

When one compares these incidents and the culpability of the venue to the murders at the Alrosa Villa, there is no comparison. Common sense dictates that any public facility must be prepared and alert to basic safety issues. An armed

---

[1] Final Thoughts footnotes begin on page 312.

gunman leaping over a fence and entering the building intent on killing someone is an entirely different situation.

With that fact in mind, one has to react realistically to the viability of each safety threat. What occurred at the Alrosa Villa was an extreme, unimaginable event; the proof of which is demonstrated by the fact that venue security across the United States hasn't significantly changed since the killings. Nor has there been any serious outcry from artists or the touring music industry for change to prevent a similar occurrence.

Since the murders, several bands have opted not to play at the Alrosa Villa. Some have called for the closing, or even the destruction of the venue. Those who subscribe to such a radical reaction are blinded by emotion and focus only on the evil of the killer. They fail to recognize the Alrosa Villa as a site where great courage, honor and compassion took center stage. Bulldoze the Alrosa Villa and The Beast wins. However, a viable music venue, where music fans can come to rock, celebrate life and contemplate the courage of Jeff Thompson, Erin Halk and Nathan Bray, is a triumph of good over evil. I, for one, can't imagine not rebuilding The World Trade Center, nor could I imagine Dallas without the introspection of the Texas School Book Depository Sixth Floor Museum.

One day, Anthony Bray, Nathan Bray's infant son, will seek the details of his father's final moments. I hope that when the time is right, if he feels the desire, his mother will be able to take him to the Alrosa Villa and perhaps to visit a memorial honoring the courage of his father and the other fine men we lost. A neglected, vacant, weed-filled lot would deny Anthony and others that option.

In the press, the larger-than-life persona, celebrity status and unfathomable death of Dimebag Darrell Abbott eclipsed the lives and courage of Jeff Thompson, Erin Halk and Nathan Bray. In the weeks after the murders, the names of these heroes slipped to footnote status in the papers, magazines and television. One needs to look no further than the 2006 VH1 documentary, "Pantera: Behind the Music" for proof. With the events at the Alrosa Villa featured heavily in the show, the killer is shown onstage, his name and image prominently used. *Sadly, there is not a single mention* of Erin Halk, Nate Bray or Jeff Thompson. Only with the credits are their names displayed, but for mere seconds on a split screen, sharing the space with scrolling advertisements. The failure to acknowledge the sacrifices of these three men in the body of the production was a missed opportunity to honor these heroes and not the perpetrator, in the popular media.

In the two years that have passed since the events at Alrosa Villa, in addition to their friends and families, it has been the heavy-metal community that have sustained and revered the memories and actions of Jeff Thompson, Erin Halk and Nathan Bray. It has been the metal community that has tried to provide some solace to their families. It has been metal fans and musicians who have organized benefit concerts and events such as "*The Ride for Dime*" to sustain the memories of the fine people killed at the Alrosa Villa.

As this book comes to an end, it's our responsibility to remember the courage, the heroism, the great riffs and the great times. It's also time to look at the big picture. The lessons taught by the events of December 8, 2004 are clear and simple; life is fragile and can end in the blink of an eye. Consequently, never hesitate to let those you love know your feelings, and, like Frank Thompson, never close the door. As with Kerri Bray, love your children and make them your priority. Finally, live your life with passion and, like Margie Carvour; endeavor to do something good for someone each day.

Footnotes

When writing a true story, there are many facts that might not belong in the context of the events, but none the less may be of interest to the reader. When the first draft was finished, I had several hundred footnotes. During the editing process, many of the proofreaders voiced their mixed feelings with so many. It was unanimous that everybody felt they were important, but many felt some could easily be added to the text. Others felt the inclusion of footnotes in each chapter disrupted the flow of the story. By the fourth draft we had eliminated over half of all footnotes by including them in the text. For the remaining footnotes I decided to follow the expert advice of my editors and proofreaders to include them in a section at the end of the book.

Most readers want to follow through the story page by page. For this type of reader, I suggest that you absorb the book, then read these footnotes for further investigation after you have read the chapters.

If you are the type of reader who insists on devouring every bit of information as it comes to you, might I suggest an extra book mark be placed in this Footnotes section. You'll be coming here often as you make your way through "A Vulgar Display Of Power: Courage And Carnage At The Alrosa Villa."

Footnotes from Chapter 2. Walk

1, page 8. -At this stage in his career Darrell Abbott's nickname was "Diamond" Darrell. In 1992 his nickname changed to "Dimebag" Darrell.

2, page 10. -Over his career Dimebag had close business relationships for years with Washburn Guitars and eventually Dean Guitars.

Footnotes from Chapter 3. I'm Broken

1, page 21. -Martino is not the true last name of the family. It has been altered to protect their privacy.

2, page 23. -The names of Mary's sons have been changed to maintain their privacy.

Footnotes from Chapter 4. Erin Halk

1, page 48 -*Semper Fidelis, or "Semper Fi," is the Latin motto of the U.S. Marine Corps. It means "Always Faithful."*

Footnotes from Chapter 5. Clash With Reality

1, page 60. -The court records do not indicate exactly what happened on Feb. 17, 1993. However, it would almost certainly involve either his brothers or his mother. His mother stated that she didn't remember the incident or the circumstances surrounding it.

2, page 60. -Based on the contents of his juvenile record it appears this adjudication was caused by his poor school grades which had fallen to well below average. The court and juvenile records do not indicate exactly what violation was committed.

3, page 62. -Marsha's notes in Gales probation file show the compassion and effort she and her colleagues expended on him. They also demonstrate her frustration. The note, written to Judge Brady reads: "*Just this past Wednesday, I, along with his school counselor, arranged for Nathan to go to Walmart to purchase an entire new clothing outfit; jeans, shirt, jacket, socks and underwear. He also just received a very expensive pair of glasses due to the extra work of the school counselor and me. Obviously Nathan isn't caring about anything. HELP! - Marsha*"

4, page 63. -With facility overcrowding, limited budgets and heavy caseloads, this tendency toward leniency by the courts in juvenile cases is not abnormal. From a "legal" perspective, Gale could have been placed into the custody of the juvenile system until he was 18 years old. Bayliss believes that had that happened he would have gravitated toward the career criminals in the system. She believes that had Nathan spent any long time periods in the juvenile detention facility or jail, any opportunities for rehabilitation would have been negated.

5, page 64. -In the world of mental health, these types of voices are known as "Command Auditory Hallucinations."

6, page 66. -Mary Clark went out of her way to express that her son really believed in his own mind that *Pantera* stole his lyrics.

Footnotes from Chapter 7. Psycho Holiday

1, page 97. -Several individuals who wished to remain anonymous indicated to the author that Gale had expressed a desire to kill *Marilyn Manson*.

    Marilyn Manson is the stage name for a performer named Brian Warner. *Manson* is recognized for presenting a garish, occasionally trans-gendered, corpse-like appearance. His hard rock/metal music contains dark, menacing lyrics coupled with outrageous on-stage behavior. In 1999 his music was incorrectly blamed as a potential motivator behind the mass killings at Columbine High School. From all indications and despite his on-stage persona, Warner/*Manson* appears to be a well-educated, articulate, highly creative individual who does not endorse violence.

2, page 99. -In the movie, Full Metal Jacket, Private Leonard Lawrence "Gomer Pyle," played to perfection by actor Vincent D'Onofrio, is probably a very close representation of Gale during his time in Marine recruit training...to a point. Set during the Vietnam War decade of the 1960s, "Gomer Pyle" is tormented and pushed by the profane, insensitive senior drill instructor. Eventually "Gomer Pyle" slips into madness. He kills his drill instructor then kills himself with his service rifle.

3, page 102. -When Gale enlisted in the USMC his DD Form 1966, shows he requested a duty position in equipment/vehicle repair. Gale was lucky because while he was free to request the position, there was no guarantee from the Marines that he would be trained in that specialty.

4, page 104. -Mandated by the Brady Handgun Violence Prevention Act (Brady Act) of 1993, Public Law 103-159, the National Instant Criminal Background Check System (NICS) was established for Federal Firearms Licensees (FFLs) to contact by telephone, or other electronic means, for information to be supplied immediately on whether the transfer of a firearm would be in violation of Section 922 (g) or (n) of Title 18, United States Code, or state law. The Brady Act is a public record and is available from many sources including the Internet at www.atf.treas.gov.

5, page 104. -If a "delayed" response is received the seller is not prohibited from selling the weapon. If the issue is not resolved within three days the seller would then have the choice to sell or not sell the weapon.

The author contacted the FBI's NICS Operation's Center in Clarksburg, West Virginia. The person I contacted related that juvenile records were considered in the adjudication process. According to that individual, (who would not reveal their name), if Gale had been convicted of a felony, even as a juvenile, the NICS check should have revealed that and his application to purchase a handgun should have been declined. When I pressed the individual about how a person with a conviction for a felony could have been "approved" for a purchase, she uncomfortably related that "well, we're very busy here." She then deferred to the State liaison and said she would transfer my call. Instead the line disconnected. I attempted to call back but no one would answer the phone. Further research indicated that background checks for gun buyers from Ohio only extend to the federal portion of the check. State and local criminal records are not checked.

6, page 105. -At the time of the Alrosa Villa murders, much of the media skirted over the specifics of the firearms purchase. Consequently while researching this book the vast majority of people the author interviewed or spoke with were under the impression that Gale's mother purchased, picked up and had the gun waiting for him under the Christmas tree.

7, page 107. -Milieu Therapy or "life space therapy" is a planned treatment environment in which everyday events and interactions are therapeutically designed for the purpose of enhancing social skills and building confidence.

The MMPI and the MCMI are tests which help paint a picture of the individual's personality and create a psychological profile of the patient.

Schizophrenia is one of the most damaging of all mental disorders. It causes those afflicted to lose touch with reality. They begin to hear, see, or feel things that aren't really there (hallucinations) or become convinced of things that simply aren't true (delusions). In the paranoid form of this disorder, they develop delusions of persecution or personal grandeur. The first signs of paranoid schizophrenia usually surface between the ages of 15 and 34. There is no cure, but the disorder can be controlled with medications.

8, page 108. -In medicine, a Prodrome is an early symptom indicating the development of a disease, or indicating that a disease attack is imminent.

9, page 119. -Read Lt. Col. Dave Grossman's insightful contribution on page 313.

Footnotes from Chapter 8. Mayhem

1, page 128. -For those not familiar with the military, when one speaks of armor in relation to the Army, it means tanks.

2, page 141. -Shannon's description of Jeff Thompson's conduct was nearly identical to the author's experience of meeting and spending time with his father, Frank Thompson. Frank is a true southern gentleman and clearly so was his son.

3, page 145. -According to Linda McAlister, Jeff was so much larger than actor Chuck Norris that he and Norris were never seen in the same scene.

4, page 148. -The author extends his thanks to Nelson Stewart for his permission to extract this story from his written memoirs of Jeff Thompson.

5, page 151. -Michael "Mongo" Smith is currently a member of two great bands; *The Hill Billy Orchestra* and the ZZ Top Tribute band, *Tres Hombres.*

6, page 154. -Dave Williams was nicknamed "Stage" by Dimebag due to William's enthusiastic performances and ability to fire up the crowds. Williams died unexpectedly in 2002 while on tour with Ozzfest. Dimebag, who had true affinity for Williams, had a portrait of the vocalist and the words "always with me" tattooed on his left shin.

7, page 157. -Crown Royal® and Coca-Cola® are the ingredients of the famed Dimebag concoction called a "Black Tooth Grin." The drink was a favorite among Dimebag and his close friends.

8, page 164. -According to Frank Thompson, *Damageplan* paid Jeff $700 per week. Apparently there was no formal contract for services.

Footnotes from Chapter 9. F'n Hostile

1, page 174. -Kevin McMeans not only attended the *Superjoint Ritual* show at the Alrosa Villa, he was also present for the *Damageplan* show on December 8, 2004.

2, page 178. -After the tragedy at the Alrosa Villa, Anselmo would state that his comments were taken out of context and that the quote was an off the cuff statement made after the interview was over. This appears to be false. Through an intermediary, Vinnie Paul Abbott provided the author an audio copy of the interview. Based on the recording of the interview, Anselmo's comments and quotes were accurately represented in *Metal Hammer* and other media outlets that wrote about the interview.

3, page 178. -The Columbus Police Department did gain permission from Mary Clark, Nathan Gale's mother, to remove and inspect her home computer. They conducted a search of the drives and found no indication that Gale had been in contact or had ever attempted communication with Anselmo.

After the murders, the Columbus Police tried to locate Anselmo for an interview. However, he never returned their phone calls. Eventually the police simply gave up; he was nowhere to be found.

Footnotes from Chapter 10. The Alrosa Villa

1, page 194. -In an interview with Cautela, he indicated he spent more money on security personnel and devices such as the barrier, than he paid to hire the band. Cautela also apparently made an error when calculating his costs and should have been charging $15.00 for tickets.

2, page 196. -The details of this conversation were obtained during an interview with Rick Cautela where he explained that most "larger" rock bands normally bring up security issues. He said *Damageplan*'s manager Chris Paluska didn't ask many questions or request specific security actions. Unfortunately, Paluska did not reply to the author's request for an interview on his perspective.

Footnotes from Chapter 11. By Demons Be Driven

1, page 208. For clarity and consistency, all descriptions of left and right will be from the perspective of a person on the stage facing the audience.

2, page 246. -The wadding is a plastic device inside a shotgun shell that separates the propellant (gunpowder) from the projectiles. It cradles the nine 00 buck shot pellets. Normally, as the round is fired the wadding flies out of the barrel and lands harmlessly on the ground. The fact that it struck Gale in the cheek and was embedded there is a testament to just how close Officer Niggemeyer was.

Footnotes from Chapter 12. Shattered

1, page 254. -The VH1 TV production of *Pantera: Behind the Music* gives the impression that Niggemeyer advanced on Gale from the front of the stage prior to shooting him. The footage that shows Niggemeyer with his shotgun shouldered while advancing across the stage was taken after Niggemeyer had dispatched the suspect. This is just one example of the "creative editing" used in the TV production of *Pantera: Behind the Music*.

2, page 257. -Intubation is the term used for inserting a tube into the mouth and throat of a victim to help them maintain an airway.

3, page 266. -Readers may remember that Jason Jewett had secured the guitar and returned it to a crew member.

Footnotes from Chapter 13. Cemetery Gates

1, page 283. -In the VH1 production of "*Pantera: Behind the Music*," Dime's long-time companion, Rita Haney, stated that she told Anselmo that if he showed up at the funeral she would "blow his head off."

2, page 283. -Apparently the "Kiss Kasket" was developed as a marketing tool or promotional gimmick, rather than a true product. Gene Simmons heard of the request and one was provided.

3, page 283. -Zakk Wylde told the author that Dime was the first person he knew of to be buried wearing the *Black Label Society* colors.

4, page 283. -This guitar was said to be the yellow striped "Frankenstein" guitar that Eddie assembled from parts. Eddie Van Halen is seen holding this guitar on the back of the seminal album "Van Halen II."

5, page 284. -In 2005 there was a parting of the ways between the Rogues. Bryan Blaylock and Jimmy Mitchell left the group and started a new band called "Scottish Mayhem" in honor of Jeff Thompson.

6, page 285. -For a very moving and detailed account of Mayhem's funeral, readers may wish to read Sharon Wothke's posting about the funeral at http://www.therogues.com/Mayhem/memories.html.

Footnotes from Final Thoughts

1, page 301. -Regarding security at the Alrosa Villa, Anthrax Guitarist Scott Ian, in an interview with *Marquee Magazine*, was quoted as saying *"I absolutely think the club should be responsible for what happened. There is no excuse for a club not to have appropriate security. Many people have said that Gale was causing trouble earlier in the evening. If that club would have had appropriate security, things may have turned out different."* His quote prompts several questions. First, where did Ian get his facts, and second, was he aware that one of the venue's security personnel died while trying to protect everyone in the club? Finally, what constitutes "appropriate security?"

Contribution by Lt. Col. Dave Grossman

In correspondence with Lt. Col. Dave Grossman, author of *"On Killing"* I put forward my idea that Gale had perhaps co-opted the message in his book to help condition and prepare himself to kill. Grossman asked if there was any indication of video game use. When I replied that there was, he found the idea intriguing and perhaps plausible. Grossman then recounted the rampage of 14-year-old Michael Carneal, who perpetrated a school shooting in Paducah, KY in 1997. Regarding Carneal, Grossman wrote:

The effectiveness of this kind of operant conditioning in the video game "Murder Trainers" can be seen in the Paducah, KY school shooting, where I acted as a consultant in the trial of Michael Carneal, a 14 year-old boy who stole a gun from a neighbor's house, brought it to school, and fired eight shots at a student prayer group as they were breaking up.

Prior to stealing that gun, Michael had never fired a pistol in his life. He had fired a few shots from a .22 caliber rifle in summer camp once, but aside from that, his parents had completely protected him from exposure to real guns. The FBI says that the average experienced, qualified law enforcement officer, in the average shootout, at an average range of seven yards, hits with less than one bullet in five. The stress of the situation, the moving targets, and the horrendous trauma of taking a human life, all add up to a situation in which a hit rate of less than 20% is the norm.

So how many hits did Michael Carneal get? He fired eight shots; he got eight hits, on eight different kids. Five of them were headshots, and the other three were upper torso. The result was three dead and one paralyzed for life. As I train law enforcement officers, I often tell them about this, and they are stunned. Nowhere in the annals of law enforcement or military or criminal history can we find an equivalent achievement. And this from a boy who had never fired a pistol before in his life!

How did Michael Carneal acquire this astounding, superhuman killing ability? Practice. Like a pilot in a flight simulator or a child in a fire drill, Michael Carneal, at the tender age of 14, had practiced killing literally thousands of human beings. His "simulator" and his "drills" were in the point-and-shoot video games he played in the video arcades and in the comfort of his own home.

Most people don't understand how expensive ammunition is; 9mm pistol bullets cost over 25 cents each. But a child in a video arcade can put 25 cents into a video game and get hundreds, even thousands of shots, all with convenient targets that will fall and die when you hit them. This tremendous cost effectiveness is why the military and law enforcement communities use "video marksmanship training simulators" to supplement their own training. And the most pervasive simulator that the U.S. Army uses is made by Nintendo.

When Michael Carneal was on his killing spree, he never moved his feet, he never fired far to the right or left, never far up or down. He simply fired once at everything that popped up on his "screen." It is not natural to fire once at each target. The normal, almost universal response is to fire at a target until it drops and then move to the next target. But many video games teach you to fire at each target only once. (If you are good, you won't even wait for the target to fall, you simply shoot once and move quickly to the next target.) And many video games give bonus points for...headshots.

-*Lt. Col. Dave Grossman*

Questions, Answers, Opinions

As I worked on this book, I kept track of the questions people asked me as I interviewed them or discussed the project. As I wrote the text, I tried to answer most of these questions. However, what follows are questions I was unable to incorporate into the story, or which merited a more detailed response.

Question: How could the killer pass an instant background check to purchase a handgun with his criminal history and documented drug use?
The "vision" for the NICS instant background check is a one-stop, "clearing house" to check the suitability of a gun buyer. However, apparently, Ohio does not participate in the program, so it does not share state or local arrest or offense records with the NICS. Consequently, when the NICS ran its background check on Gale, it only looked at federal crimes. Gale had no federal offenses, so his application was approved. If Ohio was a participant in the program, Gale's state arrest records and criminal history might well have prevented him from purchasing a handgun.

Question: Was the killer stalking the band earlier in the day, before the concert?
Several media reports made within days after the incident claim that Gale was seen at the rear of the Alrosa Villa at various times throughout the day, asking the whereabouts of the band. These "sightings" run the gamut from early afternoon until just after 10 pm. The afternoon and early evening sightings are dubious, as Gale was positively known to have been in Marysville at 6:30 pm. The drive time from Gale's 5th Street apartment in Marysville to the Alrosa Villa is between 45 to 60 minutes, depending on traffic conditions. Several Damageplan crewmembers stated that they saw Gale near the tour bus around 10 pm.

Question: Why didn't the killer simply purchase a ticket and walk into the Alrosa Villa if there were no searches being done on patrons entering the venue?
Due to the location of the public access door and the ticket booth, it wasn't possible to see what security precautions, if any, were being conducted. When a person entered the venue, they walked down a short hallway and took a 90-degree, right hand turn to pass the ticket booth. Once a person took that 90-degree, right hand turn they were out of sight of anyone outside.

Question: Did the killer have help climbing over the privacy fence to break into the Alrosa Villa?
There were several reports that a couple of patrons inside the patio saw Gale struggling to climb the fence and assisted him over the top. I was never able to determine if this was a factual recount of events, or simply a sensational myth.

Question: How did the killer know that he could easily gain access to the stage at the Alrosa Villa?
During the course of writing this book, I asked myself the same question. I found no one who conclusively knew if the killer had ever been to the Alrosa Villa prior to December 8th, 2004. With that in mind, I retraced the path he took that evening. I did it when the venue was vacant, and I later did it again while a band was performing. In my opinion, and based on witness statements, Gale seemed to know where he was going. As I retraced his steps, especially while a band was performing, I wasn't able to easily discern whether or not one could simply walk around the public address speakers. The light and shadows during a performance give the impression that the PA speakers go all the way to the wall. Consequently, I came to the conclusion that, at some time prior to the murders, Gale had either been to the venue for a show, or had intentionally "canvassed" the building.

Question: Why didn't the killer shoot Vinnie Paul Abbott when he crossed the front of the stage?
First and foremost, I believe Dimebag Darrell was Gale's primary target. The killer was on a mission and he most likely prioritized his victims. Dimebag epitomized Pantera, and that made him the killer's number one target. In addition, when the gunman strode past Vinnie Paul, Vinnie was flailing away at the drums and surrounded by cymbals, making him a very difficult moving target.

Question: Would pat-down searches or metal detectors have prevented the killer from accomplishing his murderous mission?
No, they would not have made a difference since he didn't use the public entrance. Instead, he jumped a fence and entered through a side door. Owing to that fact, any security precautions at the front door were inconsequential.

Question: What could the Alrosa Villa have done differently to prevent the killer's assault?
Gale's actions are without precedent and it's difficult to rationally assign blame to anyone or any institution other than the gunman.

Question: Why are there so many varying accounts of the incident from witnesses?
The witness accounts of the tragedy at Alrosa Villa are textbook examples of how different people perceive things. There were approximately 250 witness statements taken from people at the Alrosa on the night of the incident, and nearly as many accounts of what had happened. For example: Gale's weapon was constructed of stainless steel, so it had a dull silver appearance. Witness descriptions of the gun's color covered the full spectrum: black, silver, gold, bronze and blue.

Typically, people who witness such a traumatic event absorb very little of it. Disbelief and denial of what they are seeing tends to muddy the waters of their memories. Also, most people don't really see the entire incident, and more importantly, while the incident is happening, they are not "trying to remember" what they saw. Instead the focus is normally on self-preservation. In this incident, minutes after the assault, hundreds of witnesses were in the parking lot "sharing" their experiences, comparing notes. Consequently, many patrons were influenced by what they heard from others, rather than what they saw themselves. One also must take into account that alcohol may have clouded the memories of some of those interviewed.

Even trained observers, such as police officers are not immune to the kind of tunnel vision that can occur during traumatic incidents. Officer James Niggemeyer related to me that a few days after the shooting he saw the video taken from the stage. On the video, Charles Cochran tells him, "Hey, you had to do it, you saved a man's life." Niggemeyer said he had absolutely no recollection of those comments.

Question: If the killer fired randomly into the crowd, why weren't there more injuries?
This is a myth. Several people stated that Gale was shooting into the audience. Of course, this information spread like wildfire through the witnesses gathered outside the venue. Within 20-minutes of the shooting, Columbus TV and radio stations were broadcasting live from the scene. One of the reporters apparently heard this rumor and reported it. In the days that followed, almost all media accounts of the shooting made reference to the killer shooting into the audience. The fact is, we know that the gunman fired 14 shots, and each shot was specifically targeted, and each struck its intended target.

Question: Several people claim that, after Dimebag was shot, he whispered some "final words" to a witness at the Alrosa Villa. Is this true?
This is a bogus story fabricated by a witness who exaggerated his role at the Alrosa Villa. Dimebag's injuries were incredibly grave and based on the paramedic's statements and the

coroner's report; the second or third bullet almost certainly killed him instantly.

Question: What happens to all the property and evidence in the case?
Since this case was a homicide, the evidence will be kept and maintained indefinitely. In addition, any property with blood on it can't be returned because it's considered a biohazard. Items of jewelry and other valuables were returned to their rightful owners.

Question: Was the killer on a suicide mission?
It's very difficult to know. For example, in his apartment, he had a 2005 calendar and also had been working on memorizing a "sales pitch" for a new job at a home improvement store. On the other hand, he apparently left an incomplete will and a life insurance policy in plain sight.

Question: What does the future hold for the Alrosa Villa?
There are several lawsuits pending against the venue, and the stigma attached to it being the site where Dimebag was murdered has impacted its ability to bring in national acts.

Question: Had Damageplan filed charges against Gale in April, could that have prevented the murders?
If Damageplan had filed charges against Gale in April, whether or not it would have prevented the murders at Alrosa Villa would be a matter of pure speculation. But, had Damageplan filed charges, the potential exists that PERHAPS Nathan Gale's visions, voices and ideations about Pantera would have come to light, thus exposing him as a threat to the band and its members.

Question: Might Damageplan's charges against Gale have resulted in confiscation of his registered gun, or caused him to be enrolled in therapy, and thus forced him back on his medication?
Again, this question is a matter of pure speculation. Even if

Gale had been arrested for damage to property or for trespassing, he apparently wasn't armed at the time of the Bogarts incident. Consequently, I doubt any action would have been taken regarding his legal right to own or maintain a firearm.

On the topic of therapy or medication, there are so many variables about what could have, or might have happened had he been arrested, that it's nearly impossible to speculate. Much would have depended on how he "behaved" while in custody or when dealing with the court.

Question: What is paranoid schizophrenia?
While most people have heard of the condition, few really understand it. In popular use, many people immediately think of the movie "Sybil" and incorrectly assume that a schizophrenic is someone with multiple personalities. In fact, it does not. According to the website, www.schizophrenia.com, the condition is a chronic, severe, and disabling brain disease. Approximately one percent of the population develops schizophrenia during their lifetime – more than two million Americans suffer from it in a given year.

Although schizophrenia affects men and women with equal frequency, the disorder often appears earlier in men, usually in the late teens or early twenties. Women are generally affected in the twenties to early thirties. People with schizophrenia often suffer terrifying symptoms, such as hearing internal voices not heard by others, or believing that other people are reading their minds, controlling their thoughts, or plotting to harm them. These symptoms may leave them fearful and withdrawn. Their speech and behavior can be so disorganized that they may be incomprehensible, or frightening to others.

Available treatments can relieve many symptoms, but most people living with schizophrenia continue to suffer some symptoms of the illness throughout their lives. It has been estimated that no more than one in five individuals suffering from the disease ever completely recovers from it.

Question: Are people who suffer from paranoid schizophrenia prone to violence?
No. Most people with schizophrenia do not commit violent crimes. Typically, they are withdrawn and prefer to be left alone. Substance abuse significantly raises the rate of violence in people with schizophrenia, but also in those who do not have any mental illness. People with paranoid and psychotic symptoms, which can become worse if medications are discontinued, may also be at higher risk for violent behavior. When violence does occur, it is most frequently targeted at family members and friends, and more often takes place at home.

You can learn more about Schizophrenia.

The vast majority of the information provided about paranoid schizophrenia was obtained from the website www.schizophrenia.com. The site is an exceptional resource for people suffering from the condition and for friends and family members trying to understand its complexities.

There are a multitude of additional resources available to people interested in learning about this condition. Some links on the Internet include:

National Alliance for the Mentally III (NAMI)
Colonial Place Three
2107 Wilson Blvd., Suite 300
Arlington, VA 22201-3042
Phone: 1-800-950-NAMI (6264) or (703) 524-7600
Internet: http://www.nami.org

National Mental Health Association (NMHA)
2001 N. Beauregard Street, 12th Floor
Alexandria, VA 22311
Phone: 1-800-969-6942 or (703) 684-7722
TTY-800-443-5959
Internet: http://www.nmha.org

National Mental Health Consumers' Self-Help Clearinghouse
1211 Chestnut Street, Suite 1000
Philadelphia, PA 19107
Phone: 1-800-553-4key (4539) or (215) 751-1810
Internet: http://www.mhselfhelp.org/index2.html

National Alliance for Research on Schizophrenia and Depression (NARSAD)
60 Cutter Mill Road, Suite 404
Great Neck, NY 11021
Phone: (516) 829-0091
Infoline 1-800-829-8289
Internet: http://www.narsad.org

National Institute of Mental Health (NIMH)
Office of Communication and Public Liaison
Information Resources and Inquiries Branch
6001 Executive Boulevard, Rm. 8184, MSC 9663
Bethesda, MD 20892-9663
Phone: 301-443-4513
Fax: 301-443-4279
E-mail: nimhinfo@nih.gov
Fax back system: Mental Health FAX4U at 301-443-5158
Web site address: http://www.nimh.nih.gov/

Bibliography

Beck, Aaron. *A Day In The Nightlife*, The Columbus Dispatch, February 2000

Unattributed. *What Might Have Been: More On Club Security*, MTV News, December 2004

Unattributed, *A Bizarre Twist in Dimebag Darrell Death*, www.blogcritics.org, December 2004

Unattributed. *Dimebag's Killer's Mother Speaks Out: I Bought Him That Gun*, www.blabbermouth.com, December 2004

Lyttle, Eric. *While My Guitar Gently Weeps*, Columbus Monthly, March 2005

Zahlaway, Jon. *Hatebreed, Damageplan, Drowning Pool head up Headbangers Ball Tour*, www.livedaily.com, March, 2004

Michalski, Art. *Witness to a Tragedy*, www.detroitbuzz.com, December, 2004

Futty, John. *An account of the events of Dec. 8, 2004*, The Columbus Dispatch, January 16, 2005

Futty, John. *Police Confirm Dimebag's Murderer Was Dragged Off Damageplan Stage in Cincinnati*, The Columbus Dispatch, April 2005

Kuenning, K. *2 Ohio Roadies Come Forward With Detailed Account of Nightclub Shooting*, *www.roadie.net*, December 2004

Futty, John. *Dimebag's Murder Was Not Motivated By Pantera's Breakup*, The Columbus Dispatch, October 2005

Grossman, Dave, *On Killing: The Psychological Cost of Learning to Kill in War and Society*, Little, Brown and Co, 1995

Norris, Chris. *The Revenge of Crazy Nate*. Blender Magazine, April, 2005.

Kaufman, Gil. *Dimebag's Killer Was Stranger in His Neighborly Hometown*, MTV News, December 2004

Ross, Bobbi Jr. *Mom of Concert Killer: He was Sick*, CBS News, December 2004

Unattributed. *Dimebag Death – More News and Reaction*, www.blogcritics.org, December 2004

Unattributed. *Shooter was Ex-Marine*, Rolling Stone, December 2004

Riley, John. *Deconstructing The Past of an Isolated Man*, www.newsday.com, December 2004

Sowinski, Greg. *Columbus Shooter Played Football for Lima Thunder*, The Lima News, December 2004

Norton, T. J. *Diagnosis and Synopsis of Nathan Gales Mental Health Evaluation and Condition*, Naval Hospital, Camp Lejune, March, 2003

Zacharia, Holly, *Gunman Possibly Mentally Ill*, The Columbus Dispatch, Jan 16, 2005

Daviet, Brandon. *Anthrax Reunites Its Classic Lineup Putting Belladonna in Front of the Mic*, Marquee Magazine, January 2006

Other Resources

Dozens of unpublished letters and lyrics written by the killer himself.

Department of Veterans Affairs, *Military Personnel Records* for Nathan M. Gale from Feb 2, 2002 through Nov 30, 2003.

Department of Veterans Affairs, *Military Medical Records Chronological Record of Medical Care* for Nathan M. Gale from Feb 2, 2002 through Nov 30, 2003.

Department of Veterans Affairs, *Military Dental Records Chronological Record of Medical Care* for Nathan M. Gale from Feb 2, 2002 through Nov 30, 2003.

Certificate of Release or Discharge from Active Duty, DD Form 214, Nathan Gale

Disability Evaluation Findings of the Physical Evaluation Board in the case of PFC Nathan M. Gale, USMC

Logan County Court of Common Pleas *Juvenile Criminal History of Nathan M. Gale*

Logan County Court of Common Pleas *Juvenile Probation Records for Nathan M. Gale*

Marysville Ohio Division of Police *Arrest History and Case File for Nathan M. Gale*

Audio Interview: *Phil Anselmo Interview with Metal Hammer Magazine Writer*. December 2004

Columbus Police Department, *Color Photographs of Police Involved Shooting #2004-16, 12-8-04, Alrosa Villa*

Columbus Police Department *Firearms Board of Inquiry,*

Police Officer J. Niggemeyer, June 2005

Columbus Police Department *Police Preliminary Investigation, December 2004*

Columbus Police Department *Police Involved Shooting/Homicide Investigation Results, November, 2005*

Cincinnati Police Department Criminal Investigation Section *Incident Report from 5 April, 2004 at Bogarts in Cincinnati, Ohio.*

U.S. Department of Defense *Enlistment Document for Nathan M. Gale* 7 February, 2002

Cook County Illinios, Office of the County Clerk *Birth Certificate for Nathan M. Gale*, 11 September 1979

Department of the Treasury, Firearms Transaction Record *Nathan M. Gale Purchase of Beretta 92F Serial Number BER319253*

Columbus Police Department *Diagram of Alrosa Villa Homicide Crime Scene, from Dec. 8, 2004*

Columbus Police Department *Crime Scene Photo/Evidence Collection Documents*

Columbus Police Department *Forensic Evidence Request Documents*

Columbus Police Department *Crime Laboratory Reports on Remington 870 Shotgun and Beretta F92 Semi-Automatic Pistol*.

Columbus Police Department *Discharged Firearms Report*

Columbus Police Department *Recovered Firearm / Ammunition Evidence Documents*

Columbus Police Department *Property and Evidence Transfer Documents*

Franklin County Ohio Coroner's Report: *Finding of Fact and Verdict, Gale, Nathan Miles*

Franklin County Ohio Coroner's Report: *Finding of Fact and Verdict, Abbott, Darrell Lance*

Franklin County Ohio Coroner's Report: *Finding of Fact and Verdict, Bray, Nathan Anthony*

Franklin County Ohio Coroner's Report: *Finding of Fact and Verdict, Thompson, Jeffery Allen*

Franklin County Ohio Coroner's Report: *Finding of Fact and Verdict, Halk, Erin Alexander*

Franklin County Ohio Coroner's Office: *Property Slips*

Columbus Police Department, *Video Taken by Damageplan, Dec. 8, 2004 Alrosa Villa*

Columbus Police Department, *Crime Scene Video, Dec. 9, 2004 Alrosa Villa*

Columbus Police Department, *Audio Tape Interviews of witnesses at Alrosa Villa*

Appendix

Alrosa Villa Witnesses Dec. 8, 2004

This is not a complete list of everyone at the Alrosa Villa that evening. The people listed here provided statements to the Columbus Police Department.

Abbott, Vince P
Adkins, Shane
Alderman, Justin R
Alfrey, Jonathan
Anderson, Stephen

Babcock, Steve
Babin, Steven C
Baer, Aaron J
Baer, Zachariah T
Ball Joshua E
Ball, Thomas O
Barnes, Aaron
Bateman, Clint E
Beller, Jason
Beller, Katie
Benner, Aaron D
Blagg, Shawn L
Blair, Matthew
Blankenship, Andrew
Blevins, Andrea
Bloomfield, Justin
Boggs, Jeremy
Bowen, Jessica
Brecheisen, Wyatt
Brenstuhl, Laura
Brenstuhl, Lynn
Brown, Mark
Brown, Matthew
Bryant, Tim
Burnett, Travis
Byers, Jeffrey H

Caron, Roger
Caron, Tiffany
Carter, Heidi
Caudill, Gerald W
Caudill, Justin E
Chappelle, Thomas C

Clark, Billy
Clark, Christine
Clark, Dave
Clark, Nathan T
Clemmons, David A
Climer, James
Clouser, Kevin
Colopy, Michael
Combs, Brandon
Conner, Christopher J
Crace, Daniel
Craiglow, Michael A
Cummins, Michelle

Daly, Storm
Dameron, Joe
D'andrea, Christopher
Davis, Christopher
Deel, Jessica
Denney, Joshua
Dexter, Troy
Dietz, Greg P
Dorr, Barak,
Drake, Josh
Duke, Jameson
Dumas, Tim S.
Dunford, Danny Jr
Dunkin, Michael C

Elisa, Jessica
Elisa, Tim
Ellis, Amber

Farrier, Aaron
Fielder, Brian K
Flesch, Mike A
Flutie, Randy
Fluty, William II
Flynn, Julie M

Forbes, Heidi
Forrest, Leon
Forsythe, Blake A
Fout, Charles W
Fraley, Chris

Gallagher, Nicholas
Gibbens, David D
Gibson, Randy
Givens, David
Graham, John
Graves, Derek A
Graves, Jamie
Greene, Jeff
Gruver, Eric

Hainer, Brian C
Hale, Kimbery
Hamlin, Thomas
Hankinson, Michael
Hannah, Sarah R.
Hardin, Geno
Hardin, Tyler
Harsh, Ryan M
Hatfield, Kristy
Heiberger, Nathan
Heiden, Joe
Heischman, Jon R.
Henson, Todd
Henson, Traci
Henthorn, Allison
Heskett, Amy
Hiles, Jennifer
Hollinger, Elizabeth
Hopper, Ryan W
Horsley, Jason
Humphries, Michael
Hunter, John
Hunter, Scott

Jeffers, William T
Jewett, Jason D
Johns, Doug
Jones, Jessie J
Jones, Kevin E
Jordan, Michael
Kakaha, Robert
Karist, Brandon
Karist, Richie
Kaylor, Chad
Kellog, Karen
Kent, Brian M
Kerr, Barney
Kerr, Brian
King, Amanda
Koziki, Brian
Kruer, Jason A
Lachman, Patrock
Lahr, Joseph
Lambert, Jason
Law, Nikki D
Leivengood, Siri
Levings, Crystal
Lilley, Christopher S
Loper, Shawn

Magers, Marlana K
Maines, Stephanie R
Mara, Joseph
Mara, Michael
Mason, Matthew A
Matthews, Stephanie
Mauk, Chris
Maynard, Bryan S
McCain, Andrew
McGregor, Andrew
McGregor, Mary Kate
McGuire, Eric
McKelvey, Troy
McMeans, Kevin J
Mead, Jennifer E
Meravy, Andy
Moffat, Kenneth
Moore, Corey
Moore, David
Moore, Jennifer
Moore, Keith
Moore, Linda
Moore, Roberta
Moore, Shane
Mucciardi, Brian P
Muirhead, John

Nemeth, Jason F

Obar, Rich
Ockovic, John
O'Keefe, Desiree
Ollom, Adam R
Osborne, Joseph
Owens, Christopher

Pardo, Chris
Parker, Seth
Parsons, Eric
Patrick, Scott
Pattin, Justin A
Perry, Stephen J
Petty, Anson M.
Phillips, Debra
Phillips, Franklin
Pierce, Seymour
Poindexter, Braden

Quinteros, Livia

Radde, Matt
Rainey, Matt
Reed, Penny
Rhodes, Dustin
Rhodes, Earl E.
Rivers, Jonathan
Roberts, Lisa

Saleski, Jared
Sanchez, Christopher
Sanders, Gary II
Saunders, Joshua
Schrote, Tristan
Scott, Andrew
Scott, Bryan
Scott, Roger W.
Seabolt, Edward
Seffens, Dorothy
Sexton, Cindy
Sexton, Kenneth
Shafeffer, Aaron
Shaffer, Jason
Shearer, Jessica
Shine, Patrick A
Short, Heidi
Simcox, Roland
Slone, Christina
Smith, Kala
Snapp, Tasia J
Solinger, Cory R.

Speakman, Robert
Sprague, Joshua D
Spring, Corey
Springer, Crystal
Stacy, Amanda K
Stake, Michael
Steake, Greg
Studerbaker, Joe
Tanler, Brandy L
Tayne, Billy
Tayne, Jenny
Thompson, Brandon
Trischler, Elizabeth
Trot, Joanna
"Tubbs"

Vanfossen, James
Vanover, Adam R
Vines, Amy Ann
Walker, Todd M
Ward, Alicia
Ward, Dustin
Watkins, Chad
Watkins, Chris
Weaver, William S
Weber, Jeremiah M
Weir, J. Daniel
Welch, Jensen B
Welliveo, Heath
Welliver, Heath
Welliver, Timothy W
Wessler, Jerry L Jr
Wharton, Michael
Whitcomb, Corey
Whitcomb, David
Wild, Ryan
Wile, Ryan
Williams, Heather
Williams, Keith
Williams, Tyson R
Wilt, Mike
Wilt, Valerie
Woodruff, Marvin L

Alrosa Villa Employee Dec. 8, 2004

Bowens, Henry
Bryant, Tim
Carpenter, Mitch
Cautela, John
Cautela, Rick
Chappelle, Stephen
Cochran, Charles
Colasante, Diane
Coontz, Robert S
Graham, David
Halk, Erin
Jenkins, Ronald
Lewis, Emily
Melchiorre, Ryan
Miller, Eric
Moore, Roberta
Morris, John W
Ockovic, John
Reimund, Dean
Shannon, David
Sheets, David
Shultz, Robert T
Tejasakulsin, Vit
Walters, Brandon
Weitz, Danny
Wilkins, William
Zink, Patricia

Responding Columbus Police Personnel Dec. 8, 2004

Ackley, Jeff	PO
Adkins, G.	PO
Blubaugh, David	PO
Bonn, Shawn	PO
Bowman, Gary A	Detective
Burich, Chris	PO
Carney, Brian	Detective
Castle, Michael	Detective
Clark, David	Sergeant
Close, Brent	PO
Cormack	PO
Cox, Edward	Detective
Croom, Dana	Detective
Crum, Ricky	PO
Dilello, Aisha	PO
Farbacher, Dana	Sergeant
Ferencz, Kevin	PO
Fineran, William	Lieutenant
Fulton, Jay	Detective
Gillette, William	Detective
Gingery, Steven A	Detective
Glasure, Stephen	Detective
Goss, Wayne	Detective
Gubernath, Jeff	Detective
Hendrick, Tim	Detective
Heinzman	PO
Hogue, Robert	Sergeant
Jackson, Thomas E	Detective
Jacobs, Roer	Detective
Justice, Kathie	Detective
Ladley, Sandra	Detective
Landis, Jeremy	PO
Lang, William	PO
Lares, Dave	PO
Lawson, Ken	Detective
Love, Ronald	Detective
Mathias, N.	PO
Mays, Jeff	PO
McCann, Michael	Detective

McClary, Terry	Detective
McConnell, Terry	Sergeant
McCoskey, James	Detective
McGahhey, Daniel	Detective
Miller, William	Detective
Mounts, Timothy G	Detective
Myers, Kevin	Detective
Niggemeyer, James	PO
Norman, Dana	Sergeant
Paley, Philip	Detective
Parker, Charles	PO
Partlow, Stanley	Commander
Pickrell, Daniel	PO
Pilya, Eric	Detective
Pptak, Richard	PO
Pribe, T.	PO
Ptak, Richard	PO
Ramey, David	Detective
Redman, Russell	Detective
Reed, Ky	PO
Reese, Larry	Detective
Rond, Christopher	Detective
Sacksteder, Jeffrey	Sergeant
Schrader, James	Lieutenant
Secrest, Mike	PO
Sheehan, James	PO
Sheline, Brian	Detective
Shope, Steven A	PO
Shuttleworth, Jeff	PO
Smith, M	Det
Snyder, William	Detective
Sprague, Jason	Detective
Stumph, Bryon	PO
Taliaferro, Yvonne	Detective
Tobin, Paul	PO
Tucker, Michael	PO
Vanderbilt, P.	PO
Wachalec, Robert	Detective
Waldenga, Charles	PO
Warrick, Stephen	PO
Weeks, John	Detective
Weis, John	Detective
Young, Althea	Detective

Responding Fire Fighters & Paramedic Personnel

Clinton Township Fire Department
Chris Biasella, Fire Figjhter
Kellie Ruetsch, Fire Fighter

Columbus Fire Department
Chris Blair, EMS-11 Capt.
Ryan Brzezinski, Fire Fighter Lt.
T.J. Casa, Fire Fighter
Bryan Coss, Fire Fighter
Sam Cox, Deputy Chief
Curt Dewey, Fire Fighter
Jim Gray, Fire Fighter
Bryan Groff, Fire Fighter
Andy Halderman, Fire Fighter
J.J. Hingst, Fire Fighter
Matt Johnson, Fire Fighter
Scott Krummel, Fire Fighter, Capt.
Steve Lamb, EMS-12 Lt.
Mark Lawless, Battalion Chief
Sean Malone, Fire Fighter
Melissa Mohler, Fire Fighter
Scott Moore, Fire Fighter
Ed Rose, Fire Fighter
Don Salsbury, Fire Fighter, Lt.
Rick Schoch, EMS-13 Lt.
Charles Sendelbach, Fire Fighter
John Throckmonton, Fire Fighter
Tony Tinnermann, Fire Fighter
Mark Williams, Fire Fighter

Worthington Fire Department
Chris Craig, Paramedic
Eric Erhardt, Paramedic
Joe Pichert, Paramedic
Ty Steward, Paramedic

Officer James Niggemeyer
Awards/Recognition (2005)

NRA Officer of the Year
International Association of Chief's of Police (IACP) and Parade magazine Officer of the Year honorable mention.
National Association of Chief's of Police (NACP) Silver Star for Bravery
Ohio Attorney Generals Ohio Distinguished Law Enforcement Valor award
City of Columbus Mayors award of excellence
Columbus Division of Police Medal of Valor
Central Ohio Crime Stoppers Special Recognition award
American Legion 12th District Council Law Officer of the Year award
Fraternal Order of Police Associates (FOPA) Capital City Lodge #5 Officer of the Year
Ohio Tactical Officers Association (OTOA) Valor award
America's Most Wanted All-Star finalist

Metal fan, James Niggemeyer & Doom Crew Member, Deege Dunford "flash metal" on the side stage during a *Black Label Society* Concert. Photo by Chris A.

About the Author

Chris A. Photo courtesy of Jeff "Stinger" Brown.

Chris Armold (Chris A.) is a writer, photographer, guitar player, businessman and retired USAF Security Police Master Sergeant. Throughout his career, Chris has interviewed and or photographed the likes of *Alice Cooper, Ted Nugent, Joe Bonamassa, Zakk Wylde, Nick Catanese, Eric Loy, Yngvie Malmsteen, Rob Zombie, Johnny A., B.B. King, Mark Knopfler, Godsmack, Disturbed* and many, many more. In 2005, Zakk

Wylde made Chris a "patched" member of the *Black Label Society's* "Doom Crew."

While serving his 20-year career in the U.S. Air Force, on assignments that took him from the cornfields of Indiana to the halls of the Pentagon, Chris explored the Normandy Beaches- the site of the historic D-Day invasion, and volunteered at several military museums in England. While stationed in the Upper Peninsula of Michigan, Chris covered the Green Bay Packers as a freelance writer and photographer for "The Packer Report."

In 1999, Chris retired from the military and started a small business in Miamisburg, Ohio. A rock 'n' roll and heavy-metal fan for 35-years, Chris has attended hundreds of concerts and has seen some of the world's greatest rock and metal acts. In 2004, he became a freelance writer and photographer for the Ohio publication, "Guitar Digest."

Chris holds a Bachelor's degree in Criminal Justice and a Dual –Master's degree in Public Administration and Human Resource Development. He has been married to his incredibly tolerant wife, Connie, for 24 years. Chris and Connie live in Ohio with their three cats, six canaries, a turtle, a fish, and a black and white Pomeranian named Zakk.

Chris Armold uses the abbreviated "Chris A." for his music writing and photography works, but uses his full name when writing about military subjects. A Vulgar Display of Power: Courage and Carnage at the Alrosa Villa is Chris A.'s third book. A proud military historian, his other titles include: Steel Pots, The History of America's Steel Combat Helmets, and Painted Steel, Steel Pots Volume II.

You can e-mail the author at chrisa@core.com

On MySpace at www.myspace.com/rockwriter and www.myspace.com/avdop

The official book website is www.AVDOP.com

The publisher website is www.MJSPublications.com

Order Additional Copies Of This Book

A VULGAR DISPLAY OF POWER

COURAGE AND CARNAGE AT THE ALROSA VILLA

As you close the final page of this book,
please remember and never forget...

Jeffery Thompson
Darrell Abbott
Nathan Bray
Erin Halk

THE END